Acting Across Borders

Acting Across Borders

Mobility and Identity in Italian Cinema

Alberto Zambenedetti

EDINBURGH
University Press

A Lina, Marilisa, Denise e Violetta

Edinburgh University Press is one of the leading university presses in the UK. We publish academic books and journals in our selected subject areas across the humanities and social sciences, combining cutting-edge scholarship with high editorial and production values to produce academic works of lasting importance. For more information visit our website: edinburghuniversitypress.com

© Alberto Zambenedetti, 2021, 2022

Edinburgh University Press Ltd
The Tun – Holyrood Road
12(2f) Jackson's Entry
Edinburgh EH8 8PJ

First published in hardback by Edinburgh University Press 2021

Typeset in Monotype Ehrhardt by
Servis Filmsetting Ltd, Stockport, Cheshire

A CIP record for this book is available from the British Library

ISBN 978 1 4744 3986 2 (hardback)
ISBN 978 1 4744 3987 9 (paperback)
ISBN 978 1 4744 3988 6 (webready PDF)
ISBN 978 1 4744 3989 3 (epub)

The right of Alberto Zambenedetti to be identified as the author of this work has been asserted in accordance with the Copyright, Designs and Patents Act 1988, and the Copyright and Related Rights Regulations 2003 (SI No. 2498).

Contents

List of Figures	vi
Acknowledgements	vii
Introduction: Acting Across Borders	1

PART ONE: AMEDEO NAZZARI

	Introduction to Part One: Amedeo Nazzari's Many Im/mobilities	15
1.	Flying: Empire Cinema's (Aero)Mobilities	23
2.	Returning: Im/mobility and Immigrant's Nostalgia	37
3.	Fighting: Wartime Im/mobility in *Harlem*	61
4.	Romancing: Postwar Im/mobilities in Raffaello Matarazzo's Melodramas	85
5.	Migrating: The Pathology of Im/mobility	99
	Conclusion to Part One: Driving the *Flâneuse*: *Le notti di Cabiria*	105

PART TWO: ALBERTO SORDI

	Introduction to Part Two: Alberto Sordi's Mobile Comedies	113
6.	Vacationing: The Rise of the Travelling Comedian	123
7.	Working: 'L'Italia è una Repubblica Democratica, fondata sul lavoro'	139
8.	Killing: Criminal Mobilities	161
9.	Exploring: Italian Identity Abroad	176
10.	Drilling: (Auto)Mobile Satires of Global Petroculture	194
	Conclusion to Part Two: Driving Across (Screen) Borders	202

Filmography	208
Bibliography	214
Index	227

Figures

1.1 and 1.2	A foreign cityscape speaks of a faraway home in *Luciano Serra pilota*	29
1.3	Italian bilocations: liquid surfaces and cinematic cartographies in *Montevergine*	45
1.4	Mediating cinematic im/mobility: impermeable borders, porous time in *Montevergine*	47
1.5	ENIC letter to the Sottosegretariato Stampa Spettacolo e Turismo	63
1.6 and 1.7	Report by DGC Director Eitel Monaco to the Minister of Popular Culture Gaetano Polverelli	67, 68
1.8 and 1.9	Amedeo's mediated im/mobility: reading the news and listening to the radio broadcast of Tommaso's final fight	69
1.10 and 1.11	Gendered mediated mobilities: Elena and Lina	93
1.12 and 1.13	Amedeo Nazzari's pre- and postwar vehicular stardom	106
2.1 and 2.2	Celebrity automobility	114, 115
2.3 and 2.4	Families in transit: social mobility via transportation technology	133
2.5	Moving forward, driving east	149
2.6	Italian cinema on Australian (dolly) tracks	157
2.7 and 2.8	Criminal mobilities through the (cinematic) transatlantic gaze	168
2.9 and 2.10	Acting across cinematic traditions: Richard Conte's transatlantic gaze	173
2.11 and 2.12	Fracturing the (national) self	178
2.13 and 2.14	The imperial seeing-man in the cinematic mirror	187
2.15	Strategies of (mediated) self-stereotyping	197
2.16	Satirizing (American) petroculture: pushing the Model T	199
2.17	Stacking the iconic deck: Catholicism, *Romanitas*, Verdi, Fellini, and Sordi	206

Acknowledgements

Acting Across Borders began as a PhD dissertation at New York University, which I completed under the enlightened advisement of Ruth Ben-Ghiat almost a decade ago. It has since transformed numerous times, shaped by conversations with colleagues, students, friends, and family members; it has evolved into this book, which bears little resemblance to its first incarnation, and better reflects the direction my academic interests took in the intervening time. I am sincerely grateful to the many people who have helped me along the long and tortuous route. First and foremost, I thank my life partner and toughest editor, Denise Birkhofer, who stood by me through years of uncertainty and confusion, consoling me through the loss of my father Umberto and my grandmother Lina, and encouraging me to not give up. I thank my former colleagues at the College of Staten Island, where my academic career began: Valeria Belmonti, Chiara Ferrari, Giancarlo Lombardi, Jane Marcus-Delgado, Gerry Milligan, and Paola Ureni; you will always have a special place in my heart. At Oberlin College I was fortunate to work alongside the wonderful faculty of the Cinema Studies programme: Grace An, Rian Brown-Orso, William Patrick Day, Doron Galili, Burke Hilsabeck, Jeff Pence, and Geoff Pingree, who were always willing to share a coffee and lend an ear to my ramblings about the mobility of Italian actors. The University of Toronto, where I hope to have found a permanent home, is brimming with incredible talent, such as the graduate students who generously contributed to my graduate seminar 'Diversity and Mobility in Italian Cinema', where many of these ideas were first put to the test with the help of the distinguished filmmaker and activist Fred Kuwornu. I am also grateful to the postdoctoral fellows I have had the privilege to meet and work with, *in primis* the extraordinary Jessica L. Harris, who co-taught an iteration of this course, but also Damiano Acciarino, Matteo Brera, Marco Faini, Luca Fiorentini, Eleonora Lima, Marco Malvestio, Andrea Parasiliti, and Jessica L. Whitehead; I have learned a great deal from all of you, and you all own a piece of this book, whether you like it or not. A special thanks goes to the co-organizers of the Jackman Humanities Institute Working Group 'Im/migration, Mobilities, and Circulation' for giving me the opportunity to expand my knowledge of Mobility Studies: Laura Bisaillon, Elizabeth Harney, and Rachel Silvey.

In the Department of Italian Studies, I am truly fortunate to be surrounded by colleagues of the stature of Elisa Brilli, Andrea Lanza, Eloisa Morra, Franco Pierno, Manuela Scarci, Luca Somigli, and Nicholas Terpstra, who have all patiently listened to me talk about Amedeo Nazzari. I am also thankful to those who have since left: Salvatore Bancheri, Konrad Eisenbichler, and Francesco Guardiani. At the Cinema Studies Institute, Kass Banning, James Cahill, Corinn Columpar, Lauren C. Cramer, Angelica Fenner, Charlie Keil, Alice Maurice, Brian Price, Scott Richmond, Sara Saljoughi, Nicholas Sammond, Meghan Sutherland, Bart Testa, and Elizabeth Wijaya have been generously learning way too much about Alberto Sordi. I also wish to acknowledge the present and past administrative staff of both units, Denise Ing, Liz Laurenco, Lucinda Li, Elsie Nisonen, Tony Pi, Andrea Santos, and Anna Vanek, for their continuous support.

I am truly grateful to all the friends, family members, and colleagues who selflessly lent their time to this project, snapping into action when conducting research remotely was impossible for many reasons, including during the Covid-19 pandemic: Angela Dalle Vacche, Jessica Goethals, Matt Hauske, Kate Johnson, Pamela Kerpius, Carlo Montanaro, Nicolò Mainardi, Christina Stewart, and my dear brother Lorenzo Zambenedetti. Much gratitude to those who invited me to share my research at their institutions: Luca Caminati, Christine Daigle, Barbara Garbin, and Charles Leavitt. Finally, I am forever indebted to Gillian Leslie, Senior Commissioning Editor at Edinburgh University Press, who has believed in this project from the start and has patiently awaited its manuscript, and to Fiona Conn for transforming it into such a beautiful book. I am also thankful for the extensive and kind editorial support I received from Patrick Marshall, which was generously sponsored by the Cinema Studies Institute, and from Eliza Wright.

Research for this project was carried out in a number of archives in Italy, and North and South America, many of which I was able to visit over the years thanks to the financial assistance of the University of Toronto Faculty Association and the Department of Italian Studies. These include Archivio Storico delle Arti Contemporanee of La Biennale di Venezia, Archivio Carlo Montanaro, Biblioteca Luigi Chiarini and Cineteca Nazionale at the Centro Sperimentale di Cinematografia, the Ryerson Image Centre, Mediateca Toscana, Cineteca del Friuli, the Film Library of the Museum of Modern Art, Biblioteca Museo del Cine Pablo Ducrós Hicken, Cineteca del Friuli, Bibliomediateca Mario Gromo of the Museo Nazionale del

Cinema di Torino, Biblioteca Renzo Renzi of the Cineteca di Bologna, the Oberlin College Archives, the University of Toronto Media Archives, Archivio centrale di Stato, Biblioteca Nazionale Centrale di Firenze, and others I am surely forgetting. I wish to thank all the dedicated librarians, archivists, conservators, curators, and collectors who assisted me in this endeavour; without your knowledge and expertise, this book would not exist.

INTRODUCTION: ACTING ACROSS BORDERS

> Every story is a travel story – a spatial practice.
>
> Michel de Certeau (1988: 115)

In the December 1915 issue of the biweekly magazine *La Vita Cinematografica*, prolific actor and director Febo Mari (born Alfredo Giovanni Leopoldo Rodriguez, 1884–1939) launched into a radical eulogy for the relatively new cinematic art, which he positioned *en par* with Italy's storied performing traditions, the theatre and the opera, arguing that:

> We need to proclaim a crusade for the acknowledgement and the uplifting of the art of our century. Once we will arrive at our destination, its patron, the tenth Muse, will reveal herself. But she will be nude, brandishing a torch, and she will have one name: Truth. (*La Vita Cinematografica* 1915: 135)[1]

Mari's own innovative filmmaking practices supported this passionate plea for cinema's dignity and its elevation to the status of high art, capable as it was, in his view, of immortalizing and rendering life by virtue of its own mechanical apparatus. Most importantly, Mari's faith in the medium was grounded in its ability to transcend the need for any language beyond its own visual lexicon and syntax: 'When a work is well-conceived and well-written by its author, well-understood and well-expressed by its actors, any written word is superfluous. [. . .] When screenings will abolish *titles* and *subtitles*, the cinematographic art will be close to its destination' (1915: 135; emphasis in the original). Of course, it is not solely the photographic image's ability to return and reveal physical reality that leads Mari to trust in the new medium's representational and affective abilities, but also his own background in the dramatic arts; to him, cinema's 'truthfulness' was based on the unique marriage of photographic realism and naturalistic acting. In fact, Mari would have the distinct honour to direct and act alongside 'the divine' Eleonora Duse (1858–1924) in *Cenere* (1917), the only moving picture in which she appeared. Duse's instinctive acting style was based on naturalism and improvisation, with a pronounced engagement of the body and the absence of stage make-up. Although inclusive of the figure of the actor, Mari's call for a cinematic art independent from the written word clearly anticipated many discussions on the ontology of the medium – from Bazin to Zavattini, from Kracauer to Deleuze, from Pasolini to Greenaway.

Mari's own articulation of a cinematic expression that relied entirely on images led him to the daring and innovative notion that his 1915 picture *L'emigrante/The Emigrant* (Itala Film) should be distributed entirely without intertitles. Unfortunately, the revolutionary solution recommended by the director was curtailed by the distributors, who argued that exhibitors would not want to screen the film in its wordless form, and pressured Itala Film to insert traditional explanatory slides.[2] While Mari's proposal did not come to pass, its historical significance is still worth discussing, especially in relation to the film that would have pioneered it, which was also the first Italian feature centring on the issue of emigration to South America. *L'emigrante* starred stage actor Ermete Zacconi (1857–1948) – also a practitioner of naturalist acting – in the titular role of an elderly man who leaves his wife and daughter and crosses the Atlantic Ocean in search of lucrative employment abroad. Instead, he encounters only hardship and exploitation; after he recovers from a workplace accident that leaves him disabled, the emigrant returns home to his daughter and her new husband.[3] The film opens *in medias res*: a second-hand dealer is buying the family's modest furniture, and the emigrant's wife (Enrichetta Sabatini) is visibly dissatisfied with the puny sum he offers. The surviving fragment of *L'emigrante* housed at the Museo Nazionale del Cinema in Turin contains the contentious intertitles, and the one accompanying this scene reads 'A junk dealer strips the humble home for the price of the trip', highlighting the unfairness of the transaction, but not adding any particular nuance to the images.[4] Meanwhile, the protagonist is at the barber, where he discusses his transatlantic move with other aspiring emigrants. On the wall behind the group is a poster for Transatlantica Italiana Società Anonima di Navigazione, the company that from 1897 to 1934 (when it closed its doors) transported many immigrants to Brazil and Argentina first, and then expanded its routes to North America including the ports of New York City and Boston. This sophisticated alternate editing pattern, which is carried out without titles signalling the transitions between the two locales, speaks of Mari's refined understanding of the medium's spatial and narrative capabilities, despite the fact that *L'emigrante* was only his second directorial project after the 1913 short *Il critico/The Critic*.

Mari's invective against cinema's perceived subservience to Italy's traditional performing arts is occasioned by the release of this (potentially) groundbreaking film and the dispute surrounding its distribution. Undoubtably significant for its technical achievements, *L'emigrante* is even more important because it signals Italian cinema's growing sociological concerns by connecting the experience of homegrown poverty with the many labour issues encountered by those who leave the country seeking fortune abroad.[5] To put it into staggering numbers, over fourteen million Italians emigrated between 1875 and 1915, more than four million between 1916 and 1945, and another seven million between 1946 and 1975. In addition, it is estimated that more than nine million people migrated internally between 1955 and 1971, with a peak of 800,000 Southerners relocating annually to the North of Italy during the economic boom (1958–63). As Donna Gabaccia puts it, 'the residents of the Italian peninsula and its nearest largest islands have been among the most migratory of peoples on the earth'[6] (2000: 1). In her canonical book, the cultural historian argues that the range and breadth of Italian mobility has been so wide and multifarious that simply defining it as 'Italian migration' or even 'Italian diaspora' does not account for its many permutations. In fact, territorial and cultural displacement have contributed to shaping Italian identity at least since unification, and are still of paramount importance in debates over national and regional affiliation, to such an extent that they often problematically transfer onto immigrants and second-generation Italians, both in public discourse and in the arts.[7] The impact of this extraordinary human mobility on the cultural production of Italy and its diasporic communities alike has been enormous.[8] For instance, in his seminal book *Italy in Early American Cinema* (2010), film historian Giorgio Bertellini thoroughly examines the lively cultural exchange between these faraway lands in the early days of American cinema, demonstrating that cinematic representations of the migrant experience can be traced back to the inception of the medium itself, and that their iconography was grounded in aesthetic paradigms rooted in landscape painting and its articulation of the Italian South.

In other words, from early *actualités* to contemporary virtual reality installations, image-based media have been utilized to capture and represent people who move and the technologies they employ to do so; this book is an intervention in the scholarly conversation about the cinema devoted to such mobilities. In particular, I would like to suggest that the Italian film industry has continued to share Mari's concern for mobilities throughout its long and hallowed history; furthermore, I contend that this interest has given rise to a veritable filmic tradition that, if not unique to the Italian national cinema, occupies a particularly prominent position among its extensive filmography and disparate genres.

By virtue of the country's history, narratives of migration and displacement undoubtedly emerge as the most significant of the four 'socio-spatial practices of mobility' defined by sociologist John Urry, which include corporal mobility, object mobility, imaginative travel, and virtual travel (2000: 4). Additionally, in recent years, a growing number of film scholars and cultural historians have taken a more holistic view of human mobility, expanding the field by turning their attention to the place occupied by infrastructure (Restivo 2002), vehicular transport (Fullwood 2015), and politics (Ben-Ghiat and Hom 2016) in the visual (if not exclusively cinematic) articulation of Italian mobilities. Their contributions have been enormously valuable in exploring the broader implications of the public and social discourse surrounding a cinema interested in the effects of increased mobility, and they coincide with the consolidation of mobility studies (or mobilities) as both a scholarly discipline and a methodological framework.[9]

Ultimately, I argue that 'Italian cinematic mobilities' participated in the creation, the circulation, and the critique of ideas pertaining to 'the nation' – broadly construed as an assembly of people with ties (ethnic, juridical, or otherwise) to a particular land or idea thereof. Of course, I do not equate cinema with society, and I remain sceptical of approaches to film studies that draw rigid parallels between the screen and the public square. What I wish to probe are the strong and problematic associations of certain 'cinematic bodies' (by which I mean clusters of signs animated by the medium into recognizable human figures) with notions of a shared national 'identity' that transcends the screen. Of course I am aware that, by virtue of the broad strokes with which these 'bodies' are painted as an abstract 'average' citizen, they also entail conscious and unconscious exclusions that ultimately undermine their ability to truly capture society – or to capture 'true' society. In fact, I suggest that the two issues (mobility and national 'identity') are entwined since, according to Sandro Mezzadra, 'the act of creating a national territory (and tracing its boundaries, as they are legally defined by the "material constitution" of a state), has always involved dealing with the intersecting movement of bodies in a given space, with the management of mobility' (2012: 40). By extension, the *creation* (not the comprehension) of a shared national 'identity' (imagined or otherwise) that is bound to, but not confined by, said territory also entails interrogating the movements of the bodies within, across, and beyond its boundaries. Ultimately, as Michel de Certeau argued, the production of spatial meaning, which in this case is also social and political, is always accompanied by 'the actions of historical *subjects*' and their movements (1988: 118; emphasis in the original).

Given the enormous number of titles dealing with Italian cinematic mobilities, I have chosen to narrow the scope of my intervention by anchoring it to the respective oeuvres of two *male* actors, Amedeo Nazzari and Alberto Sordi.[10] In my view, these performers lend themselves to a discussion of how processes of identity formation are both described and actuated on-screen, especially when activated by corporal, vehicular, imaginative, or virtual movement. I concur with Catherine O'Rawe when she writes that

> the Italian cinema is concerned to mark and reinforce the limits of [a] gendered terrain, but of course what is significant is not just the degree to which this is successful, but also the visible traces left of the effort and labor of marking and delimiting this terrain. [. . .] [T]hese screen representations of men are the textual effects of concern about masculinity and gender that are circulating in Italian culture. (O'Rawe 2014: 8–9)

The choice to discuss a selection of Nazzari's films in this book's first part is determined by the actor's singular position as a representative of the changing political and social realities in the years straddling the Second World War; as Ernesto Nicosia writes, throughout his career

> Nazzari is always the new man, the man who is about to be born, who is about to gain awareness of himself and of his new (or renewed) needs to achieve freedom and justice. In this sense he anticipates, he pioneers a model of behaviour that others will try to adopt. It is not him that proposes himself as a model, it is others who see him that way. (Nicosia 2007: 7)

As I will discuss in the introduction to the book's second part, I chose Alberto Sordi's films for reasons that are similar and yet opposite to Nazzari's; while the latter was seen as a model for the other to imitate, the former became emblematic of a widespread mediocrity that many saw as descriptive of the Italian postwar bourgeoisie. Enrico Giacovelli notes that

> If Totò was overall a mask, Alberto Sordi was a face that became a mirror; and as mirrors do, he transformed the way Italians saw and saw themselves more than the great Totò ever did, because he acted outside the rules. (Giacovelli 2003: 32)[11]

But if Sordi was indeed a mirror, I contend that the image he reflected was simultaneously truthful and distorted: he was not, in fact, a faithful reproduction of an imagined 'average Italian', as many have written, but a diviner of the cruel, callous, and cowardly underbelly of a theoretical 'nation' that, in fact, hoped not to resemble him. Sordi's greatness both as actor and, later on, as director lies precisely in his profound understanding of this paradox, which is proper to the cinematic medium.[12]

While Nazzari and Sordi may seem an unlikely pairing for a book that interrogates what I term Italian cinematic mobilities, a cursory glance at their respective filmographies will reveal that both actors are associated with various types of *movement*, from peripatetic to vehicular, motivated by leisure or by labour or economic reasons, forced or voluntary, with a destination, nomadic, or even exploratory. For this reason, the films I have chosen to analyse are grouped together by the 'actions' performed by their protagonists as they cross physical or metaphorical borders, including those circumscribed by the screen's edges. Of course, the act of crossing is itself one that involves motion, and in film it is often articulated in spatial and cognitive terms through physical structures (doors, portals, public squares, and the like) and cinematic devices (cuts, tracking shots, dollies, fades, and so on); as Marco Bertozzi underscores,

> The trope of the crossing of the city's limits appears in Febo Mari [sic] *L'emigrante* [*The Emigrant*, Itala, 1915]. On the eve of his departure for Latin America, a peasant visits the nearby city of Turin for last-minute shopping and is assaulted by two robbers. To his eyes, the cityscape is a different world, a place of inexplicable activities and innumerable dangers. The incident furthers his sense of geographical and cultural estrangement from the urban environment. (Bertozzi 2000: 327)

Additionally, the scene speaks of the uneven cultural and economic development that continued to occasion mobility across the country and beyond for at least another sixty years, and to which many more films are devoted.[13]

In essence, I am suggesting that the case of *L'emigrante* can be understood as a blueprint for the kind of analysis on which I embark here, as it stands as one of the first incarnations (and interrogations) of Italian cinematic mobilities.[14] Mari anchored his cine-sociological investigation of emigration to Zacconi's acting and to the representational abilities of the medium. Similarly, I argue that much can be learned about the 'on-screen' construction of Italian national identity by analysing the many titles in which Nazzari and Sordi 'acted across borders'. I should note that my work is indebted to the scholars that have interrogated Italian film stardom (Landy 2008), from the Fascist years (Gundle 2013) to contemporary cinema (O'Rawe 2014), some of whom focus precisely on the 'stars' in question (Ranieri 1955; Gubitosi 1998); however, this book remains 'adjacent' to star studies rather than fully belonging to them. My interest is not to intervene in the discourse about Nazzari's and Sordi's stardom, but rather to bring into play their figures in a larger conversation about Italian cinematic mobilities. For the same reasons, it should also be clear that this is not a book about acting, at least not in the way intended by scholarship that focuses on screen performance.[15] In the introductions to Parts One and Two, I provide detailed descriptions of how each chapter is anchored to an action verb, and clarify how Nazzari's and Sordi's respective performances in the films treated therein are tethered to such actions.

As I journey though the manifestations of Italian cinematic mobilities in Nazzari's and Sordi's illustrious careers, I encounter many significant junctures in the history of the national film industry, from its complicated relationship with the Fascist dictatorship to the postwar period, from Neorealism to the golden age, from the rise of domestic genres to their internal crises. I rely on the accounts by film historians operating on both sides of the Atlantic for the necessary contextualizations, mobilizing their work to show how the national cinema's strengths have sometimes coincided with its weaknesses; in times of oppression and dictatorship, the studio system has flourished and delivered many high-quality pictures whose politics were bankrupt; in times of war, intellectual filmmakers working with limited means produced the short-lived but massively influential Neorealism; in times of freedom and democracy, the irreverent eye of satirists and comedians held up a mirror to society and politics, showing how paradoxical the inescapable humanity of an increasingly dehumanizing world truly is. Italian cinema is rarely ahistorical and almost never apolitical, qualities that have sometimes plagued its box office returns but that have helped establish its reputation as an art house staple. The film industry has participated in the history of the nation, providing commentaries and political opposition, promoting sociocultural awareness and activism, as well as constantly critiquing Italy's and Italians' many idiosyncrasies. Ultimately, with this book I wish to demonstrate that Italian cinema's active involvement in the shaping of the nation's understanding of itself and its political structures is particularly poignant when the artistic medium engages with the extraordinary mobility of the Italian people.

Notes

1. Titled 'Thus Spoke Febo Mari', the interview is brimming with enlightened observations about the medium, ranging from the specificity of its mechanical materiality to recommendations for actors on how to best perform for the camera. Unless otherwise noted, all translations of Italian-language sources are mine.
2. In the same December 1915 special issue of *La Vita Cinematografica*, we find this note by the magazine's editorial staff: 'At the last moment *Itala Film* shares a piece of news that astonishes us: some film buyers, contending that movie theatres' proprietors (luckily not the ones in Turin) refuse to screen

L'emigrante without titles and subtitles, forced the company to add them, or they would not collect the copies they ordered! We refrain from commenting, because we would use scorching words for these speculators who are incapable of understanding what is beautiful and new. To them, cinema must remain at a primitive state, because they treat moviegoers as a bunch of imbeciles and ignoramuses! Here in Turin, as in Genoa, Spezia, etc., *L'emigrante* was screened without titles, and the audience was very pleased, appreciating the innovation; why is such a thing impossible in other cities?' (1915: 138). I cannot help but fantasize about the kind of Italian film history we would be studying today, had Mari's vision prevailed over the exhibitors' conservatism.

3. The print housed in the cinematheque of the Museo Nazionale del Cinema ends with an intertitle announcing the emigrant's return: 'In the old house, Antonio can forget the past and find the lost happiness beside the happy couple.' Given that the font is different from the one used on the previous titles, that the Itala Film watermark is missing, and that the emigrant is referred to as Antonio for the first time, we can safely conclude that the title was added at a later moment, after the original finale went missing. In fact, according to the blurb on the Museo's Vimeo page, 'accounts from the time allow us to reconstruct the tragic epilogue, in which the wife dies and the daughter is seduced by a rich count'. See <https://vimeo.com/96091714> (last accessed 17 August 2020).

4. We could see Umberto Paradisi's *Dagli Appennini alle Ande / From the Apennines to the Andes* (1916) as the formal opposite of *L'emigrante*. An adaptation of the penultimate story in Edmondo De Amicis's *Cuore* (1886), in which young Marco seeks passage to Argentina to be reunited with his ill mother, the film wholeheartedly embraces its literary source material, a fact that becomes clear precisely in the treatment of the intertitles. In the fragment of *L'emigrante* housed in the cinematheque of the Museo Nazionale del Cinema, the intertitles are used sparingly, and almost exclusively to convey simple spatial and temporal information; this seems to be in tune with Mari's directorial philosophy, which placed more stock on Zacconi's performance (his gestures and facial expressions) to convey pathos than it did on the titles. Conversely, *Dagli Appennini alle Ande* features many intertitles that exhibit very strong literary qualities, priming a certain emotional response in the viewer; the pathos is found in the interplay between word and image, in the internal rhyming of the two forms and not, as in *L'emigrante*, on the immediacy of Zacconi's naturalistic performance. Moreover, Paradisi's film utilizes anti-naturalistic solutions like multiple exposures, irises, and dissolves that call attention to the constructed nature of the medium as well as to its storytelling devices, rather than naturalistically concealing them as in *L'emigrante*.

5. Many books have been devoted to the cinema of Italian emigration; see, for instance, Sanfilippo (2009); Corrado and Mariottini (2013). Also of interest are Bertonelli and Lombardi Satriani (1991); Gianferrara (1988); Cicognetti and Servetti (2003).

6. The figures I quote come from Gabaccia's *Italy's Many Diasporas* (2000). According to Gabaccia, 'migration rarely created a national or united Italian diaspora. But it did create many temporary, and changing, diasporas of peoples with identities and loyalties poorly summed up by the national term, Italian' (2000: 5–6). See also Alberto Bonaguidi's essay on internal migration (1990).
 7. I analyse how these false equivalences mar cinematic representations of migrants in 'New Coinages for Old Phenomena: From *Terrone* to *Extracomunitario* and Beyond' (Zambenedetti 2010).
 8. Historian Mark Choate reports that 'on the remote frontiers of Brazil and Argentina, Italian schools flourished as the only option for Italian and many non-Italian families, who willingly paid for their children's education' (2008: 117). See also Ipsen (2007).
 9. I am referring here to the increasing interest across a variety of disciplines (anthropology, sociology, geography, migration and cultural studies, and so on) to examine *movement* in its wide variety of manifestations and mediations by building on the conceptual roots of the 'spatial turn'. See Sheller and Urry (2006).
10. As Tim Cresswell and Tanu Priya Uteng note, 'Understanding the ways in which *mobilities* and *gender* intersect is undoubtedly complex given that both concepts are infused with meaning, power and contested understandings. The concept of gender does not operate in a "binary" form. It is never given but constructed through performative reiteration. The resultant interpretations of gender are also historically, geographically, culturally and politically different, enabling a certain slippage between the different realms in terms of how genders are "read". This point is central to an analysis of how mobilities enables/disables/modifies gendered practices. We can use mobility both as an *archive* and *present indicator* of discourses, practices, identities, questions, conflicts and contestations to understand its gendered nuances' (2008: 1–2; emphasis in the original). Cinematic mobilities behave similarly, but in addition to that, they intersect with gendered discourses proper to the medium and its industry, such as stardom, race, and age. In this book I choose to focus on two male actors in an effort to limit the scope of my analysis to case studies that can be effectively compared using a shared methodological framework. Again, I relate to O'Rawe's approach when she writes that 'Emphasis on the performative dimensions of on-screen and off-screen masculinities, allied to readings of screen performance that highlight the ways in which it is shaped by mise-en-scène, editing, cinematography, and sound, helps us to understand how star bodies might articulate or make visible preoccupations with masculinity that may be circulating in a culture, and also shape those preoccupations in specific directions' (2014: 13).
11. Totò is the stage name of Antonio de Curtis (1898–1967), one of the most popular Italian performers of the twentieth century.

12. According to Maurizio Grande, 'The self-destructing cynicism of the types embodied by Sordi recalls a central function of the comedian discussed by Bakhtin: "we deride to forget". In the case of Alberto Sordi, the action is even more disturbing because it hinges on the ambivalence of a brutal, savage, sarcastic derision that is shorn of any preoccupation of absorption into reality' (Grande and Caldinon 2003: 109)
13. For instance, in Luigi Comencini's 1974 *Delitto d'amore/Crime of Love*, a handsome Milanese factory worker (Giuliano Gemma) courts a colleague who has migrated to Italy's industrial capital from Sicily. Because of her traditional values, which are out of place in the progressive Northern city, Carmela Santoro (Stefania Sandrelli) initially rejects the forward Nullo Branzi. Eventually, the two become romantically involved, provoking the ire of her protective family. When their relationship seems doomed by their cultural differences, tragedy befalls the couple: the factory's unsafe working conditions cause Carmela to become fatally ill. Faced with misfortune, the families set aside their petty feud and Nullo marries Carmela on her deathbed. As Sandro Mezzadra notes, 'Amid the spectacular processes of industrialization and modernization that took place in the 1960s, antisouthern racism [. . .] cast itself as a functional "supplement" of the management – or the "domestication," one could say – of internal migrations, a traumatic experience of mobility that radically changed not only the composition of the working class in Italy but also the country's social and cultural landscape in general' (2012: 41). Framed in a story of internal migration, *Delitto d'amore*'s political tenor speaks to the debate over factory safety and the lack of safeguards to prevent work-related injury and illness, which was part of a larger set of issues related to the end of the economic boom: according to David Forgacs, 'attempts by employers to stay profitable by intensifying the rate of exploitation in the mass production industries led, in Italy as elsewhere, to acute workplace conflicts [. . .] centered as much on control of the pace of production as the quality of work as on wage demands' (1990: 136). Lina Wertmüller's fifth feature film, *Mimì metallurgico ferito nell'onore/The Seduction of Mimi* (1972), a story of internal migration and organized crime told from the point of view of the titular character, satirizes many of the same issues.
14. The relationship between silent cinema and Italian cinematic mobilities is suggested in Paolo and Vittorio Taviani's *Good Morning Babilonia/Good Morning Babylon* (1987), in which the brothers Nicola (Vincent Spano) and Andrea Bonanno (Joaquim De Almeida) emigrate in the attempt to earn enough money to restore the prestige of the family business, a traditional laboratory of stonemasonry and artistic restoration run by their elderly father. The brothers' talent and refined craftsmanship brings them to work on the set design of D. W. Griffith's *Intolerance* (1916), but their success, their unity, and their very lives are obliterated by the First World War. In this two-pronged allegory of cinema and the Italian diaspora, the Tavianis

use metacinematic language and Brechtian gestures to depart from any realistic representation of either topic. In their postmodern appropriation of silent cinema, they opt for formal opacity – as opposed to Mari's transparent naturalism. The very journey of the talented artisans is depicted in a stylized, highly theatrical fashion: the ship is suggested by metonymical shots of the sea, the chimneys, and the portholes, but it is never shown. Even the sociopolitical implications of the brothers' migration are summarized by graffiti that reads 'Addio Italia' (Farewell, Italy) and 'Porca Italia' (Italy, you swine), rather than being discussed in all their complexity. Pier Marco De Santi explains that 'the tragedy of emigration is rendered in a theatrical fashion, in a sort of existential religiosity that achieves the melodic and memorial heights of a choral chant [. . .] that travels like a prayer for human solidarity towards the indifferent American landscape' (1998: 138). In *Good Morning Babilonia*, everything is connoted using rhetorical figures, which exposes the artificiality of the cinematic medium as well as the storytelling devices the directors use. For instance, when the brothers first settle in the New World, their job is to feed pigs in a desolate desert landscape, in which their skin is scorched by the sun and their very existence is threatened by ravenous vultures. Far from being realistic, the scene offers a powerful allegorical treatment of the plight of Italian immigrants in the United States, but as the Tavianis themselves point out, it is also a commentary on early twentieth-century Italy: 'The emphasis we would like to place is on the fact that two craftsmen *have* to emigrate in order to exercise their craft and to that extent it is also a film about Italy at that time' (Taviani and Taviani 1987: 16; emphasis in the original).
15. See, for instance, Naremore (1988); Klevan (2004); De Benedictis (2005); Baron and Carnicke (2006); Pomerance and Stevens (2018).

Part One

Amedeo Nazzari

Introduction to Part One: Amedeo Nazzari's Many Im/mobilities

In Ignazio Silone's 1934 novel *Fontamara*, ill-tempered peasant Berardo Viola prepares to emigrate to America by selling his land, paying off his debts, and buying his passage papers:

> But before he left there came a new law [...] suspending all emigration. And so Berardo had to stay in Fontamara, like an unleashed dog that doesn't know what to do with its freedom and desperately circles around the good thing it has lost. (Silone 1960: 78)

No longer able to work on his property, Berardo must turn to manual labour, which is made scarce by the same policies limiting the mobility of labourers.[1] He sets out to leave the fictional Abruzzo town to seek work in the nearby Cammarese, but his attempt to travel to the county seat is thwarted by the Carabinieri, who tell him that he cannot work outside his place of residence unless he is able to produce mysterious papers ('la tessera' – the card). 'That's the new rule on internal emigration', they explain. Unable to see how this provision would apply to his case, Berardo replies, 'I wasn't going to Cammarese for internal emigration, but to find work' (Silone 1960: 98).[2] Silone's character's inability to understand that those reasons are indeed the same is perhaps *Fontamara*'s most direct indictment of Fascist policies regarding human mobility. Depriving him of the opportunity to find employment wherever it is available is an obvious infringement of Berardo's civil liberties, but even more important is the man's powerlessness before draconian laws he is ill-equipped to comprehend. Education, or lack thereof, is one of the novel's main themes, which Silone suggests is the root of all the injustices that are perpetrated by policymakers and law enforcement against the town's inhabitants. Silone also underscores how the Fascist government was preoccupied with the mobility of the Italian people throughout its twenty-one-year existence. The famous adage that 'Mussolini made the trains run on time' is, albeit historically untrue, one of the most resilient myths about the regime. This concern is evident in many of the government's projects, from capillary interventions, such as the creation of garden cities and seaside colonies, to large-scale operations, such as the colonial effort and involvement with diaspora communities overseas. As I will discuss in the first three chapters of this book, the film industry is not an exception to this interest; far from it. I should note that the relationship between Fascism and the entertainment industry has a long and complicated history that has received much scholarly attention, with a significant spike in contributions in the last three decades.[3] I shall not attempt to disentangle the intricate web of individual and collective responsibilities that, according to many scholars, forced Italian cinema in the 1930s to operate in close relation to the regime; rather, my goal is to discuss how the film industry, which was undeniably besieged by political pressures, portrayed human mobility in this decade, and to insert these representations into a larger history that began before the regime and continued long after it, as Ignazio Silone's novel and personal history make salient.

The first part of this book is anchored to the broad-shouldered frame of Amedeo Nazzari (1907–79), quite possibly one of the first true leading men to materialize in the Italian film industry alongside Vittorio De Sica (1901–74).[4] Standing at 1.86 metres tall,[5] the elegant, dark-haired and moustachioed Nazzari was 'a product of the history of Italian cinema, of its constant efforts to signify and represent the Italian nation' (Gubitosi 1998: 15). Over his long career, the prolific actor created an on-screen character who was heroic but human, exceptional yet flawed, sensitive to the seductions of material wealth but (almost always) ultimately following the straight and narrow path to moral and spiritual fortitude: 'Nazzari was clamorously, ostentatiously but also calmly, a positive character', Masolino d'Amico writes about him (2007: 11). While the character's roots are firmly planted in Nazzari's Fascist-era work, the actor was able to navigate the treacherous ideological waters of Neorealism with signature performances like gruff partisan fighter Captain De Palma in Alessandro Blasetti's *Un giorno nella vita/A Day in the Life* (1946) and troubled POW-cum-gangster Ernesto in Alberto Lattuada's 1946 *Il bandito/The Bandit*. He emerged from the postwar period starring opposite Greek-Italian leading lady Yvonne Sanson (1925–2003) in Raffaello Matarazzo's melodramas *Catene/Chains* (1949), *Tormento/Torment* (1950), *I figli di nessuno/Nobody's Children* (1951), and *L'angelo bianco/The White Angel* (1955),[6] at the same time appearing in a variety of costume dramas that consolidated his stardom and allowed him to stretch his acting muscles. As I discuss in the concluding pages of Part One, in 1957 Federico Fellini famously harnessed the actor's popularity, by then in slow but inevitable decline, casting him for the thinly disguised role of Alberto Lazzari in *Le notti di Cabiria/Nights of Cabiria*. In this film, Nazzari delivers a memorable performance in which his character's exceptional automobility[7] and social status are counterbalanced with emotional vacuity and casual sexism.

Through an examination of a selection of Nazzari's work between 1938 and 1943 in Chapters 1–3, I will show how the film industry reflected regime politics about human mobility, highlighting how mass entertainment reinforced, at times in very problematic and contradictory ways, the government's overall discouraging stance towards emigration and internal migration when motivated by individual agency rather than official decree. Of course, not all films produced during this period necessarily fall in line with regime policies, yet the examples discussed here exhibit a high degree of consonance, if not compliance, with Mussolini's overall stance on mobility. The Duce was voicing his concerns with demographic issues as early as 18 November 1922, framing emigration in terms of a giant loss of human capital: 'The question of emigration worries us particularly. [. . .] The Government intends to act by conciliating the demographic needs of the nation while energetically caring for our emigrants, who are both workers and Italians' (Mussolini 1951–63: XIX, 29).

The focus of each chapter is largely thematized by a corresponding action verb: Chapter 1 focuses on the (aero)mobility of *Luciano Serra pilota/Luciano Serra, Pilot* (Goffredo Alessandrini, 1938), in which Nazzari reunites with the director that had given him his 'military' breakout performance in *Cavalleria/Cavalry* (1936). A film about a former First World War pilot disappearing during a transatlantic flight from South America to Italy and resurfacing in Italian East Africa, *Luciano Serra pilota* is an example of what Ruth Ben-Ghiat (2015) has termed 'Italian Fascism's Empire Cinema',[8] a sub-genre which frequently engages with the subject of human mobility to exorcize fears of both literal and figurative desertion. In many of these films, liminal spaces such as the colonies in Italian East Africa and Libya provide the background for a territorially displaced, but ideologically compliant, nationalist return or repatriation.[9]

In Chapter 2 I will analyse two films in which Nazzari plays an *americano*,[10] or a migrant who returns from North or South America and reintegrates (or struggles to do so) into Italian society: *Montevergine (La grande luce)* by Carlo Campogalliani (1939) and *La bisbetica domata/The Taming of the Shrew* by Ferdinando Maria Poggioli (1942). As we shall see, these character types appear in a variety of films that differ greatly in terms of genre, setting, or even prestige. *Americani* are not to be confused with actual (pretend) Americans, whom Nazzari does play in *Centomila dollari/A Hundred Thousand Dollars* (Mario Camerini, 1940) and *Dopo divorzieremo/Then We'll Get a Divorce* (Nunzio Malasomma, 1940).[11]

Chapter 3, which is the last one dealing with Nazzari's Fascist-era work, is devoted to an in-depth analysis of Carmine Gallone's boxing picture *Harlem* (1943). A film entirely devoted to the *bonifica umana*[12] (human reclamation) of Italian citizens living abroad, *Harlem* represents the last bout of propagandist cinema's decade-long struggle against the representation of emigrants as belonging to the disenfranchised working class – a common assumption, given that even Mussolini in the speech quoted above conflates Italian migrants and workers. In an attempt to dislodge this image from the national consciousness, *Harlem* casts the most glamorous stars of the moment, Vivi Gioi, Massimo Girotti, and Amedeo Nazzari. I will also briefly discuss how *Harlem*'s ideological alignment with Fascism clashes with some other films of the same period, which to varying degrees displayed an awareness of the forthcoming changes in Italy's cinematic and political landscape; in fact, the rise of Neorealism was preceded by a few titles[13] that contributed to returning the industry's focus onto the real struggles of the lower classes, after a decade of *telefoni bianchi* had attempted to reframe the issues, aligning them with party politics and actively functioning as a means to manufacture the public's consent.[14]

Chapter 4 is devoted to Nazzari's collaborations with Italian cinema's undisputed king of postwar melodrama, Raffaello Matarazzo, with whom the Sardinian star collaborated on eight feature films. In this chapter, I will trace the evolution of Nazzari's on-screen persona via his characters' various im/mobilities, articulated as they were by (cinematic) border crossings, vehicular transport, iterated captivities, and most importantly, romance. Sociologist Jan Nederveen Pieterse explains that 'the migration movements which make up demographic globalization can engender absentee patriotism and long-distance nationalism' (Pieterse 1997: 49); in Chapter 5, I will discuss Dino Risi's *Il gaucho* (1964), in which Nazzari plays an Italian migrant for whom such manifestations of loyalty towards his motherland assume pathological dimensions.

Notes

1. As Silone explains, these policies had disastrous effects on the town's economy: 'We had never seen such lazy young people before. At one period they went off to look for work as soon as they were sixteen years old. Some of them went to Latium, some to Puglia, and the most eager of them went to America. Many of them left their fiancées for four, six and even ten years; the girl swore to be faithful and she married him when he got back. Others

got married the day before the boy left, and after the first night of love they were separated for four, six and even ten years. And when they got back, they found their children already grown up – and sometimes they found several of various ages. But the ban on emigration had interrupted the departure of the young people. They were obliged to remain at Fontamara, so that there was less work for everyone. The anti-emigration law meant that it was impossible to save the little nest egg that would rescue the ancestral land from the debts and mortgages, that would permit some improvements, that would permit the substitution of a new donkey for the old or dead one, that would make possible buying a pig, two goats, or a bed in which to put a wife' (1960: 87).
2. In Carlo Lizzani's 1980 eponymous film adaptation of the novel, Berardo (Michele Placido) is pulled off the train on which he is travelling to be questioned by a *maresciallo* (marshal). Interestingly, in this interaction the word 'emigrazione' (emigration) is replaced with 'immigrazione' (immigration), thus emphasizing not Berardo's desire to leave Fontamara, which Silone underscores throughout the novel, but his inability to enter (and assimilate into) a community other than his native one.
3. See, for instance, Mancini (1985); Landy (1988); Hay (1987); Argentieri (2003); Zagarrio (2004); Ricci (2008); Ben-Ghiat (2015).
4. Landy (2008) and Gundle (2013) add the lean Fosco Giachetti (1900–74) to this short list.
5. In *Il gaucho*, Nazzari's and Gassman's height is the source of a politically charged joke: at the airport, Maruchelli comments on Ravicchio's stature, asking, 'How tall are you?' The dumbfounded Ravicchio replies, 'I don't know, 1.90 . . .' Maruchelli responds, 'Just like me! The beautiful Italian race, strong, vital, exuberant!' Of course, Maruchelli's reference to an Italian 'race' is loaded with Fascist overtones, an unspoken attribute of this character that Scola confirms in the interview accompanying the film's DVD release by Cecchi Gori Home Video.
6. For an enlightening discussion of the series' conservative ethos, see Günsberg (2005: 19–59). Maria Elena D'Amelio discusses Nazzari's transition from Fascist hero to melodramatic *pater familias* in her brilliant essay 'The Ideal Man: Amedeo Nazzari, Fatherhood, and Italy's Melodramatic Masculinity' (2018).
7. I borrow the concept from Alan Walks, who writes that 'Automobility is conceptualized as a complex, path-dependent non-linear system with its own evolving coherent logic of movement, production, and consumption (Sheller and Urry 2000). This encourages a melding of the functions and practices of autonomous humans with machines (cars, trucks, etc.), thus creating new social hybrid "car-drivers" that are co-constituted by the roads, signs, cultural practices, and daily activities that bind them (ibid.). Automobility constitutes a historical assemblage of social, economic, cultural, and technological-material practices, and the power relations that they have spawned' (2015: 5).

8. Ben-Ghiat writes: 'I use this term to refer to Italian features and documentaries on imperial themes made between 1936 and 1943' (2015: xv). For more scholarship on Italian colonial cinema, see Ben-Ghiat and Fuller (2005: 179–91); Bertellini (2003); Boggio (2003); Baratieri (2005).
9. See Zambenedetti (2012), particularly chapter 2.4. Although these narratives are primarily male, female returners appear in Guido Brignone's *Sotto la croce del Sud / Under the Southern Cross* (1938) and Goffredo Alessandrini's *Giarabub* (1942), which feature 'lost women' whose character arcs can be understood in terms of displaced return migrations. For more on *Sotto la croce del Sud*, see also Ben-Ghiat (1996).
10. On returning *americani*, see Choate (2008: 8). Also, in his 1992 memoir *Unto the Sons* the late Italian American 'New Journalist' Gay Talese offers an account of *americani* and their 'white widows'. The similarities between Ignazio Silone's account of *americani* in *Fontamara* and Talese's reconstruction of the history of his diasporic family are striking.
11. In *Dopo divorzieremo*, Nazzari plays an impecunious violinist opposite Vivi Gioi, who went on to star as Massimo Girotti's Italian American love interest in *Harlem*. Malasomma's film is entirely set in the United States, a relatively frequent screenwriting trick that allowed for more risqué situations and dialogue. For more on the multifarious implications of Italian heartthrobs playing American characters, see Ricci (2008: 150–5).
12. I use this term to refer to the specific practice on the part of Italian authorities of (re)claiming Italians living outside Fascism's immediate sphere of influence as belonging to their fatherland and not to their adoptive homes – a rhetorical gesture that hinged on the perceptible traction of nationalist sentiments in diasporic communities. This expression dates back to liberal Italy and was widely employed in the medical sciences, in eugenics, and in the literature on the criminal justice system: see, for instance, Negri (1909); Pende (1933); Grandi (1941). In her cultural history of Italian Fascism, Ruth Ben-Ghiat expands on the metonymical uses of this term: 'The campaigns for agricultural reclamation (*bonifica agricola*), human reclamation (*bonifica umana*), and cultural reclamation (*bonifica della cultura*), together with the anti-Jewish laws, are seen here as different facets and phases of a comprehensive project to combat degeneration and radically renew Italian society' (2001: 4). The scholar underscores that the film industry was invited to be complicit in these processes, particularly in the case of *bonifica umana*, for which mass entertainment proved to be an extraordinary vehicle of persuasion. She writes: 'Freddi placed the CSC within the context of fascism's "organic reordering" of Italian society, and Chiarini reminded younger Italians that their films were to contribute to the "great work of human reclamation" (bonifica umana) that the regime had undertaken' (Ben-Ghiat 2001: 92).
13. For instance, *Avanti c'è posto . . . / Before the Postman* (1942) and *Campo de' fiori / The Peddler and the Lady*, both directed by Mario Bonnard; *Tragica notte / Tragic Night* (Mario Soldati, 1942); *Fari nella nebbia* (Gianni

Franciolini, 1942); *4 passi fra le nuvole/Four Steps in the Clouds* (Alessandro Blasetti, 1942); *L'ultima carrozzella/The Last Wagon* (Mario Mattoli, 1943); and, of course, *Ossessione/Obsession* (Luchino Visconti, 1943).

14. *Telefoni bianchi* (white telephones) were films in which masquerades of wealth and nobility often provided the main source of comic and romantic situations. Notable examples are *Gli uomini, che mascalzoni!/Men, What Rascals!* (Mario Camerini, 1932) and *La contessa di Parma/The Duchess of Parma* (Alessandro Blasetti, 1937). For more on *telefoni bianchi*, see Casadio et al. (1991); Casadio (1989); Bruni (2013); Innocenti (1999); Maurri (1981); Mida and Quaglietti (1980); Savio (1975).

CHAPTER 1

Flying:
Empire Cinema's (Aero)Mobilities

A cultural project that participated in the numerous initiatives of nation formation promoted by the regime, empire cinema also interfaced with a variety of discourses pertaining to human mobility – understood as a broad category encompassing various permutations of movement of singular or plural bodies across physical and political geographies. The Fascist militarization of society implied the organized shifting of large groups of people, from the deployment of military personnel at home and abroad, to the ritual mass gatherings for official celebrations; from the employment of labour force in the colonial efforts, to the displacement of rural communities to build and populate the *città di fondazione*[1] – itself a form of internal colonization. Concurrently, the forces of modernity reshaped social participation and leisure activities, making room in people's schedules for weekend outings,[2] which were propelled by the improvement of railway transportation and the development of the automotive highway network, but also of night-time entertainment – moviegoing being the most important activity to the present discussion.

Italy's seashore, countryside, and mountain slopes were often the elected sites for the negotiation of political consensus: a cursory look at the many summer camps and winter activities created in the 1920s and 1930s confirms the regime's interest in moving people in a controlled fashion, certainly as soldiers and colonists, but also as vacationers.[3] In this scenario, the physical and discursive centrality of the peninsula is counterbalanced by a complementary interest in Italy's many decentred communities and their respective narratives, from the Little Italies of North America to the colonies in Libya and Italian East Africa: in official policies and in the cinema, the 'margin' becomes a particularly significant site (both locational and ideological) for the interrogation of individual and collective mobilities.

Amedeo Nazzari's career-defining performance as Luciano Serra[4] must be understood in the context of a concerted effort to promote the homecoming (physical and/or spiritual) of those citizens who had figuratively 'escaped' the ideological reach of Fascism by virtue of their individual mobility. *Luciano Serra pilota/Luciano Serra, Pilot* (Goffredo Alessandrini, 1938) constitutes a particularly effective example of a cultural artefact operating within this project, since its narrative connects two different geographies and mobilities: Italian emigration to South America and the Second Italo-Ethiopian War.

Since colonialism posited Africa as an empty space, a blank canvas upon which fantasies of domination could be projected, colonizers found themselves unencumbered, freed from traditional burdens and responsibilities that might have hindered their mobility. However, the larger imperial project was predicated upon ethnic nationalism, whose underpinning notions were language, kinship, and land. Therefore, during the Fascist dictatorship the potentially energizing sense of freedom made possible by mobility was necessarily contained within such parameters. Paradoxically, while the colonial enterprise hinged on the readiness of men and women to travel away from home, and therefore to become mobile, land was also an implicitly embedding commodity whose exploitation was predicated on stasis. Botanical metaphors, which prescribe the existence of soil, are particularly revealing of this philosophical impasse: colonialists must 'deracinate' (uproot) themselves in order to 'take root' (settle) elsewhere. Human mobility runs counter to such narratives, emphasizing the transient, the nomadic, the disembedded: Fascism's empire cinema attempts to resolve this contradiction by temporarily lifting it away from the fixity of land, using notions of kinship and folk as ideological vaulting poles over the Atlantic Ocean and the Mediterranean Sea. It is within this deeply modern framework that the colonial returners can transcend their physical body, and perform a moral and ethical motion that may or may not be also physical. Luciano Serra is the epitome of this ideological, yet deterritorialized return. As Ruth Ben-Ghiat writes,

> *Il grande appello* and *Luciano Serra pilota* present the Italian colonies as redemptive spaces for their male protagonists, whose lives abroad (French colonial Djibouti and Brazil, respectively) were marked by loneliness and humiliation. Both films contrast these itinerant men with their militarized sons, commenting on the passage from a generation of migrant laborers to a generation who went only where the Fascist state sent them and from an impulsive individualism to a mind-set devoid of personal desire. (Ben-Ghiat 2015: 79)

In both films, as well as in *Sotto la croce del Sud/Under the Southern Cross* by Guido Brignone (1938) and Goffredo Alessandrini's *Giarabub* (1942), acts of heroism or self-effacement ultimately reinscribe mobile subjects within the ranks of citizenship, retrieving their national affiliation through meaningful displays of loyalty that may include self-sacrifice and even immolation.[5]

On 5 May 1936, commenting on the news of Addis Ababa's capitulation to the Italian invasion, Mussolini declared:

> Ethiopia is Italian! Truly Italian, occupied as it is by our victorious army; rightfully Italian, because with Rome's gladius is it civilisation that triumphs over barbarity, justice that trumps the cruel arbiter, the redemption of the meek triumphing over millenary slavery. (Mussolini 1951–63: XXVII: 265)

According to the Duce's worldview, Ethiopian land had to be considered a direct extension of Italy, the southern tip of an empire that was supposedly coming together under his leadership, after the Liberal government's failure to secure Italy's 'place in the sun' during the colonial scramble. Consequently, any inter-African mobility of Italian citizens that had its ending point in either Libya or Italian East Africa would be, though continentally displaced, a form of homecoming.

Directed in 1938 by Goffredo Alessandrini, *Luciano Serra pilota* is the film that exhibits the most comprehensive approach to human mobility in all of Italian Fascism's empire cinema, and perhaps even of Fascist-era cinema in general.[6] Earlier titles had connected patriotism and mobility, linking return migration to the accomplishments of the revolution, such as *Camicia nera/Black Shirt* (Giovacchino Forzano, 1933) and *Passaporto rosso/Red Passport* (Guido Brignone, 1935). As I have noted elsewhere, Mario Camerini's *Il grande appello/The Great Appeal* (1936) certainly constitutes a template for *Luciano Serra pilota* for its focus on the Second Italo-Ethiopian War, its story of intergenerational patriotism, and its engagement with colonial mobilities.[7] Arguably, *Il grande appello* is also the better motion picture, benefitting as it does from Camerini's nimble direction and Mario Soldati's contributions to the screenplay. Yet, *Luciano Serra pilota*'s 'two-pronged' approach to Italian mobility is what distinguishes it from the rest: the film combines the diaspora with colonialism, exposing the perils of Italian emigration while simultaneously praising return migration, which it interprets as both a physical (transatlantic) journey and a spiritual one – deterritorialized and utterly patriotic. This innovative framework is synthesized in the arc of the film's eponymous protagonist, which combines that of the ambitious emigrant who leaves the country to follow his dreams and find his fortune with that of the disillusioned returnee who is ready to atone and immolate himself for his family and his fatherland.

It is 1921. Luciano Serra is a legendary First World War veteran, who now struggles to get work taking tourists for leisure flights around Lake Como on his seaplane.[8] Luciano is married to Sandra (Germana Paolieri) and they have a son, Aldo (Roberto Villa). While the boy has inherited his father's adventurous streak, his wife is critical of the man's stubborn attachment to his profession, and pleads with Luciano to accept the position her father (Egisto Olivieri) offers him in his textiles factory. Instead, Luciano is hired by an American couple and decides to relocate overseas, pledging to return only when he will have regained his rightful place in society. Sandra and Aldo do not follow him, in compliance with her father's wishes. Luciano is unable to return to his family for many years. In the meantime, he works as a commercial pilot in South America, transporting unusual and dangerous cargo – including a circus lion. The opportunity to make history finally presents itself in 1931: Serra is to fly a plane over the Atlantic Ocean, from Rio de Janeiro to Rome.[9] The arduous flight is financed by the unscrupulous impresario José Ribera (Guglielmo Sinaz). Unfortunately, Serra cannot complete the crossing, and he is reported missing. In 1935, the jaded man resurfaces in Africa, where he hides his real identity behind a fake moniker. His son Aldo, now a grown man, has become a pilot himself, unknowingly fighting in Abyssinia alongside his estranged father. During a mission, Aldo's plane is forced to make an emergency landing; in the thick of battle, Luciano learns that his son is stranded behind enemy lines, and without hesitation he goes to his rescue. The hero manages to reach Aldo's plane before the Abyssinians and he flies it back to base, but both men are severely wounded. Strained by the effort of bringing his son back to safety, Luciano perishes and is posthumously awarded a medal of honour.

As I have discussed, *Luciano Serra pilota* is, first and foremost, 'the most successful and striking example of the type of propaganda that the Fascist regime regarded as most effective in the field of a feature film' (Gundle 2013: 184). It is not surprising that the project was very dear to Vittorio Mussolini who, as an unspecified reviewer in *Bianco e Nero* reports,

> having fought in Africa as an aviator, was inclined to make a movie inspired by his own history and the figure of a *typically* Italian aviator, who is full of enthusiasm for his profession, which he understands almost as a need, a mission, an instinct. (*Bianco e Nero* 1938: 12; my emphasis)

Vittorio's experience in the bombing squad *Testa di Leone* is channelled in the film through Luciano's longing for the days in which skilled daredevil pilots like himself were in high demand. Against such a 'typically Italian' (according to the Fascist ethos) idea of aviation, the picture contrasts two dishonourable, cowardly attitudes: Nardini's (Sandra's father) and Ribera's. If the former is interested in keeping his daughter happy by choosing the safest option for her life (i.e. by trying to muscle Luciano into an 'emasculating' office job), Ribera's goal is to profit off his skin. Loaded with the visual markers of dishonesty (white boater hat, cigar, and profuse sweating), the unctuous José Ribera is first introduced as he bets on a rigged boxing match between a white and a black fighter, only to lose his money. In the film's rhetoric, his figure epitomizes everything that is supposedly wrong with America,[10] which is depicted as a land of false promises from the very beginning.

Back in Como, when Luciano voices his wish to migrate, albeit reluctantly, his friend Major Franco Morelli (Mario Ferrari), who will later accept Aldo into the pilot-training programme, tries to discourage him from leaving: 'Over there you will find good reasons to come back in five or six months', forecasting a return that will take the most adventurous of routes. Years later, Luciano has indeed become a personality abroad, but not for the right reasons; far from being the respected pilot he once was, he has acquired a 'carny notoriety', as the aforementioned *Bianco e Nero* reviewer describes him (1938: 14). As Major Morelli predicted, America is cruel to righteous Italians like Luciano and his loyal mechanic, Mario (Felice Romano), who on the eve of the historic transatlantic flight delivers a speech that confirms the pointlessness of their migration, which has not been accompanied by upward mobility:

> I left a mechanic, and I stayed a mechanic. It would have been better to just be a mechanic in Italy, in my country, at least I would have been among my people. But if you give up on the flight now, who's ever going to leave this place?

John Urry discusses the entanglement between physical and social mobility, noting that 'it is increasingly understood how various mobilities fragment national societies through the emergence of local, regional, subnational, networked, diaspora and global economies, identities and citizenships' (2007: 185–6). Mario's bitter assessment of his life as a mobile subject who has failed to attain social mobility reflects the film's overall stance against this fragmentation.[11] The scene comes after the pilot has discovered that Ribera has not been straight with him. In fact, the impresario has been unable to secure financing for the flight, and Serra is ready to abandon the plan. However, a letter from Italy arrives, and Luciano reads it while Mario speaks these lines, the camera cutting between medium shots and close-ups of an increasingly distraught Serra. As he later explains to the mechanic, his son Aldo is requesting his permission to follow in his father's footsteps and enrol into the aviation academy. He hands the letter to Mario and moves to stand by the window, his medium close-up lit by a flashing light. Extra-diegetic music swells as Nazzari's left eye-line points off-screen right, followed by a cut to a reverse bird's-eye view of the skyline of a papier mâché metropolis (Figure 1.1). The subjective shot reveals that the light source is a neon sign on top of a building spelling out, in capital letters, the word 'ITALIA' (Figure 1.2). Coupled with the foreign cityscape, the proleptic sign triggers the pilot's resolve to move forward with the flight. At the airport, Serra is reached by an anxious Ribera who tries to stop him with the help of the local police, but the pilot manages to take off. A print-reel montage informs the viewer of the flight's progress through bad weather, intercut with Serra's growingly worried close-up. The sequence ends with shots of the seas that, allegedly, swallow the man forever.

Nazzari's ability to move rapidly between different emotional registers is showcased in this sequence, from his impassioned description of his son Aldo (the camera being positioned at a slightly higher angle, thus softening his facial features) to the almost brooding close-up by the window – the camera switching to a lower angle, allowing the actor to fill the frame with his physicality. As *Cavalleria* (1936) and *Luciano Serra pilota* show, Alessandrini was keen on capturing Nazzari's stronger side, undoubtedly establishing the foundations of his persona:

> Nazzari, it has been said, represented a super-Italian; he was an Italian as Italians would have liked to be. They were happy to see themselves in him; men wanted to be him and women wanted their men to be like him. (Gundle 2013: 190)

While this is certainly true, it would be a mistake to understand Nazzari's on-screen persona as monolithic: as this sequence shows, the actor was capable of sudden outpourings of emotion without compromising the stoicism required by this particular brand of (one might say *Fascist*) masculinity.[12] In the few words he devotes to Nazzari in his book on acting, Maurizio De Benedictis underscores that the actor's upright posture and firm facial expressions could mutate into a partially concealed interior pain.[13]

As I will discuss to a greater degree in the next chapter, the actor was also capable of putting his heroic side in inverted commas, to some degree parodying his early roles, as he does in *Centomila dollari / A Hundred Thousand Dollars* (Mario Camerini, 1940), which directly evokes Serra's transatlantic attempt: in this film, Nazzari plays an eccentric American millionaire, Mr Woods, who will stop at nothing to run his business. After he falls in love with Hungarian phone operator Lily Zilay (Assia Noris), Mr Woods recklessly steals an aircraft in Brussels and attempts to fly to Budapest in

FLYING 29

Figures 1.1 and 1.2 A foreign cityscape speaks of a faraway home in *Luciano Serra pilota*.

the midst of a storm to stop Lily's wedding.[14] The print-reel montage that accompanies the reckless flight is a crescendo of negative assessments of Mr Woods' sanity: 'Woods' plane is lost in the storm'; 'Woods mad? The latest news'; 'Too much work! Says Mr Barton, Woods' secretary'; and finally, 'Millionaire Woods MAD!' Marcia Landy argues that in Fascist-era film 'The aviator thus serves as a modern reincarnation of the traditional romantic hero, transported in space and time by both the camera and the airplane' (2008: 66).[15] To this doubly technologically enhanced mobility we must add another layer: the use of the print-reel montage in these scenes produces an account of the event which is both synchronous (the headlines appear on-screen while the action they chronicle is happening) and asynchronous (the newspapers are printed and reach their audiences after the event). As Peter Adey notes, this is yet another form of mediated mobility, which was first addressed by Marshall McLuhan when he registered the temporal cleavage caused by the 'speeding up' of communication technology (to which the news cycle is inevitably tethered) vis-à-vis the slower pace of innovation in transportation infrastructure (2017: 209–10). The print-reel montage is thus another mediation of Serra's and Woods' already extraordinary mobility via the physical medium of the aircraft and its affective articulation through the cinema.

In the romantic comedy *Centomila dollari*, the aircraft functions as a technologically advanced surrogate for the proverbial white horse, allowing Mr Woods to rescue Lily from a loveless marriage. In *Luciano Serra pilota*, the romantic ethos is consonant with the protagonist's hubris, marked by his indefatigable struggle to be reinstated in the figurative pantheon of aviators, and his inability to settle for a humble family life and to let go of his ambition in the film's first act. Ironically, these heroics are also what disqualify him from a peaceful, territorialized reassimilation into Italian society. For Serra, the only way to redeem himself is not through another stunt, such as the bombastic transatlantic flight, but through a spiritual homecoming that requires him to resume his parental duties, national realignment, and ultimately immolation – significantly, the equally hubristic Mr Woods also chooses love over money.

Borrowing from Nina Glick Schiller, I argue that Serra's return migration is motivated by long-distance nationalism,

> a set of identity claims and practices that connect people living in various geographical locations to a specific territory that they see as their ancestral home. Actions taken by long-distance nationalists on behalf of this reputed ancestral home may include voting, demonstrating, lobbying, contributing money, creating works of art, fighting, killing, and dying. (Glick Schiller 2004: 570)

It is not coincidental that when Serra resurfaces under the moniker of Alberto Conti, he is on a train headed to the front. As a protagonist whose character arc is constructed through his superior mastering of mediating (vehicular) technologies, Serra must be constantly on the move to claim a cinematic existence. A volunteer in the African conflict, he explains: 'No, no. My name is not Alberto Conti. I had promised many things to my real name. [. . .] I had promised him nothing less than glory. We both ended up at the bottom of the ocean. He drowned. And I . . . I am here.' The sea waters that doom Serra's transatlantic crossing, a shot of which ends the sequence described above, also redeem him: his pride and individualism are clearly washed off in this nationalistic baptismal font, from which he is reborn as a man and, most importantly, as a contributing member to the colonial effort. While his return migration physically overshoots Italy, his spiritual re-entering into the Italian *Volk* earns him greater purpose: it is on the battlefield that he is allowed to redeem himself as a father and as an Italian, both roles he had deserted many years prior. As Landy writes regarding conversion narratives in Italian film during the Fascist era, 'The conversion motif is central to the war narrative, involving the protagonist's conflict between pleasure and commitment to national aspirations' (1998: 158). It is only after Serra shifts his focus and puts his talents at the service of the colonial enterprise that he achieves greatness. Yet, this is posthumous: as James Hay notes, 'the imperative is dramatized through the death of a father figure, who bestows on his son a legacy with which to live' (1987: 183). Tainted by pride, a character flaw that is also a cardinal sin, Serra can reintegrate into Italian society only as exemplum of extraordinary courage, whose memory is more valuable to the country than his actual life, which is altogether too mobile and cosmopolitan to serve as a model for the Fascist combatant. As Saulo Cwerner writes,

> The new mobilities paradigm allows us to look at aeromobilities in their relations with various social networks and systems, therefore grounding or embedding them in processes whereby these mobilities, and their own distinctive spaces, networks, systems and environments, are effectively produced, reproduced, performed and regulated. (Cwerner 2009: 3–4)

In the context of my survey of Italian film history understood *through* motion, the examination of screen aeromobilities brings these processes to the surface, underscoring ideological continuities between seemingly disparate eras, such as those between *Luciano Serra pilota* and Giuseppe Masini's *Il cielo brucia/The Sky Burns* (1958), in which Nazzari reprises the role of a singularly heroic aviator with a complicated past. Set in the tumultuous years straddling the Second World War and reconstruction

(1940–52), the film centres on the adventures of a group of pilots flying the Savoia-Marchetti SM.79 *Sparviero*, a three-engined aircraft also known as 'il gobbo maledetto' (damned hunchback) due to its fuselage's distinctive hump. At the outset of the film, Captain Carlo Casati (Amedeo Nazzari) is in Libya, where he reluctantly takes command of the 143rd squadron. During a mission, his plane is forced to land behind enemy lines, and he takes refuge in a former Italian colonial village, now occupied by the English forces. Anna (Faith Domergue), an Italian colonist widow, takes in the wounded man, nurses him back to health, and eventually becomes his wife. The film snakes through several aerial missions, splicing together footage from actual wartime air and land combat, studio shots, and practical special effects created using models of the iconic planes. Eventually it focuses on the armistice between Italy and the Allied forces of 8 September 1943, when Casati decides to fly to the South and join forces with his former enemies against the Germans. After the war, Casati is in charge of Italy's flight academy, and is ordered to retire the last surviving SM.79. Before he can pass on these instructions, he climbs into the cockpit for one last mission: flying a sick child to a hospital in the midst of a hurricane.

If *Luciano Serra pilota* envisioned the spiritual homecoming of a prodigal aviator, effectively reinscribing him into an imaginative Italian-cum-Fascist *Volk*, the strangely anachronistic revisionism of *Il cielo brucia* does more than absolve its protagonist of his wartime sins: it equates unrepentant Fascists with partisans, vaulting over the struggles of the resistance and their cinematic memorialization by Italian Neorealism. In resuming the role of the aviator, Nazzari effectively resuscitates Serra, extending his character arc into the *pater familias* he will play in the Raffaello Matarazzo melodramas I discuss in Chapter 4. But the film's problematic exonerations from political responsibilities are not limited to its protagonist; indeed, they are extended to all combatants, regardless of their role in the war. In fact, while Nazzari is ultimately the hero, successfully mastering both the quintessential features of aeromobility – 'altitude and speed', as Cwerner continues (Cwerner 2009: 4) – *and* navigating the ideological quandaries of Italy's transition to democracy, he is not the character tasked with dispensing forgiveness. This burden falls on Lieutenant Marchi (Fausto Tozzi), whose plane is downed in combat. Adrift on a raft, he rescues another Italian pilot he finds floating in the sea. Marchi has followed Casati to the South and joined the Allied forces, while his unexpected companion continued to fight alongside the Germans. Feeling their end approaching, the Lieutenant offers words of reconciliation to his fellow Italian, despite their political division: 'Remember, we are all fighting for the same idea. We'll have to start over, but together we'll manage', concluding that 'We'll have to forgive, on both sides.' The men perish at sea, and when their bodies are washed ashore, they are buried together in the name of a reconciliation that, unfortunately, is as historically myopic as it is cinematically dated.

Notes

1. For an account of how these projects are still relevant to contemporary Italian mobility, see Pennacchi (2008).
2. Mario Camerini's romantic comedies showcase many of the social activities organized by the Opera Nazionale Dopolavoro; *I grandi magazzini/ Department Store* (1939) contains a direct reference to 'i treni della neve', railway transport to ski resorts on the Alps. For more, see Canella and Giuntini (2009).
3. See, for instance, Betti (1984); Bazzoffia et al. (2003); Capomolla et al. (2008); Wall and De Martino (1988); De Grazia (1981); Falasca-Zamponi (1997); Mainardi (2004); Nicoloso (2008); Thompson (1991).
4. Pruzzo and Lancia comment on the perfect match between role and performer: 'the eponymous protagonist is not a one-dimensional hero who would burst into the skies of glory. This flying madman, optimistic with regards to resources and technology, and headstrong in his convictions, is a man with his own problems and a troubled family. He is certainly brave: strong in the body and bold in his choices, but also aware and ponderous, and gifted with an intelligence that is not complacent, but that seeks simplicity and does not hide the natural likability even when the actor's mask is tense. In other words, Nazzari. And Nazzari is ready, the movie grows with his name' (1983: 47–8).
5. Ben-Ghiat's discussion of *Il grande appello* (2015: 80–96) is consonant with my description of the many deterritorialized, 'spiritual' returners of Fascist-era cinema.
6. Mussolini's direct involvement with the making of the film is also evidenced in an anecdote told by Maria Evelina Buffa: 'During *Luciano Serra pilota*'s production, Mussolini visited the set (his son Vittorio was the film's supervisor). The film still did not have a title. The duce asked: "What's the protagonist's name?" "Luciano Serra." "And what does he do?" "He's a pilot." There was the title. What imagination! Much has been said about this "regime" film. In part, it was certainly instrumental as propaganda for the strong man who defied danger! But the character was not that prototype of virility that Fascism liked. How much tenderness in Luciano Serra, fearless pilot who cries because he has to leave his son . . .' (2008: 72).
7. See Zambenedetti (2012: 116–25). On *Il grande appello* and the trope of the 'Prodigal Father', which to some degree applies to *Luciano Serra pilota* as well, see Landy (1998: 192–4).
8. For an extended discussion of this film in relation to Fascism's empire cinema, see Ben-Ghiat (2015: 96–117).

9. Many sources (Pruzzo and Lancia 1983: 46; Rosselli and Pampaloni 2005: 78; Gundle 2013: 184) erroneously report Luciano's flight as a Buenos Aires–Rome journey, which is certainly more coherent with the film's fictional 'South America', where the language spoken is a simplified Spanish (not Portuguese) and the shady impresarios have Hispanic names. However, the copy I was able to view at Archivio Storico delle Arti Contemporanee of the Biennale di Venezia contained a print-reel montage that reported Rio de Janeiro as the point of departure. This sequence ends with the close-up of a hand tracing the route on a map from the Brazilian city to Rome. On the one hand, the shortening of the transatlantic flight by approximately 1,200 miles would seem a perfectly valid reason for this choice; on the other, this incongruity between countries might be a simple mistake, the Carioca city being inexplicably at odds with the rest of the picture. This might not be the only discrepancy in the geography of Luciano's emigration. In fact, the pilot is first hired by the Thomsons, an American couple with ostensibly English names. Presumably, he would follow them to the United States; even Nardini's bitter farewell to Luciano seems to indicate this: 'Dear Serra, I can only wish you a safe journey, and good luck in dollar country!' Ben-Ghiat, who argues unequivocally that the route is Rio–Rome, notes that the Grand Hotel scenes also created some confusion: 'Its Hollywood-inspired elegant dancing couples, platinum-haired women, white columns, and ballroom floor led Antonioni to mistake Stresa for Hollywood in his review of the film; he stated erroneously that Luciano first went to North America before landing in South America' (2015: 102). How he ends up flying circus animals in a generic 'South America' remains a mystery.
10. Let us not forget that, in condemning Italian emigration to the new continent, Fascist-era cinema did not differentiate between North and South America. Moreover, 'Alessandrini had worked in the United States, but most of all he knew America via the cinema, so in his imagination the image of the States could extend to the entirety of the American continent' (Gubitosi 1998: 30).
11. The recent rise of populism and the resurgence of extreme right-wing politics in the West could be a symptom of a widespread fear before the perceived fragmentation of nation states described by Urry (2007).
12. When writing about the goals of the totalitarian approach to nation building, Philip Morgan maintains that 'the Fascists wanted to create an Italy made in their own image, a nation of ready-made warriors, physically fit, mentally agile, disciplined, courageous and obedient, committed believers and fighters in the cause of the nation. To achieve this, Fascist propaganda and indoctrination projected a series of images and models of the kind of conduct and behavior for the "new" Italian to emulate' (2004: 132).
13. De Benedictis notices this emotional range across the actor's career, arguing that Nazzari's heroic persona begins to crumble in *La donna della montagna / The Mountain Woman* (Renato Castellani, 1944), in which he plays a grieving widower: 'Here too the brash self-assuredness transmutes into a petri-

fied, otherworldly pain, even if moderately mitigated by a new love' (2005: 110).
14. According to Gundle, this has to do with Nazzari's star text: 'As often occurred with Hollywood stars, his films included nods or occasional amusing reference to previous roles (as when the former aviator Serra, in his guise as Woods, grabs the controls of a plane and diverts its course in *Centomila dollari*)' (2013: 198).
15. Nazzari plays an aviator once more in *Giorni felici* (Gianni Franciolini, 1942): 'It doesn't matter that, in the story, the charming aviator with whom the young women fall in love is named Michele; we all know he is the perfect embodiment of Nazzari, the actor. That image that was shaped by his own myth with a certain cross-section of the audience, especially with women', comment Pruzzo and Lancia (1983: 86), again stressing the importance of the relationship between Nazzari's persona and his roles.

CHAPTER 2

Returning: Im/mobility and Immigrant's Nostalgia

During his swift ascent to stardom in the mid- to late 1930s, Amedeo Nazzari played a variety of im/mobile characters in several genre pictures. He also lent his long stride and cheeky smile to a number of 'American' characters (a curious case of Italian cinema masquerading as foreign film), from the aforementioned workaholic businessman Mr Woods in *Centomila dollari* (Mario Camerini, 1940), to the womanizing violinist in *Dopo divorzieremo* (Nunzio Malasomma, 1940). Malasomma also directed him in *Cose dell'altro mondo* (1939), in which he plays a police inspector disguised as a gangster against the background of a (fictional) United States penitentiary.[1] These characters are of course different (and present the film historian with interpretive challenges of their own) from the Italian mobile subjects who come back from either North or South America, in accord with the historical narrative of the global diaspora, and who upon their return are quickly branded as *americani*.[2]

In this chapter, I will discuss a peculiar feature that can be observed in a cross-section of characters played by Nazzari during Fascism and beyond: that of being im/mobile, or of moving from a state of mobility at the beginning of the narrative to one of immobility at the end. Of course, the ideological reasons for this transition are entirely apparent in the films made during the Fascist regime. However, I will show that this quality will transfer onto Nazzari's postwar efforts – particularly those directed by Raffaello Matarazzo, a discussion of which will occupy Chapter 4 – and anticipates *Il gaucho*'s emotionally troubled engineer (Ing.) Maruchelli, whom I discuss in Chapter 5. In particular, the present chapter focuses on an array of films that feature Nazzari as a return migrant and an im/mobile character, zooming in on two very different titles: *Montevergine (La grande luce)* (Carlo Campogalliani, 1939)[3] and *La bisbetica domata/ The Taming of the Shrew* (Ferdinando Maria Poggioli, 1942). While the former is a rural family melodrama set in the early years of the twentieth century, the latter is the 'spiritual' sixth instalment in a series of romantic comedies and *telefoni bianchi* in which the actor plays opposite Lilia Silvi, a small-framed, highly energetic performer who excelled at trading barbs with the imposing Nazzari and at awakening his dormant comic timing.[4] Arguably, at least in the early years of his career in film, Nazzari was at his finest when sparring with the quick-tongued Silvi, who was trained as a dancer and could make up for Nazzari's physical stiffness, a quality that served him well when he was required to cut a statuesquely heroic figure, but that ultimately got in the way when he was cast in roles that demanded a certain agility and looseness in the limbs: Stephen Gundle reports that 'According to Lilia Silvi, he danced badly and he was tone deaf. Despite playing a musician, he is unconvincing in the musical *Dopo divorzieremo*' (2013: 198).

Before delving into *Montevergine* and *La bisbetica domata*, I shall briefly discuss two more films in which Nazzari's characters are singularly im/mobile without being migrants returning to Italy: first, the paper-thin romance *È sbarcato un marinaio* (Piero Ballerini, 1940), in which the Sardinian actor stars opposite Doris Duranti in the role of Gianni, a strapping sailor ever torn between the security of a land-bound love nest and the call of an adventurous life at sea – a predicament that, with the addition of a small child to complete the family portrait, Nazzari will face again in Raffaello Matarazzo's *Malinconico autunno / Melancholic Autumn* (1958). Heavily indebted to the 1938 poetic realist masterwork *Le Quai des brumes / Port of Shadows* (Marcel Carné), *È sbarcato un marinaio* purges the original narrative of its subversive potential, transforming the embittered deserter played by Jean Gabin into a cheerful seaman with a weak spot for tall blondes, as he puts it, and replacing the rebellious seventeen-year-old Nelly (Michèle Morgan) with a more age-appropriate Duranti – also named Nelly. Lovestruck, Gianni decides to settle down with the woman he meets at an amusement park, but when he suffers an accident and is temporarily incapacitated, Nelly has to find work. The woman falls prey to ruthless impresario Gomez (Enrico Glori), who furnishes her with a blonde wig and employs her in his titillating 'mermaid show', an attraction of dubious morality. When Gianni finds out, he decides to resume his travels, arguing that 'A ship, old friend, must be out at sea, and the sailor on the ship.'[5] However, labouring under the misapprehension that Gianni murdered Gomez out of jealousy and that the sailor is now trying to flee aboard a ship, the police stop him and temporarily imprison him. All is well in the end, when Gianni is freed and is reunited with a pregnant Nelly. Gone from the Italian romance are the sexual predator Zabel (Michel Simon) and the emasculated gangster Lucien (Pierre Brasseur), as well as the foggy atmospheres of Eugen Schüfftan's cinematography, which made *Le Quai des brumes* a ponderous meditation on human nature in the face of Europe's steep descent into moral bankruptcy. What remains is the port setting, a protagonist donning a sailor cap, and a general concern for a masculinity that, in the case of the Italian film, is simplistically predicated on a tension between mobility (appropriate for the young and unattached) and immobility (as a foundational property of the reproductive family unit that was so essential to Fascist biopolitics).

Second, it is also worth mentioning the singular case of the dual-language *Sancta Maria/La muchacha de Moscú* (*Saint Maria*, 1941), one of the titles directed by Edgar Neville during his two-year stay in Rome.[6] Based on the novel *Sancta Maria* by the Fascist writer Guido Milanesi (1875–1956), this rare film was made in Spanish and in Italian for the respective markets; the Italian version was supervised by Pier Luigi Faraldo. Nazzari plays Paolo Wronski, a Russian émigré who meets Nadia (Conchita Montes), a young Soviet journalist, on a cruise ship. The voyage soon turns into tragedy when a fire breaks out aboard the ship and Paolo saves Nadia's life. Billed as the first Italian anti-Bolshevik film, *Sancta Maria* is a straightforward romance, but its religious themes are quickly foregrounded: when the devout Paolo falls ill with leprosy, the atheist Nadia changes her ways and gives in to the Christian faith, praying to the Madonna of Pompeii for a recovery that will bring them back together. Of course, Nadia's conversion is to be understood in both religious and political terms: as Torre points out (2015: 162), if the model for *È sbarcato un marinaio* was French poetic realism, *Sancta Maria* is indebted to both Ernst Lubitsch's 1939 *Ninotchka* (another narrative of conversion from communism to capitalism) and to *Ben-Hur: A Tale of the Christ* (Fred Niblo, 1925), in which Jesus cures the protagonist's mother and sister of their leprosy. What is most relevant to this discussion, however, is the fact that Paolo chooses to seclude himself because he believes he is highly contagious. Once again, Nazzari's character moves from an initial state of extreme mobility (at the film's inception he is an émigré aboard a ship) to one of immobility and confinement, but that eventually leads to a romantic (and in this case, religious) reconciliation, generating another reproductive (and ideologically conforming) family unit.

The return migrant appeared so frequently in Fascist-era cinema that it can almost be considered a stock character: the subtle variations of his[7] backstory ran the gamut of human mobility, and Nazzari was far from the only actor to star in this role. On one end of the spectrum is Vittorio De Sica as the elegant Mr Brown, a first-generation Italian American car dealer (Bruni is the surname before its anglicization) travelling to Italy on business and reconnecting with his ancestral culture in *Due cuori felici/*

Two Happy Hearts (Baldassarre Negroni, 1932).[8] On the opposite end is the stoic-faced farmer Pietro Gori (Mario Ferrari) in Mario Baffico's *Terra di nessuno/No Man's Land* (1939), an oddly enlightened returnee with peculiar ideas on private property, land ownership, and community building.[9] While the tuxedoed Mr Brown is chaperoned into Italian society and culture by the charms of Anna Rosi (Rina Franchetti), whose side he will decide never to leave again, Gori is set apart from the rest of the characters precisely by his past and his experiences abroad, and this chasm dooms his prospects of reconciliation with his country and its people.

The heterogeneous array of films made during Fascism employed this character in its many incarnations, arguably to reinforce the regime's overall opposition to all kinds of unsanctioned human mobility, as the perils that doom Luciano Serra's migration (and deterritorialized return) exemplify.[10] Of course, totalitarianism required that the energies provided by able-bodied men be funnelled into projects of public interest, such as land reclamation and the building of satellite cities, agriculture, and the military. By writing this character into very diverse narratives that do not necessarily accommodate him easily, screenwriters inevitably resorted to similar rhetorical strategies across settings and genres: at times a disillusioned, jaded, or otherwise 'tainted' individual, at other times quirky, creative, even outright eccentric, the return migrant is a person who strives to find a way back into Italian society, having realized that his travels and cosmopolitan experiences simply cannot give him the happiness and wholesomeness that his (native or ancestral) country can offer him.[11] Generally speaking, when the character is secondary and serves as the protagonist's foil, this quest can be malicious and at the expense of others (as it will be for Paolo Verdesi in *Montevergine*); when the returnee is the protagonist or a supporting character allied with him, the choice to go back is simply a logical action following the composed realization that (Fascist) Italy is a good place for finding employment, meeting a spouse, raising a family, or even retiring. Such is the case, for example, for the returning family in *Camicia nera* (Giovacchino Forzano, 1933), the quintessential example of a propagandist film bent on providing a template for this kind (the right kind, according to the film's politics) of human mobility.

Often these characters present some interesting similarities: many start out as working-class people who left the country and made their fortune abroad, primarily prior to their appearance in the film in which they are featured. Armed with the experience acquired in this perennially offscreen world (an apparent visual symptom of Fascist-era cinema's stunted, often studio-bound mobility),[12] they carry with them the mystique of the exotic places they have visited, and they are enveloped in a strange aura of cosmopolitan knowledge. This is certainly the case for *Terra di nessuno*'s Pietro Gori, but also for John, the character played by Gugliemo Sinaz in Corrado D'Errico's *L'argine* (1938), whose mobility is circular: he leaves rural Italy in his youth; spends most of his adult life roaming around the world looking for his fortune (all of this happening before the story begins); returns to urban Italy, which proves to be still too pretentious for his taste; and finally retires to his rural hometown. When they have been successful in their travels, which is true in the majority of cases, they have acquired aggressive business skills. Initially, cynicism and a dubious moral status may accompany them, but since their arc prescribes some form of return (in most cases permanent) to the homeland, these negative characteristics are eventually curbed. Be it physical or simply ethical (as in the case of Luciano Serra), their return migration is always accompanied by the rejection of affectation and decadent behaviour, in lieu of which most of these characters proudly embrace their 'wholesome' Italian roots.[13]

In 1939, Carlo Campogalliani directed Amedeo Nazzari in two films: the remarkable peasant melodrama *Montevergine (La grande luce)*, and the less successful brigand adventure *La notte delle beffe*. Both period pieces, the films came into dialogue with *Strapaese*, the coeval literary and cultural movement that advocated a return to folklore and regional cultures, and that supported the populist and traditionalist side of the Fascist doctrine.[14] Walter L. Adamson describes it as

> an idiosyncratic, self-styled vision of a new regionally based Italy that would restore its public-minded citizenry, revive qualitative experience through close proximity to the land and to artisan traditions, and suppress those commercial distractions responsible for the softness and unmitigated materialism of the modern bourgeoisie. (Adamson 2001: 245–6)

Gathering around the periodicals *Il Selvaggio*, edited by Mino Maccari, and Leo Longanesi's *L'Italiano*, *Strapaesani* artists and intellectuals like Ardengo Soffici, Curzio Malaparte, and Ottone Rosai advocated 'a "return to order" that put a synthesis of classical and modern aesthetic values at the service of a Fascist politics' (Adamson 2001: 242).[15] The movement's xenophobic tendencies often translated into blatant anti-transalpine and anti-American slogans, while also calling for a 'return to the rural' in labour, leisure, and cuisine, as the following stanzas from Mino Maccari's 1928 *Il trastullo di Strapaese* demonstrate:

> A burp of your local priest is worth more
> Than America and its arrogance

Behind the last Italian
There are centuries of history [. . .]

Nightclubs and the Charleston
Make you lose your marbles
Oh Italian go back to dancing the trescone
and to eating omasum

Oh Italian go back to your clods
Do not trust the customs of France
Keep eating bread and onions
And you'll keep your belly at bay (Maccari 1928: 11)[16]

In the same way, *Montevergine* displays strong anti-modernist sentiments that translate into an approach to human mobility promoting an idealized return to one's roots based on feelings of longing and immigrant's nostalgia; in fact, the film exemplifies the two possible trajectories of *americani* who return to a rural setting (like *Terra di nessuno*'s Pietro Gori). Featuring a screenplay by Vittorio Malpassuti and Campogalliani himself, from a story by Guido Paolucci, *Montevergine* begins in 1912, and is set in a rural town in the Campania region located by the Montevergine sanctuary to the Virgin Mary.[17] The film's protagonist is Rocco Moretti (Amedeo Nazzari), a cobbler who flees to South America when he is unjustly accused of drunkenly murdering a townsman. Rocco is tried in absentia and is sentenced to twenty years in prison. Two years later a witness comes forth with the truth: the protagonist is acquitted, again in absentia, and he is allowed to return home safely. However, the unrequited affection of his South American employer Donna Manuela (Ivana Claar) jeopardizes his repatriation: the woman frames him for smuggling drugs, and Rocco must spend ten years in a Peruvian prison.[18] In 1924, Rocco is finally able to travel back home, only to learn that the architect of his doom, the return migrant Pietro Verdesi (Carlo Duse), is meddling with his daughter's plan to marry a decent young man, Alberto (Andrea Checchi). Armed with a knife, Rocco follows Verdesi to the Montevergine sanctuary, where the Virgin intercedes[19] to dissuade him from seeking revenge and opens his heart to forgiveness.

Originally titled simply *Montevergine*, but renamed *La grande luce* for distribution, the film was awarded the Coppa del Partito Nazionale Fascista (Fascist National Party Cup) at the VII Venice International Film Festival. A dark melodrama with marked Catholic overtones, the film received an overall positive review by Umberto Barbaro, who praised it in the pages of *Bianco e Nero* as 'The finest Italian film presented at the festival' (1939: 7). Gian Piero Brunetta briefly summarizes the film's main themes and rhetorical strategies:

> The film is an exemplary interpretation of the culture of a society whose values are tied to an archaic Catholicism; to a ruralist ideology as the locus for the preservation of such values; to an exalted nationalism and a consolatory displacement that covers up the theme of mass emigration. (The South American countries where the protagonist, Amedeo Nazzari, lives for a few years are depicted as places of vice, corruption, evil.) The topology of popular melodrama (*home-fatherland* vs. *elsewhere*) is binary. (Brunetta 1979: 511; my emphasis)

I would argue that, in its two-pronged exploration of the theme of return migration, *Montevergine* actually achieves rather nuanced and sophisticated insight, especially when compared with other Fascist-era titles dealing with the same subject matter. From the film's inception, the villain Verdesi is characterized by the markers of an *americano* as understood by the propagandist machine. In his travels he has achieved a certain social status and wealth, as evidenced by his clothes and demeanour, yet his heart is corrupt and he is incapable of leading an honest existence without deception and trickery. At the town's fair, Verdesi harasses Sabina (Leda Gloria), Rocco's wife, who had dared to reject his marriage proposal many years prior. Being unable to possess her is what triggers Paolo's resentment towards the handsome cobbler, and his desire to ruin him. When Rocco learns about this affront he confronts Paolo in the tavern; a brawl ensues, and in the chaos the bartender Gennaro (Giovanni Dolfini) kills an innocent man. Seizing the opportunity to get rid of Rocco, Paolo unjustly accuses him, an act that immediately sends the cobbler into exile and allows for the South American subplot to begin. Verdesi's misdeeds extend to Rocco's offspring in the second part of the picture, when he tries to muscle Alberto's father, a mild-mannered farmer, into selling him his olive oil at a submarket price, while also pressuring the man to dissuade his son from romancing Rocco's daughter Lucia. Even if his actions are governed by greed and personal interest at the expense of other characters, Verdesi is spared in the end. In fact, murderous revenge in Fascist-era cinema is rarely carried out: even when characters behave in the most despicable ways (as does Gomez in *È sbarcato un marinaio*), the desirable scenario is repentance, which is promptly followed by forgiveness and the productive reintegration into society of the wayward individual – *Terra di nessuno* constituting an outlier in this frequent narrative scheme. In other words, societal peace and collective interests are almost always preferred to individual gain and personal vendettas.[20] When Rocco ascends to the sanctuary intending to kill Verdesi, divine intercession allows for the men to reconcile, one experiencing shame and regret, the other forgiveness. The film's last shot is a close-up of their hands, united in a fraternal clasp, the former rivals humbly kneeling before the altar.

Differently from almost all other Fascist-era films, the innocent and the guilty are brought together not by their allegiance to the country or the nation, but rather by the power of religion, which is celebrated here as the supreme governing principle.[21] In order to pave the way for the unusual ending, the film displays many religious symbols throughout. In particular, the character of Lucia is directly associated with the Holy Cross. When she is still a little girl (played by Vandina Guglielmi), she helps her father cross himself at the sight of the town's religious procession. Unable to protect Rocco from the misdeeds of men, with this simple gesture Lucia reminds him to keep his soul and heart pure. Reminiscent of this moment, on her first communion Rocco sends her a necklace with a crucifix from his South American exile. As Giuseppe Gubitosi reminds us in his study, Nazzari's characters are often fathers, but even when they do not have offspring of their own, they take on paternal responsibilities towards a character or a group of characters, a fact that, the scholar argues, informed Nazzari's stardom and attracted the ire of certain cross-sections of critics and spectators, especially in the latter part of his career.[22] *Montevergine* is no exception to this general rule:

> Once more, in *Montevergine* also Nazzari plays a father, and again a very affectionate one toward his daughter. At the beginning of the film, the daughter fills the scene with her charming mannerisms, she's at the centre of the home and the shop, because her father's existence revolves around her. [. . .] Later, he fulfils his educational duties by telling the child about the pilgrims who travel to the Montevergine sanctuary. In fact, Rocco's fatherhood is directly linked to his religiosity. (Gubitosi 1998: 60)

As I have discussed, Rocco's migration to South America is prompted by his flight from justice, and brings upon him many misfortunes. He passes through Argentina and finally arrives in Peru. His transatlantic journey is narrated with a simple and elegant visual device: shots of a map showing the route, with a hand pinning the final destination, are interspersed with picturesque images of water glistening and a ship rolling on the horizon (Figure 1.3).

The protagonist's spatial displacement is carried out metonymically through several ports and means of transportation – a rhetorical device that directly recalls little Marco's travels in *Dagli Appennini alle Ande/ From the Apennines to the Andes* (Umberto Paradisi, Film Artistica 'Gloria', 1916). In his seminal work on the use of cartography in cinema, Tom Conley notes that

> a map in a film prompts every spectator to consider *bilocation*, which may indeed be cause for the resurgence of debates in which film is treated in terms of issues

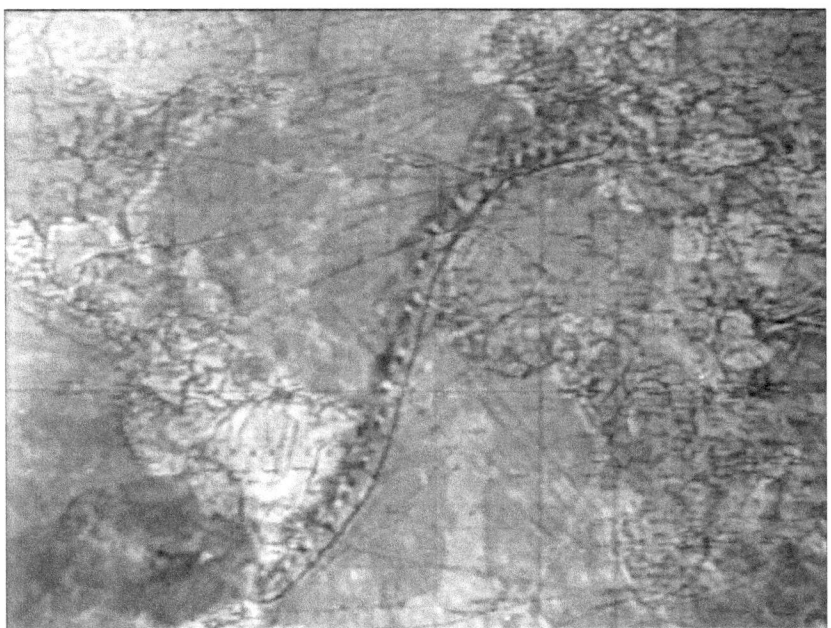

Figure 1.3 Italian bilocations: liquid surfaces and cinematic cartographies in *Montevergine*.

concerning identity. Identity can be defined in a narrow sense as the consciousness of belonging (or longing to belong) to a place and of being at a distance from it. (Conley 2007: 3)

Thus, this visual device situates the issue of identity with spectators, raising questions regarding their own position with relation to the nation (construed both in physical and in political/ideological terms). Moreover, according to the scholar, films themselves can be understood as functioning as maps, in that they perform the double gesture of building Euclidean representations of space as well as posing ontological questions, thus eliciting in the viewer a mix of curiosity for the unexplored and memory of the experienced. In the cinema examined in this chapter, the journeys are almost always signified via visual devices that provide some form of locational imaging, such as maps (*Luciano Serra pilota*), print-reel montages (*Centomila dollari*), or transportation hubs like harbours (*È sbarcato un marinaio*) and airports (*Luciano Serra pilota*, *Centomila dollari*). In scenes such as Rocco's flight in *Montevergine*, montage is the primary form of signification to indicate the passing of time and physical displacement through space: editing, therefore, becomes the means through which mobility is narrated.

At the beginning of his escape, Rocco is in Naples, by the pier where the ship is harboured, working the docks. He then boards the ship clandestinely, but he is able to befriend the boatswain, who is appreciative of the man's help. Once the ship reaches Argentina, Rocco flees the authorities again. On a train, he befriends Gonzales (Eugenio Duse), a shady trader who offers him employment in his distillery in Callao, Peru, boasting of his own professional success: 'I started with nothing, and in three years I came to own a distillery.' In cohort with Gonzales, Donna Manuela runs a cabaret where Carmencita (Elsa De Giorgi), an Italian singer with a Spanish stage name, entertains the predominantly male guests. When Rocco learns that the real nature of Gonzales's business is smuggling drugs and reselling cheap alcohol as fine imported wine, he leaves the distillery. Donna Manuela, smitten by the gallant Italian, hires him at the club as a bouncer. There, Rocco befriends the frail Carmencita. Their first encounter is triggered by the man's chivalrous attitude and national affiliation: the singer is onstage, clad in white lace that glows under the lights, and holds a fan to cover her face; even from a chromatic point of view, the woman does not belong in this sordid environment. A drunken brawl breaks out in the audience, interrupting her song. Rocco intervenes and re-establishes order, picks up Carmencita, deposits her onstage and concludes: 'I'm Italian as well. And now you can sing', respectfully addressing the chanteuse with the formal, regime-mandated pronoun *voi*.[23]

In the course of the film, we learn that both Carmencita and Rocco harbour the wish to return to Italy, and when Rocco learns that he has been retried and found innocent, he tells Carmencita, 'The hell with the distillery and having to look after the drunks. I'm returning to my town, among honest people who truly work!' Donna Manuela eavesdrops on the conversation, and in order to prevent Rocco from leaving, she plants some drugs in his suitcase. He is found out by the customs officers, and after an unsuccessful attempt at fighting his way out of the predicament, the strapping man is held at gunpoint by the guards. At first, he hangs his head in desperation, then slowly lifts his face up in camera view and looks off-screen left, his eyes desperate but hopeful, anticipating the divine intercession that will seal the narrative. This gaze will be replicated in the climactic ending, when Rocco surrenders his knife and his desire to avenge himself when kneeling before images of the Virgin Mary in the sanctuary. Music swells and the shot dissolves into ocean waves. In his imagination, Rocco travels back home. A slow dissolve introduces the cell bars that hold him captive, his hands clenching them. In superimposition, the year 1914 appears on the screen, gradually moving from the back to the foreground. A year count begins, and it quickly reaches 1924 (Figure 1.4). The

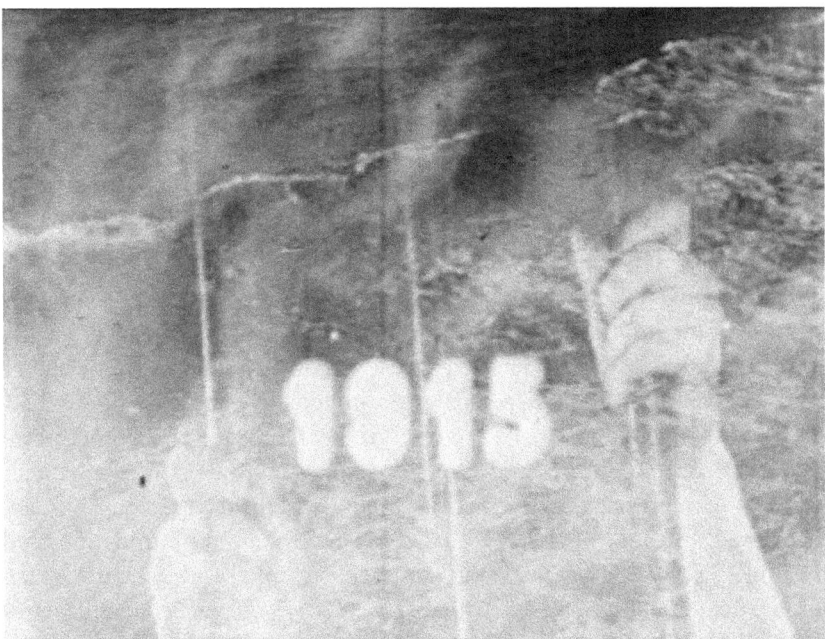

Figure 1.4 Mediating cinematic im/mobility: impermeable borders, porous time in *Montevergine*.

last number dissolves on a poster being glued to a wall, announcing the Montevergine fair and procession; an announcement for the same event had opened the film in 1912.

In her discussion of borders in contemporary film, Sarah Mekdjian argues that the manipulation of space and time that is intrinsic to cinematic devices such as editing and other visualization techniques can produce enhanced cartographies and mobile geographies that reflect the mutability of migratory patterns and their ever-changing geopolitical networks. According to the scholar,

> the displacements and migratory courses contribute, commensurately with their progression, to the evolvement of the border expanse, which constitutes itself 'along the way'. Several cinematographic techniques are reinforcing this progressive and ephemeral construction. The evanescent mention of toponymies or the appearance on the screen of illegible topographical maps translate the fundamental instability of the border expanse. (Mekdjian 2014: 797)

In other words, journeys of migration are 'imag(in)ed' in (by) the cinema: their rendering (and trans-mediation) through a series of visual techniques and manipulation of the image reflects the peculiar quality of borders of being simultaneously stable and mobile, porous and impenetrable, inclusionary and exclusionary. In *Montevergine*, Rocco is peculiarly free to enter and travel across South America: as cinematic projection of an ideologically defined idea of migrant mobilities, these boundaries are at the service of his escape and also later come to enforce his immobility – incarceration on foreign soil being the ultimate propagandist threat against emigration.

As Brunetta points out (1979: 393), the Peruvian subplot in *Montevergine* is clearly reminiscent of *Passaporto rosso* (Guido Brignone, 1935), and many characters seem almost interchangeable, which points to their ossification into this tradition of films. The virginal Carmencita is clearly modelled after Isa Miranda's schoolteacher-turned-reluctant-entertainer Maria Brunetti. *Passaporto rosso*'s unscrupulous trader, seedy impresario, and political agitator Pancho Rivera (Giulio Donadio) is split here into two characters, Gonzales and Donna Manuela. Into the single character of the fugitive Rocco Moretti are also condensed the righteous, amenable worker Antonio Spinelli (Ugo Ceseri) and the honest, unjustly exiled Gianni Casati (Filippo Scelzo) – another example of a dynamic Italian man whose mobility is eventually restricted. *Montevergine* also deviates from *Passaporto rosso*, which is ultimately a narrative of successful emigration and integration (but not assimilation), inasmuch as Rocco's fate abroad is largely negative; dishonest people take advantage of him, and he must serve jail time – a fate that, I have noted, many other Nazzari im/mobile characters suffer. In *Montevergine*, corruption is posited as the only way to succeed outside of Italy. It is safe to assume that while Rocco stands by his moral and ethical standards even abroad, Paolo Verdesi did not, and his corruption follows him home upon his return. However, Rocco's greatest mistake is lacking trust in Italy's judiciary, which results in having to serve a longer sentence (ten years instead of two) away from his beloved daughter.

As I have mentioned, echoes of *Strapaese* ethics are present in films that advocate for a return to the rural, from *Camicia nera* to *Passaporto rosso*, from *L'argine* to *Terra di nessuno* and *Montevergine*. However, both the literary movement and the listed films share the longing for a place of origin upon whose very absence their wishes are predicated. Their nostalgia is consonant with the kind described by Susan Stewart (1984), whereby they posit a return not only to Italy but to a wholesome (imagined) rural Italy as the only antidote to the decadence and moral corruption of both foreign cultures and city dwelling. Moreover, in *Camicia nera*, *L'argine*, *Terra di nessuno* and *Montevergine*, the characters' 'return to the rural' functions as wish fulfilment of fantasies of the 'future-past' described by Stewart, in an effort to ground (or to 'take root') in a reality that, as she underlines, only exists as ideological. Immigrant's nostalgia is, after all, a pathology affecting the mobile subject for whom 'the future becomes idealized, robbing the present of full psychic commitment' (Akhtar 1999: 126): unable to fully experience the present moment, the immigrant retreats into the past or daydreams about the future.

This temporal slippage can be observed in many of Nazzari's im/mobile characters, but it is present in many other manifestation of return migrants: for instance, *Terra di nessuno*'s Pietro Gori's return to the land brings to mind a specific type of *americano* described by Carlo Levi in his celebrated 1945 memoir *Cristo si è fermato a Eboli/Christ Stopped at Eboli*. Levi divides the returners into two categories that exemplify the temporal slippage described by Salman Akhtar: the peasants, who upon their return resume their former occupation and soon forget all about their sojourn in America (also exemplified by *L'argine*'s John, who resumes his duties as the town's restaurateur); and the small entrepreneurs who saved up overseas and return to open a business in their hometown (like the 'utopian' community founded by Pietro Gori). However, Levi also writes that both projects of reintegration ultimately fail: the peasants are forever doomed to destitution by an uncooperative soil, and entrepreneurs are met with resistance and envy on the part of those who stayed. Ultimately, return migrants are perennially asynchronous individuals whose former mobility is permanently embedded in their relationship with specialized language and technology. Levi chronicles that the community displays the subtle but tangible effects of its mobile citizens:

> Life at Gagliano was entirely American in regard to mechanical equipment as well as weights and measures, for the peasants spoke of pounds and inches rather than of kilograms and centimetres. The women wove on ancient looms, but they cut their threads with shiny scissors from Pittsburgh; the barber's razor was the best I ever saw anywhere in Italy, and the blue steel blades of the peasants' axes were American. The peasants had no prejudice against these modern instruments, nor did they see any contradiction between them and their ancient customs. They simply took gladly whatever came to them from New York, just as they would take gladly whatever might come from Rome. But from Rome came nothing. Nothing had ever come but the tax collector and speeches over the radio. (Levi 2006: 131–2)

In *Fontamara*, Ignazio Silone paints a similar picture, casting a shadow on the possibility of combining the Fascist and *Strapaesano* 'return to the rural' with American-style capitalist entrepreneurship in an agricultural environment based on feudalist latifundia:

> At one time the people of the mountains could at least emigrate to America. Before the great war, even people from Fontamara tried their luck in Argentina and Brazil.

> But those who were able to return to Fontamara with some bank notes between their skin and their shirt soon lost their small savings on the sterile, arid lands of their native heath, and fell back into the former lethargy, keeping the memory of their life abroad as a lost paradise. (Silone 1960: 10–11)

In Fascist-era cinema, *americani* return either as eccentric millionaires or as disillusioned individuals who have lost everything, which is consonant with Ruth Ben-Ghiat's observation that 'capitalist America [. . .] formed the biggest threat to the survival of Italian institutions and ways of life' (2001: 39), and therefore its myth needed to be deflated at every opportunity. Among the many *americani* played by Amedeo Nazzari in this decade is the protagonist of Gennaro Righelli's 1938 *Fuochi d'artificio*, a returnee who failed to find his fortune in America.[24] Nonetheless, Gerardo di Jersay takes residence in a hotel, and the rumour of his 'American-made' wealth begins to spread. Eventually, Scaramanzia (Giuseppe Porelli), Gerardo's personal secretary, makes millions on the stock market with money borrowed from his boss, who finds his fortune on his home turf.

To recapitulate, *Terra di nessuno* and *Montevergine (La grande luce)* used the vocabulary of rural melodrama to explore different permutations of return migrants' reassimilation into Italian society (as it was imagined by Fascist-era cinema): Gori starts a grassroots revolution, Verdesi embraces outright villainy to dominate his environment, while old Rocco privileges forgiveness and reconciliation. *Due cuori felici* preferred (and arguably, developed) the language of a romantic musical comedy to portray the return of a second-generation Italian American, Mr Brown, a character played by Vittorio De Sica who coyly affected foreignness by switching his /r/ to rhotic sound. In his favouring of Italy over America, De Sica's Mr Brown provides a template for Nazzari's Mr Woods, who will similarly abandon a lifestyle governed by capitalist pursuits for one of familial bliss. Although eight years separate the films, both display an anti-American attitude: yet, as Gubitosi writes, 'the interesting thing is, as far as the main character is concerned, that Woods discovers that he possesses, under his American clothing and behaviour, an Italian soul' (1998: 50).[25]

The last film in this chapter, Ferdinando Maria Poggioli's *La bisbetica domata* (1942), an abridged and uncredited adaptation of William Shakespeare's *The Taming of the Shrew* (1590–2), returns to that same comedic tone and recasts Amedeo Nazzari in the role of a return migrant.[26] A bubbly wartime musical comedy, *La bisbetica domata* is a prime example of a film in which an *americano* is shoehorned into the story for no other reason than to argue for the superiority of Italy over America and to advocate for return migrations. In fact, the picture becomes oddly political at times, with references to the ongoing conflict and the renovation of the urban landscape in which it is set. The choice to make Nazzari's character an *americano* seems rather arbitrary, in that it adds very little to the film's arc, which is precisely what makes it so interesting in the context of Fascist-era cinema's engagement with human mobility. Sergio Amidei wrote the screenplay with Poggioli, but at least three other writers contributed to the zippy dialogue: Gherardo Gherardi, Dino Falconi, and, uncredited, Giacomo Debenedetti. While the basic plot does not deviate radically from Shakespeare's original, some essential changes were made.

It is Rome, in the present day. Battista the tailor (Lauro Gazzolo) has two daughters he wants to marry off, the adorable Bianca (Rossana Montesi) and the insufferable Catina (Lilia Silvi). The flirtatious younger sister cannot be married before her venomous elder, but when the handsome Petruccio (Amedeo Nazzari) returns from America to his native Rome, the problem seems solved. He will marry Catina, allowing Bianca and Luciano (Aldo Capacci) to finally get engaged. Initially, the virago resorts to many tricks to avoid having to marry the iron-willed *americano*, but she eventually capitulates when their lives are endangered by an enemy bombing. The newlyweds spend their honeymoon in a castle, where Petruccio psychologically and physically torments his bride in order to break her spirit and curb her temper. In the meantime, three new couples form in Rome, not without much slapstick based on disguises, mistaken identities, subterfuges, and so forth. One night the castle burns down and Petruccio saves Catina's life, finally convincing her of the sincerity of his love. The couple returns to Rome, reunites with the other youths and their significant others, and the merry company sings the marital virtues of the 'tamed shrews'.

In Shakespeare's original play, Petruchio is a gentleman adventurer from Verona admittedly seeking his fortune 'farther than at home, / Where small experience grows' (1997: I.i.51–2), and his travels bring him to Padua, where he is persuaded to become Katarina's only suitor by Bianca's many wooers. Petruchio is born in English Renaissance theatre as a figure of mobility: the young man is motivated by his desire to explore and by the challenge presented by this arduous conquest, since he can already claim a privileged position from a financial point of view: 'Crowns in my purse I have and goods at home, / And so am come abroad to see the world' (II.ii.57–8). Nazzari's Petruccio's trajectory is somewhat different. Originally from Rome, the returning *americano* has made his fortune during his stay abroad before the film begins,[27] and he travels back to his native country at the news of the current war. Shakespeare conceived the character as an outsider, though not an exotic one, and set the play in the (to him) faraway land of Northern Italy. Amidei instead made Petruccio an insider with knowledge of the outside world (an emotional and psychological advantage, a measure of difference from the community in which he wishes to reassimilate), and kept the action domestic.

While the motives for Petruccio's interest in Catina's hand despite her notorious intractability remain unspecified throughout the film, the audience is given some clues into his heart by his evident attachment to his homeland. Before meeting him, we learn that while he was abroad, he kept a steady correspondence with Catina's father, never failing to renew his vow to marry her. Moreover, upon his return Petruccio marvels at the changes brought about by the recent renovations (clearly a nod to the regime's radical urban planning): 'By Jove, you have changed everything! It's incredible, it's wonderful!' Framed from below, his gaze off-screen right, Petruccio stands in awe before the results of Rome's *sventramento*.[28] Hence, Petruccio's voyage is framed as a homecoming, and even his most extravagant (and abusive) behaviour in the process of 'taming' Catina can be understood as motivated by his desire to re-enter Italian society and create a new family for himself. Perhaps a bit simplistically, and certainly not unproblematically, Gubitosi interprets the nature of their relationship as evidence of the couple's national character:

> Indeed, their relationship is typically Italian: he is authoritative, sure of himself, strong, and able to love without getting overwhelmed. She is temperamental, intolerant, sour, shrewish, that is a childish girl who must grow into an adult. And Pietruccio [sic], who has returned to Italy after having become rich and who wants to marry a fellow Italian, educates her using all means, leading her with his enthusiasm to become a real wife. (Gubitosi 1998: 63)

In many ways, Petruccio resembles Mr Brown (and by extension, Mr Woods, provided Italy is replaced with *Centomila dollari*'s fictitious Hungary): he is handsome, glamorous, rich, has the wisdom of a well-travelled man, is eager to marry an Italian woman, and enjoys Italy more than America. But Petruccio is also depicted as cagy and eccentric, if not outright sadistic and twisted, seldom explaining his quirky behaviour.[29] As Stephen Gundle notes, playing characters of this kind was not altogether uncommon for Nazzari:

> He was often haughty and solitary, ill-disposed to conversation or reflection, inflexible in his ideas and responses to people, traditionalist in his attitude to women, occasionally bullying (although his exaggerated performance as an unsympathetic lout in *La cena delle beffe* was unusual), short-tempered and self-centred. (Gundle 2013: 190)

Among his im/mobile characters, the sailor in *È sbarcato un marinaio* is occasionally misogynistic, and Mr Woods is often brusque and impatient, yet Petruccio's cruelty is unique to this character: in other words, if De Sica's gentlemanly charm in *Due cuori felici* was appropriate for 1932 audiences, by 1942 the critique of America (and of its 'false guiles') needed to cut more deeply, and Nazzari's imposing size and menacing presence in *La bisbetica domata* drive the point home.

Peter Adey writes that

> The processes which make our world work the way it does, however big and small and however imperfectly, from tourism to migration, from transport to communications, at multiple scales and hierarchies, depend upon highly uneven forms of mobility. Moreover, they rely upon and produce equally intensive and extensive forms of immobility. (Adey 2017: 11)

This inescapable reality can be observed directly in Fascist-era cinema, and in particular in the films produced during the period of 'autarchy' (1939–43) that followed the 1939 promulgation of the Alfieri Law, which progressively drove American cinema out of the Italian distribution circle. A dramatically isolated national industry[30] produced increasingly homebound films, in an ideological and aesthetic retreat that manifested itself on-screen in various ways: first, at the level of mise-en-scène, with landscapes, vistas, and panoramas created on the soundstages of Cinecittà or using stock footage (which is especially true for foreign-set films); second, at the level of plot, with characters often transitioning from diverse states of mobility (travellers, explorers, adventurers, pilots, capitalists, runaways, colonialists) to a variety of comparable immobilities (settling down, starting a family, taking root, returning to their hometown, becoming domestic). Simultaneously, Italian characters also found themselves temporarily immobilized on foreign soil, by means of forced, undesirable, or inescapable labour in a disreputable or secluded establishment, or, in the worst cases, imprisonment.

As this overview of the wide array of im/mobile characters played by Nazzari in the years between the mid-1930s and the early 1940s shows, Fascist-era cinema's preoccupation with human mobility was deeply ideological. However, as the chapter focusing on Nazzari's postwar mobility will clarify, Italy's ideological and political shift was not necessarily reflected in certain popular films, which continued to look at what lay beyond its national borders with a high degree of scepticism, if not with outright xenophobia. As a consequence, Nazzari's characters found themselves in similar circumstances, and developed along similar narrative and emotional arcs. But before I examine a sample of the actor's postwar production, namely his collaborations with director Raffaello Matarazzo, I will delve into a detailed analysis of the most egregious example of character im/mobility in late Fascist-era cinema, Carmine Gallone's 1943 *Harlem*, a film that directly attacked the United States using the Italian migrant, and the diaspora at large, as a lens through which to articulate an elaborate indictment of American society.

Notes

1. Although my take on these characters is slightly discordant from his, Steven Ricci offers a detailed analysis of the relationship between the Italian film industry during Fascism and the United States as a mighty cultural agent, especially via the cinema; see Ricci (2008: 125–55).
2. Mark Choate writes that both during the Liberal and the Fascist administrations, 'The state encouraged and welcomed all return migration, be it from patriotic loyalty, economic disappointment abroad or visits to family at home. Approximately half of Italian emigrants returned, bringing capital and experience with them. Upon return all emigrants regained Italian citizenship automatically, even if they had previously renounced it. [. . .] Those returning to their hometown from overseas were called "Americans" [*americani*] with the stereotype of wealth, independence, and exotic mystique' (2008: 8).
3. The copy I was able to examine at Cineteca del Friuli was a print of American provenance, as stated clearly in the title credits.
4. The other films being *Assenza ingiustificata/Unjustified Absence* (Max Neufeld, 1939), *Scarpe grosse* (Dino Falconi, 1940), *Dopo divorzieremo* (Nunzio Malasomma, 1940), *Scampolo* (Nunzio Malasomma, 1941), and *Giorni felici* (Gianni Franciolini, 1942). The charismatic Silvi is often cast alongside more conventionally beautiful leading actresses (Alida Valli in *Assenza ingiustificata*, Elena Altieri in *Scarpe grosse*, Vivi Gioi in *Dopo divorzieremo*, and Nice Ranieri in *Scampolo*) but in many films she ends up 'stealing' Nazzari's attention away from them by virtue of her ebullient personality.
5. The original sentence is 'Una nave, vecchio mio, deve stare sul mare, e il marinaio sulla nave.' The expression 'vecchio mio' recalls the French 'mon vieux', which is consonant with the rest of the film's references.
6. Produced by Film Bassoli, *Frente de Madrid/Carmen fra i rossi* (1939) also starred Conchita Montes, but featured different male leads: Rafael Rivelles in the Spanish version, and Fosco Giachetti in the Italian. On this film, see Nadal (1999: 121–41). With Julio Fleischner, Neville also co-supervised (and co-wrote the screenplay of) the Italian–Spanish co-production *Santa Rogelia/Il peccato di Rogelia Sanchez* (1940) by Productions Hispánica and Safic. The Spanish version was by Roberto de Ribón, and Carlo Borghesio helmed the Italian one. According to Torre (2015: 149 n. 431), in this period Neville also collaborated with director Augusto Genina on the first draft of a screenplay that would eventually become *L'assedio dell'Alcazar/The Siege of the Alcazar* (1940), also produced by Renato and Carlo Bassoli. For more on

Neville's Italian films, see Aguilar (2002: 53, 132); Carratalá (2007: 259–75); Torre (2015: 148–63).
7. As discussed, this character is almost always male, with the notable exception of Doris Duranti's Mailù (*Sotto la croce del Sud*, Guido Brignone, 1938) and Dolores (*Giarabub*, Goffredo Alessandrini, 1942).
8. The film is a remake of a German picture directed by Max Neufeld, titled *Ein bißchen Liebe für Dich (Zwei Glückliche Herzen)/A Bit of Love (Two Happy Hearts)* (1932), which is based on the play *Geschäft mit Amerika (Business with America)* by Paul Frank and Ludwig Hirschfeld. In the Italian screenplay, Aldo Vergano and Raffaello Matarazzo raise important questions regarding the national affiliation of the handsome Mr Brown, which is certainly a symptom of great interest in the diasporic communities of the New World and their relations with Italy. For more on this, see Zambenedetti (2012: 73–8). In Amleto Palermi's 1938 *Partire/Departure*, Vittorio De Sica plays Paolo Veronda, a young Neapolitan man who is itching to leave the country and seek his fortune abroad. A romantic musical comedy like *Due cuori felici*, the source of the film's humour is the initial clash and subsequent understanding between the wealthy Milanese family of entrepreneur Anteo Diana (Giovanni Barrella) and the romantic Veronda, who reluctantly finds himself employed in Diana's farm machinery company. The event that brings the two groups of characters together is an automobile accident caused by the reckless driving of Anna Diana (played by the Argentine-born María Denis). In a heart-rending scene in the harbour, Paolo sees off his friend Giovanni (Gianni Altieri) as he boards a commercial ship headed to Genoa in the hope of finding passage to Lisbon, the Portuguese Azores islands, and finally Mexico. Eventually, Giovanni returns, disappointed by the experience and in need of work. By the end of the film, this return migrant also finds himself employed by Diana. In other words, the film argues that the creation of a synergy between Italy's industrial and agricultural sector, a crucial tenet of Fascism's economic policies, is the solution to the emigration issue. Ultimately, the narrative prevents Veronda's international mobility, but rewards his loyalty to the homeland by furnishing him with a love interest (Diana's classist daughter Anna). In a way, this character can be understood as Mr Brown's mirror image. Finally, the film gently nods to De Sica's breakout performance as a mechanic and driver in Mario Camerini's 1932 *Gli uomini, che mascalzoni!*, as he is often shown behind the wheel of a convertible – his competence with automobiles allowing him to move swiftly between city and countryside. For a detailed discussion of how Vittorio De Sica's particular brand of stardom emerged in his collaborations with director Mario Camerini, see Landy (2008: 46–56) and Gundle (2013: 144–65). Bruni also devotes a chapter of his book to this film (2013: 60–73).
9. Directed by Mario Baffico, the film's screenplay is a composite of two novellas by Luigi Pirandello, *Romolo (Romulus)* and *Requiem aeternam dona eis Domine! (Grant them eternal rest, O Lord!)*. Under the pseudonym Stefano

Landi, Pirandello's son merged them into the short story *Dove l'uomo edificò* (*Where Man Built*), on which the screenplay is based. The copy I was able to examine at Mediateca Toscana was a 1985 Cineteca Nazionale restoration from an American print that was confiscated at the outbreak of the Second World War. Unfortunately, two reels were missing from the positive, and the restorers inserted intertitles to explain the plot. Judging from what the intertitles relate, it is safe to say that the missing reels would have not impacted this analysis significantly.

10. Other titles featuring returners are *La cantante dell'opera* (Nunzio Malasomma, 1933), *Non c'è bisogno di denaro* (Amleto Palermi, 1933), *L'albero di Adamo/Adam's Tree* (Mario Bonnard, 1936), *Joe il rosso* (Raffaello Matarazzo, 1936), *Fuochi d'artificio* (Gennaro Righelli, 1938), *Due milioni per un sorriso* (Mario Soldati, 1939), *Tragica notte* (Mario Soldati, 1942), and (depending on the version, as I will explain later) *Harlem* (Carmine Gallone, 1943). Steven Ricci conflates Italian returners with Italian Americans and also lists another 1936 film directed by Raffaello Matarazzo, *L'anonima Roylott*, as well as *Chi sei tu?/Who Are You?* (Gino Valori, 1939) and *Grattacieli* (Guglielmo Giannini, 1943) (2008: 142). I would contend that, although part of the same ideological attack on America (which will culminate in 1943 with *Harlem*, discussed later), returners (or *americani*) are quite different from pretend Americans: the former interface with the longer history of Italian mobility, of which they acknowledge the cultural and political magnitude, while the latter sidestep it altogether, constituting a cinema that is effectively masquerading as foreign film (Italian pictures cheekily but unconvincingly dressed up in American paraphernalia).

11. I use the masculine pronoun because in the overwhelming majority of cases this character is male.

12. The aforementioned *Partire* is a prime example of a film about geographic and social mobility without the ability to effectively represent either: the film's opening scene is very clearly shot on a soundstage (pretending to be a trattoria in the Bay of Naples), and rear-projection is used so extensively that it produces a curiously alienating effect, the actors often awkwardly pretending to walk while standing in front of a screen.

13. This admonishment against the dangers of xenophilia is not exclusively a quality of male characters: see, for instance, the romantic comedy *La contessa di Parma* (Alessandro Blasetti, 1936), in which the matronly Marta Rossi (Pina Gallini) curbs the rampant Francophilia of a fashionable Italian boutique. While much rarer, there are also cases of returning female characters, often found in empire films such as Goffredo Alessandrini's 1942 *Giarabub*, in which Doris Duranti plays the nomadic prostitute Dolores Deltalish, who experiences a narrative of conversion back to her original Italian identity of Antonietta Pieri.

14. *Strapaese* was against the forced modernization of cities that characterized much of Fascist urban policies. Interestingly, one of its most illustrious par-

ticipants, the writer Curzio Malaparte, was also involved in the creation of its specular opposite, *stracittà*, which advocated modernization and urbanization. In her seminal work on landscape in Italian postwar cinema, Noa Steimatsky summarizes the tensions between regionalism and modernism that coexisted in Fascist rhetoric, which are epitomized by the rise of these two competing (and complementary) intellectual movements. According to Steimatsky, the two polarizing trends emerged from this inherent ideological tension: 'one conspicuous regionalist movement was strapaese ("ultra-country" or simply regionalism), which coexisted alongside stracittà ("ultracity" or urbanism) as Fascist themes in response to the rapid industrialization and first full experience of modernity in the Italian 1920s and 1930s. Strapaese's regionalist cult posited itself as the pure Italian alternative to technology and to the internationalist modern culture of the city, which it understood as un-Italian and thereby un-Fascist' (2008: 186). For more on this, see Luciano Troisio (1975).

15. In his 1931 *Terra madre/Mother Earth*, Alessandro Blasetti presented the *Strapaese* ethics in a classic arrangement of Manichean dualism, borrowing its themes from F. W. Murnau's *Sunrise: A Song of Two Humans* (1927): urbanites versus peasants, new money versus old wealth, innovation versus tradition, sexual promiscuity versus abstinence and modesty. While Corrado D'Errico's *L'argine* (1938) is certainly consonant with *Strapaese*, his experimental film *Stramilano* (1930) is perhaps the most notable example of an Italian city symphony film; similarly to Walter Ruttman's 1927 masterpiece *Berlin: Die Sinfonie der Großstadt/Berlin: Symphony of a Great City*, D'Errico's *Stramilano* both celebrates and critiques the rhythms of urbanization and industrialization. For more on this, see Pucci (2012).

16.   Val più un rutto del tuo pievano
   Che l'America e la sua boria:
   Dietro l'ultimo italiano
   C'è cento secoli di storia [. . .]

   Tabarino e ciarlestone
   Ti fanno dare in ciampanelle
   O Italiano ridatti al trescone
   Torna a mangiare il centopelle

   O Italiano torna alle zolle
   Non ti fidar delle mode di Francia
   Bada a mangiare pane e cipolle
   E terrai a dovere la pancia

   I am not aware of a published translation of Maccari's 1928 text, in the absence of which I provide my best effort at it.

17. Pruzzo and Lancia opine that for its precision in the depiction of the rural setting, and its attention to labour, 'some critics would even attribute the film

with an anticipation of neorealism, which is, frankly, too much. Certainly, when it first appeared, *Montevergine* was impressive for its mastery of (film) language and the authenticity of some settings (those that are clearly Italian, not the ones related to a South America that was scrapped together using the Roman countryside)' (1983: 52).

18. In their plot summary, Pruzzo and Lancia (1983) report that Rocco escapes to Argentina, which is only partially correct, as I will discuss later.
19. This conversion narrative exhibits many similarities with the aforementioned *Sancta Maria*.
20. This may be one of the most striking differences with coeval American cinema, which consistently prefers individual action and societal retribution over rehabilitation.
21. A notable exception to this rule is the late Fascist war films, as I argue in Zambenedetti (2017).
22. This quality becomes even more prominent in the Matarazzo-directed runaway melodramas. For more on Nazzari's embodiment of the Italian *pater familias*, see D'Amelio (2018).
23. On the use of *lei* versus the Roman *tu* and *voi*, see Ruffin and D'Agostino (1997: 69–71).
24. In her anecdotal biography of her father, Maria Evelina Buffa reports that Nazzari could not travel to Eastern Italian Africa to shoot the battle scenes of *Luciano Serra pilota* because he was simultaneously shooting *Fuochi d'artificio* and the comedy of errors *La casa del peccato* (Max Neufeld, 1938) (2008: 72). It is truly an extraordinary coincidence that one of Nazzari's most mobile characters, the heroic pilot, is figuratively immobilized and confined to a studio backlot by Italy's most popular actor's shooting schedule.
25. Much like *Luciano Serra pilota*'s real-life immobility, the fact that Woods actually finds this Italianness in (pretend) Hungary is not without irony.
26. Pruzzo and Lancia note that 'the familiar story of the embittered and despotic girl who is tamed into submission by the young husband is transposed to fit modern clothes (but the film makes no mention of its illustrious author, with whose fatherland Italy is at war' (1983: 80).
27. In the first beats of Poggioli's film, the future father-in-law enquires, 'Did you manage to make a million?' Petruccio replies, 'Well, more or less.'
28. Literally, 'gutting'. It was a radical and invasive city plan that razed many houses to the ground in order to make way for roads and boulevards. For more on this, see Cederna (2006).
29. Another picture in which the 'dubious' qualities of a (pretend) American character are put to good use is *Joe il rosso* (Raffaello Matarazzo, 1936), a gangster-comedy hybrid based on the play by Dino Falconi. In this film, French aristocrat Stefano Sandelle-Lafitte (Luigi Pavese) marries the orphan Marta (Luisa Garella) while on a transatlantic journey to America. Unbeknownst to him, his bride's only surviving relative is the notorious criminal Joe Mark (Armando Falconi), aka Joe il rosso. But when a painting

goes missing from the family estate in Côte d'Azur, Marta calls upon her uncle to find it.
30. With the notable exception of Spain, whose film industry became largely intertwined with Italy's (especially at the level of personnel and co-production) following the end of the revolutionary war.

CHAPTER 3

Fighting:
Wartime Im/mobility in *Harlem*

Harlem (1943) is the last picture made under the Fascist regime to devote its entire narrative to Italian emigration to the United States. At the helm of this prestigious production was director Carmine Gallone, a veteran filmmaker who worked abroad during the interwar period, acquiring knowledge and experience in Weimar Germany, France, and Great Britain. Courted by the regime, the director eventually returned to Rome, putting his skills at the service of the freshly revamped national cinema. Because of his taste for grandiloquent sets and large, sweeping epics, Gallone is often likened to Cecil B. DeMille, and his most famous picture, *Scipione l'Africano/Scipio Africanus: The Defeat of Hannibal* (1937), reflects this grandiose aesthetic.[1] *Harlem* is stylistically and thematically different from Gallone's epic biopic of Publius Cornelius Scipio, but the director's penchant for large crowd scenes and elaborate sets is apparent in several instances; most notably, in the climactic boxing match at 'Madison Square Garden' – which, as we shall see, is really Cinecittà studio no. 5.

As film historian Pasquale Iaccio writes in his book on Gallone, *Harlem* is particularly significant because, 'based on a story of emigrants from Sorrento and set in a New York tainted with materialism and gangsterism, [it] is perhaps the only example of an anti-American film made in Italy during the war' (2003: 16). As I argued in the previous chapter, *Harlem* is not unique in this regard. However, Iaccio is correct in noting that the story combines anti-Americanism and Italian migration, and as we shall see, this is an important fact that, in the midst of the Second World War, makes *Harlem* a perniciously anachronistic film.

As is well known, in the same period a small number of films seemed to anticipate the revolution that would arrive soon after the end of the conflict with the advent of Neorealism: Mario Soldati's *Tragica notte/ Tragic Night* (1942), Alessandro Blasetti's *4 passi fra le nuvole/Four Steps in the Clouds* (1942),[2] and most of all Luchino Visconti's *Ossessione/Obsession* (1943) displayed the signs of an imminent ethical and aesthetic renewal, while others, such as *Harlem*, kept toeing the ideological line. War and colonial films, in particular, continued to be conservative, and celebrated the bravery of Italian soldiers even when defeat or death were the inevitable outcome of battle.[3] With few notable exceptions (such as *La bisbetica domata*), family dramas and romantic comedies glossed over the conflict entirely. Historical pictures and costume dramas remained focused on the glories of dead patriots and cultural icons. Not only is Gallone's film firmly lodged in this entrenched tradition, it also openly attacks the United States, which was historically one of the major destinations of the Italian diaspora for the better part of the 1930s and was still one of Italy's primary cultural interlocutors, in spite of Fascism's autarchic and isolationist policies. In sum, *Harlem* is one of the last incarnations of a worldview that was about to face its inevitable demise.[4] As Pruzzo and Lancia summarize,

> 1943 is the year of two traumatic events taking place on 25 July and 8 September. Enthusiasm, anxiety and political and military backlash naturally affect the cinema. Films were planned and never made; some were finished hastily or remained unfinished; others were destined to be finished or distributed after the war. Cinecittà shuts down: in the fall part of the film stock and the equipment travel north on bombproof wagons. The Repubblica Sociale chose Venice as a new site for the film industry; but few actors, directors, and technicians would respond to the call. (Pruzzo and Lancia 1983: 92)[5]

Harlem is the last feature film Amedeo Nazzari shot in 1943 that obtained distribution that same year.[6] Also in 1943, Nazzari starred in Nino Giannini's *L'invasore/The Invader*, which was delayed until 1949, and in *La donna della montagna/The Mountain Woman* (Renato Castellani), which was released in late 1944.

In a letter dated 3 October 1946 and addressed to the Sottosegretariato Stampa Spettacolo e Turismo, the Ente Nazionale Industrie Cinematografiche (ENIC) announced that CINES had prepared a new cut of *Harlem* for postwar redistribution. The document states that,

> thanks to opportune cuts and modifications, new dialogues and mixing, all the political and propagandist elements that informed the first edition of this film have been abolished. The new edition, which is titled 'KNOCK-OUT', retains the spectacular and artistic qualities of the earlier film, while being much nimbler. [. . .] We believe that the modest role played by the actor Osvaldo Valenti would not provoke in the audience reaction of the political kind. (Figure 1.5)[7]

The film's original 1943 cut was removed from circulation in the postwar period, and only recently rediscovered and restored.[8] A copy of *Harlem*'s *cineromanzo*[9] still survives at the Biblioteca Luigi Chiarini of the Centro Sperimentale di Cinematografia (*Harlem* 1943), and it sheds light on the

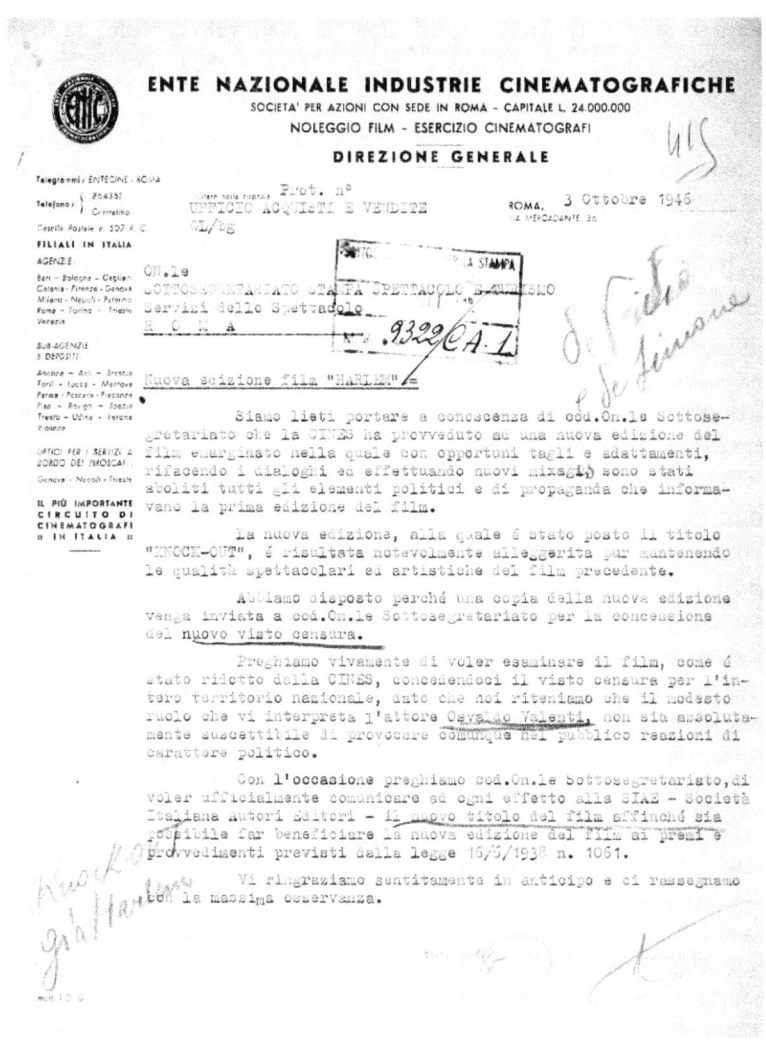

Figure 1.5 ENIC letter to the Sottosegretariato Stampa Spettacolo e Turismo. Archivio centrale dello Stato, authorization no. 1620/2020, MinCulPop, 1926–45, D.G. Cinematografia, b.7, f.164. Courtesy of the Ministero per i beni e le attività culturali e per il turismo.

many changes between the two versions. One of these is the excision of an important sequence depicting the breaking out of the Second Italo-Abyssinian War and the ensuing escalation of racial tension between the two ethnic groups, which I will discuss later.[10]

Tommaso Rossi (Massimo Girotti) is a young architect who travels to New York City in the company of his nephew Tony (Gianni Musy),[11] in order to reunite with Amedeo (Amedeo Nazzari), who is Tony's father and Tommaso's older brother. Amedeo had migrated to the United States many years prior and is now a wealthy entrepreneur and a respected member of the community. At a gala, the famous prizefighter Bob Bull[12] publicly provokes Tommaso, and to everyone's surprise the Italian migrant knocks him out with a single blow, gaining immediate popularity. Talked into trying out professional boxing, the strapping young man begins training in Ben Farrell's gym (Enrico Glori)[13] under the benevolent eye of Italian American coach Frankie Battaglia (Erminio Spalla). In the meantime, Amedeo tries to acquire Barney Palmen's cabaret joint (Luigi Almirante) and convert it into a movie theatre, in the hope of salvaging the Italian neighbourhood from the nefarious activities of his rival Chris Sherman (Osvaldo Valenti), who plans to encroach upon it and corrupt it. Tommaso makes a name for himself in the ring, but Amedeo repeatedly pleads with him to quit fighting and offers to hire him in his construction business. The brothers have a falling out when Amedeo hits his younger sibling during a quarrel. Tommaso, distressed, inebriated, and angry at his brother, turns to Sherman. The shady businessman takes advantage of the rift, and frames Amedeo for the murder of Joe Smith (Luigi Pavese). Amedeo is sent to jail, awaiting trial, and his properties are confiscated. Tommaso must fight the reigning heavyweight champion Charlie Lamb (Ludovico Longo)[14] and win the prize in order to restore Amedeo to his position within the Italian American community. But Sherman's minions kidnap Tony to keep Tommaso out of the ring. With the help of his loyal friend Pal (Enrico Viarisio) and his love interest Muriel (Vivi Gioi), Tommaso rushes to the crooks' hideout, fights them, rescues Tony, and makes it back to Madison Square Garden in time for the big match. Amedeo listens to a radio broadcast of the fight from behind bars. Cheered on by the Italians in the audience, Tommaso boxes his way to victory and collects the prize money.

The postwar cut I was able to examine at Mediateca Toscana ends with the family's merry reunion upon Amedeo's release, and refocuses the narrative onto the boxing scenes and the romance between Tommaso and Muriel, and away from the strictly anti-American propaganda of the original cut. However, as I hope to show with this analysis, the excisions are meaningful not only in the context of a discussion of institutional history (as evidenced by the recirculation during the postwar period of Fascist-era films whose political content could not be effectively disguised in the editing room), but also in the way they activate discourses of nationalism and mobility across the social and political threshold represented by the compounded historical events of the armistice, the civil war, liberation, and the ensuing transition to democracy.

As the ENIC letter confirms, many passages in *Harlem*'s dialogue were altered in the postwar cut and did not even employ the original actors' voices. One such sequence is that devoted to the Second Italo-Abyssinian War and racial tensions: this segment begins with a parade of black 'Americans' carrying pro-Abyssinian signs and pelting the 'Palazzo d'Italia' (presumably the Italian embassy) with rocks. From a medium shot of the affronted Italian seal, the film cuts to the prison where Amedeo is detained, where his guards are listening to a radio newscast of the war's latest developments: the Italian invaders are losing ground to the Ethiopians. The captors approach his cell and taunt the man, who first takes offence and jumps to his feet, but then kicks a stool and walks away defeated, hands in his pockets. The two black occupants of the neighbouring cell, however, become animated; one starts banging on his stool, and the other begins jumping up and down while holding on to the bars. The camera tracks in, framing them frontally, and then the film dissolves to a different black man holding the slatted backrest of a chair and hitting it with a liquor bottle – the inherently racist connotations of the visual match cut here are obvious. A dolly reveals that we have travelled to a busy jazz club where the nightly festivities are interrupted by news of the war. Charlie Lamb, the black boxer Tommaso will fight in the film's climax, grabs an ice bucket and begins a collection for Abyssinia. The next scene takes place at Ben Farrell's gym, where Frankie Battaglia is refereeing a training match between a white and a black pugilist; when the latter fails to obey his order to break from his opponent, and dares to call him a 'dirty Italian' to boot, the seasoned trainer knocks him out of the ring with a single punch.

As we learn from the *cineromanzo*, both versions of the film miss a sequence in which

> The news of the conflict caused a wild reaction in Harlem, New York's negro borough. Riots erupted in the streets, and the shops of our fellow citizens were targeted by the negro crowds. Thousands of honest workers, guilty only of being Italians, found themselves unemployed overnight. The police and the authorities were absolutely indifferent. (*Harlem* 1943: 29)

Instead, in the original version it is Frankie who laments this state of affairs with Farrell, who gets the idea of stoking the flames of the ethnic enmity by organizing the fight between Charlie Lamb and Tommaso Rossi. Most importantly, the film's postwar cut ends with Tommaso and Amedeo reuniting in front of the police station after the fight. However, as the print restored by the Cineteca Nazionale confirms, *Harlem* originally ended on a much more negative note; as James Hay describes:

When the young brother wins a bout against an American Negro [sic] fighter, he pays for his brother's release from jail; but soon thereafter, the older brother is shot and killed by rival gangsters. As he lays dying, he insists that his young brother give up boxing and return to Italy, since nothing good will come to him in America. (Hay 1987: 93)

In their book *Il Ventennio in celluloide*, Alberto Rosselli and Bruno Pampaloni report the same ending: 'As soon as he is released, Nazzari is cowardly killed. But before he dies, he manages to urge his pugilist brother and his friends to return to Italy' (2005: 68). In his volume on Fascist-era cinema, Guido Aristarco also writes about a return migration that was excised in the postwar print: 'With Harlem, Carmine Gallone returns to the theme of the Italian emigrant returning from America' (1996: 100). The *cineromanzo* also contains this tragic ending:

Found innocent, a few days later Amedeo was released from jail: unfortunately, he would not go far. The bullet from a machine gun pinned him to the ground, just outside the prison. In an ambush, Chris had claimed his revenge. A week later, Tommaso, Muriel, Tony and Pal left New York aboard the 'Rex' on their way to Italy: because this was their land, and in Italy they shall live, far away from that cursed country that only offered them tears, pain, and loss. (*Harlem* 1943: 30)

The film's propagandist goals are very clear even in the abridged postwar cut. As Hay notices, '*Harlem* was made during the years when *official* animosities toward America were widely proclaimed in Italy' (1987: 93; emphasis in the original), and this stance is indelible. In fact, according to Rosselli and Pampaloni, the film belongs to a 'sottogenere' (sub-genre), that was specifically conceived in an attempt to discredit the political and economic structures of enemy nations (2005: 224). Official documents confirm this thesis: a 1943 report to the Minister of Popular Culture Gaetano Polverelli by the director of the Direzione Generale per la Cinematografia[15] Eitel Monaco lauds the film for its political content:

I have attended several screenings of the film: the audience has whistled loudly, and often, at the negroes [sic], the Abyssinians, the American policemen and the gangsters, clapping frenetically for the Italians and when our hymns were chanted. Similar reports arrive from all other cities. The efficacy of popular propaganda stoking hatred toward our enemy reached by this film is great and without precedent: we suggest that HARLEM's 'formula' is considered when preparing other films. (Figures 1.6 and 1.7)

Of course, the film's true intent was not lost on contemporaneous film critics: in his June 1943 review for *Bianco e Nero*, Antonio Pietrangeli points to the aesthetic limits of *Harlem*'s skewed cinematic vision:

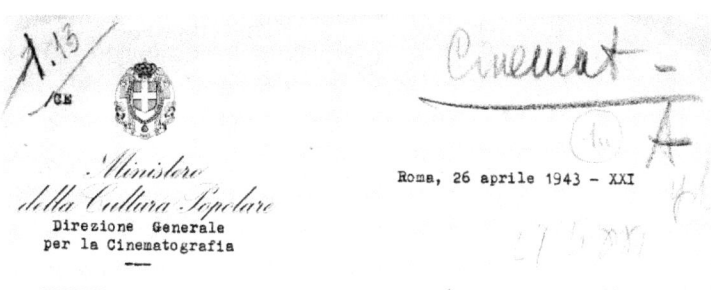

Figure 1.6 Report by DGC Director Eitel Monaco to the Minister of Popular Culture Gaetano Polverelli. Archivio centrale dello Stato, authorization no. 1620/2020, MinCulPop, 1926–45, Gabinetto, Affari Generali, b.143, f.988. Courtesy of the Ministero per i beni e le attività culturali e per il turismo.

The America in which the film is set is entirely artificial, all clichés, entirely lifted from the abstract indications of American movies. In their turn, the latter were already an obstinate and unchanging stylisation, colourless and conventional. In essence, this film's authors gave the audience a surrogate of those American films whose evocative fascinations still have a grip on our moviegoers. Therefore, the

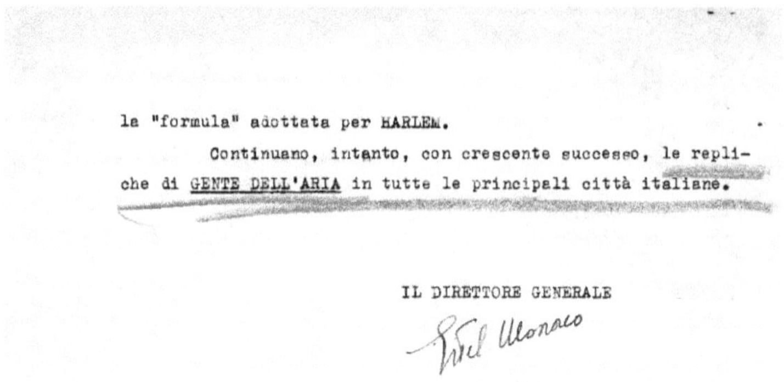

> la "formula" adottata per HARLEM.
>
> Continuano, intanto, con crescente successo, le repliche di GENTE DELL'ARIA in tutte le principali città italiane.
>
> IL DIRETTORE GENERALE
>
> *Eitel Monaco*

Figure 1.7 Report by DGC Director Eitel Monaco to the Minister of Popular Culture Gaetano Polverelli. Archivio centrale dello Stato, authorization no. 1620/2020, MinCulPop, 1926–45, Gabinetto, Affari Generali, b.143, f.988. Courtesy of the Ministero per i beni e le attività culturali e per il turismo.

> characters, the affectations, the life of the 'villains,' the situations, the developments, the solutions are copied from the American models. (Pietrangeli 1943: 34–5)

The appropriation of American motifs and scenarios was not uncommon in the 1930s and 1940s,[16] and *Harlem* is far from being the only film attempting to synthesize and combine tropes borrowed from American film with the regime's propagandist agenda. In her book on anti-Americanism in 1930s Italy, Michela Nacci gestures to American cinema as a discursive framework through which the Italian intelligentsia interrogated transatlantic relations:

> The strong identification of America with cinema played a fundamental role in the development of a negative image of American civilization. This allowed for an expression of reservations, and sometimes contempt, for a *made-in-America* culture, which in some instances were motivated by the analysis of financial indicators of the Old World and the New, in some others by the reflection on the fall of all civilizations and of the European one in particular, and finally by the historical-anthropological analysis of the *homo americanus*, with his lack of history and his constitutional infancy. (Nacci 1989: 149; emphasis in the original)

As both contemporaneous and modern critics agree, the results of this 'formula', as Eitel Monaco described it, are in reality far from perfect. However, the film remains an important document for a discussion of Italian cinematic mobilities, in that it grapples with the myths and knowledge of America that reverse migrations infused into Italian culture, while trying to actively discourage emigration by portraying the United States

Figures 1.8 and 1.9 Amedeo's mediated im/mobility: reading the news and listening to the radio broadcast of Tommaso's final fight.

in a very negative light. Moreover, the trajectory of Amedeo Nazzari's character is, unsurprisingly, consonant with the ones discussed in the previous chapter, moving from a state of social and physical mobility to one of immobility.[17] In fact, Amedeo is behind bars for the film's entire second half, learning about his brother's fortune (and misfortune) in American society primarily via newspapers and the radio (Figures 1.8 and 1.9).

Based on a novella by Giuseppe Achille, the script for *Harlem* was written by Sergio Amidei and Emilio Cecchi. Over two long journeys, the latter had spent a considerable amount of time in North and Central America in the 1930s, and commented extensively on the experience in two memoirs titled *Messico* (first published in 1932) and *America Amara* (*Bitter America*, published in 1939). If on the surface the postwar edit of *Harlem* is a glossy sports and romance film, it is clear that Cecchi's observations inform its political core. Therefore, his memoirs are a crucial tool to gain a better understanding of *Harlem*'s negative critique of US society and culture, as Giuseppe De Santis points out in his otherwise scorching review of the film. The critic and future Neorealist director praises Gallone's precise direction while condemning the screenwriters' departure from *America Amara*'s sophisticated indictment of the United States, asking, 'Why, oh why, this betrayal of factual truth on the part of someone who, at other times, could look clearly at that same truth?' (De Santis 1943: 280). Moreover, in line with the emphasis on realism that will emerge in his own cinema, De Santis suggests that a more nuanced approach to storytelling could represent an efficient way for genre cinema to be a propagandist tool: 'Presenting our audiences with the same America he saw in his book, with all its defects and also the pity it inspires, this would have been propaganda for a brighter intelligence and, more importantly, with a higher sense of humanity.'

Harlem's principal photography was carried out in Cinecittà's massive studio no. 5 (Teatro 5), the legendary facility where Federico Fellini would shoot most of his films from *La dolce vita* (1960) onward, and where Martin Scorsese would return for his *Gangs of New York* (2002).[18] In a note housed at the Archivio Carlo Montanaro, Francesco Pasinetti comments on the artificial nature of this enormous set:

> At studio 5, the largest one, where Gallone works, people come and go. It doesn't matter that the theatre is open, because we are on an ocean liner approaching New York. The City's skyscrapers are outlined against the night sky. It is an accurate reconstruction by Guido Fiorini. For once, Carmine Gallone has left behind the music, the singers, the saccharine subjects. He now wants to remake America, the boxing world. Some time ago he was looking, through his production director Jacopo Comin, for stock footage: New York Streets, city backgrounds.[19]

As the Venetian critic remarks, the film also features a number of long shots and panoramas of New York City, especially during the title credits and as a way of transitioning between scenes. This stock footage, which closely resembles the aestheticizing shots of classic city symphonies of the previous decades, unapologetically drops the viewer into the urban environment, evoking the experience of the metropolis's hustle and bustle. However, the clash between the polished studio sequences and the rough stock-footage produces the strange effect of underscoring the artificiality of the former, and the authenticity of the latter. In these brief passages, the busy American cityscape looks more like a product of rampant conurbation than cohesive urban planning, its screen texture is crowded and unappealing, the large billboards dwarf the viewer, the electric lights blind the eye rather than glowing seductively. It is the portrait of an unforgiving mid-century New York City poised to become the privileged location for stylized film noir and realist police procedurals.

The title credits open with a shot of the Chrysler building, the camera panning downward along the skyscrapers' streamlined contours, the principal players' last names rushing to the foreground in a dynamic contrast of motions. Two more panoramic shots of the city follow, moving rightward at different speeds and angles, and finally an aerial shot drifts over the dense metropolis. This vertiginous high angle, almost a bird's-eye view, replicates the sensorial experience that is so commonly associated with verticalization in American urban architecture, of which Cecchi was very openly critical.[20] About the film's opening, Pasinetti writes:

> The skyscrapers are all lit up. Leaning on the railing, the ocean liner passengers admire the view. The actor Giuseppe Addobbati has a line to say; they try it once, twice, three, seven times. Finally, even the crowd movement looks spontaneous. Ready, action![21]

While the postwar edit focuses immediately on Tommaso and Tony, the original cut opens with short exchanges between Italians from different regions remarking on New York's skyline and history. Tommaso and Tony stand on the deck of the *Rex*[22] while it quietly rolls into New York Harbor, and admire stock footage of Manhattan's skyline by night. Tommaso enquires about the skyscrapers and Tony enlightens him, pointing out the Empire State building, the Chrysler building, and the Commodore Hotel,[23] where his father Amedeo lodges. His eyes filled with admiration for the city's magnificence, Tommaso stands before the camera and points his finger at buildings that exist in the off-screen space and behind the spectators' shoulders. With his gesture, not only does he establish himself as the audience surrogate in this cinematic journey to America, he also creates relations between the diegetic and the extra-diegetic space, between studio and stock footage, between the flatness of painted backdrops and the complexity of Emilio Cecchi's account of the city.[24] Their sightseeing is interrupted by the announcement that they will not be able to disembark until morning. As they turn to face the officer giving them the news, the camera cuts to a medium-long shot of the passengers on the deck, and the stock footage that had functioned as a reverse shot for the duo's conversation is replaced by the painted backdrop of a generic metropolitan skyline. While the same backdrop had opened the original cut, in the postwar edit this abrupt transition has the effect of turning the narrative from the personal to the collective: as intended, the film becomes an opportunity to reflect on the journeys it symbolizes, conjuring up a 'Nuova Yorke' that exists as a mythologized diasporic space firmly lodged in the collective imaginary of generations of Italians.[25] Most importantly, by showing the assembly of people looking at a painted backdrop of the skyline, this shot envelops the spectator in the crowd of travellers. At least in the director's ambition, the film's cityscape operates on a cognitive as well as a visual level, functioning as what John Urry defines as

> imaginative travel, by which distant events, personalities and happenings are mundanely brought into the living room and transform everyday life. As a consequence we imagine ourselves sharing events, experiences and personalities with many others, with whom we constitute certain kinds of community. (Urry 2000: 70)

Before Tommaso and Tony can disembark the ship, they need to meet with immigration officers, who separate American passport holders from the immigrants. The first shots of this brief scene are excised in the postwar cut, which inexplicably places the boy and his uncle in different crowds. Both groups appear well fed, well groomed, and well dressed, but while Americans breeze through the inspections, immigrants are treated rudely by the officers, who accuse them of stealing jobs from the '12 million unemployed' United States citizens.[26] While the postwar cut again chooses to focus immediately on the protagonists, the original cut spends a considerable amount of time showing Europeans getting rejected or sent to Ellis Island for further screening.

From a purely historical point of view, the film here makes a precise statement on the Rossis' social status: at that time, when requesting admission to the United States, first- and second-class ocean liner passengers were questioned by immigration officers directly aboard the ship, possibly in their cabins. Conversely, steerage passengers were processed through Ellis Island, which was in use until 1954. Political scientist and sociologist William Walters argues that, when studying mobilities, 'vehicles matter because they are mobile zones of governance and contestation in their own right' (2015: 473). He advocates for a scholarship that foregrounds, rather than obfuscates, the enmeshment of transportation technology, infrastructure, geography, economics, and migration. 'Viapolitics', as Walters terms this approach, 'orients us to see migration from the middle, that is, from the angle of the vehicle and not just the state' (2015: 269). Of course, as Peter Adey notes, paying attention to vehicles and other mediated mobilities also means interrogating their function as (political and spatial) borders (2017: 212). As the analysis of this particular juncture exemplifies, I contend that Walters's invitation can be extended to a medium-specific, 'cinematic viapolitics' aimed at extending mobility studies to a metaphorical (and by definition, interstitial) 'middle' of the film.

In the original cut, it is Pal's confident intercession with the immigration officers that secures Tommaso's unhampered entry into the country. Amedeo's quick-mannered friend whispers something to the uniformed

American, who proceeds to stamp Tommaso's passport, instilling the suspicion amongst the other Italians that he surely must be a 'raccomandato' (a person having connections) – a term that hints at the possible corruption of the border police. The postwar cut removes Pal's intervention, and awards Tommaso a degree in architecture, which grants him passage despite the officer's judgemental remark that he is 'a sort of artist'. The elegant Tommaso casts an image of the Italian emigrant that goes against the grain of the stereotype of the ragged peasant looking for better days, lending itself to the postwar cut's deception, in which his lines, and those of the immigration officer, were clearly added using different voices, as they do not match the actors' lips movements.[27]

The Rossis' spatial transition between the ship and the Commodore is elided and conveniently replaced by more stock footage of New York City landmarks; dynamic wipes and upbeat music usher the characters into the hotel lobby, where the concierge, just like the officers, is fluent in Italian. The trope of speed (the same speed that Tommaso will master in the ring, and that will allow him to save the day) is introduced by Pal and Tony, who are accustomed to American ways. Even in these transitional scenes, the postwar cut prefers shorter shots and interactions, while in the original edit Pal takes the time to explain to Tommaso that American hotels do not bother checking their guests' papers, because they only care that they pay their bills – again suggesting that in the United States, profit is more important than safety and propriety. The large hotel is luxurious but functional; Tommaso marvels at the comforts of modern technology featured in his room, but Tony jokingly rebukes his uncle: Italy has the same things, so why is he so impressed? Striving to puncture the myth of technological (and by extension, military) American superiority, the film's rhetoric strangely coils around itself: by dismissing the modernity of Cinecittà's obvious set for the 'Commodore Hotel', isn't Tony unwittingly taking a shot at Italy's filmmaking crown jewel?

The Italians' position in American society is defined by contrasting them with other characters, and always at the expense of the latter. When the French-speaking bellboy drops Tommaso's luggage in his room, the well-mannered gentleman enquires with Pal about the tipping protocol. With a smile, Pal informs him that in America tipping is considered rude, and that such a gesture would offend the bellboy. However, when the same action is performed by the (presumably) African American porter, the latter lingers in the room, expecting some compensation. Tommaso promptly tips him, but not without a rather snide remark:

Tommaso: I got it. You don't get offended, do you?
Bellboy: No, no, sir, I never offend, poor negro [sic]. Thank, thank, sir!

Speaking with a very strong dialect and poor grammar,[28] to the modern viewer the porter offers a horribly offensive characterization of a black man, but it also speaks volumes on the linguistic policies and the attitudes towards the colonial subjects that were transferred to continental Italy.

This racist comparison is also evident during the climactic fight scene at 'Madison Square Garden' – an 'imagined' location that in reality is an assembly of disparate materials. In fact, for this extended sequence the film's editors Renzo Lucidi and Maria Rosada utilized stock footage of a real fight between a white and a black fighter – given the banners that are visible in these shots, they are possibly of New York City's Madison Square Garden III, which was in business from 1925 to 1968 – and original material shot in Cinecittà featuring Massimo Girotti sparring with Ludovico Longo. The difference between these materials is truly jarring: the stock footage of the massive arena is dark, raw and journalistic, while the Teatro 5 shots are well-lit, smooth and elaborately choreographed: if the opening scene on the ship had allowed the viewer's imagination to construct New York City's space and architecture, this assemblage of ill-fitting parts brutally reins it in while foregrounding the film's many limitations.

The fictional fight scenes take place in a large and ingeniously reconstructed arena populated by a racially segregated audience. After a long tracking shot establishes that the audience is predominantly black, the editors alternate between the two groups, setting up visual vignettes at the expense of the supposed African Americans. For instance, one juxtaposition shows a white woman calmly eating some candy followed by a crazed black man biting a piece of rim off his straw hat. In his foreword to Umberto Lenzi's 2009 *Terrore ad Harlem*, a crime novel inspired by the film, Gianfranco De Cataldo gossips that the black extras were 'prisoners who were detained in a nearby camp and hired for the occasion thanks to the mediation of some high-ranking regime officer temporarily enamoured with the latest *starlet*' (in Lenzi 2009: 5).[29] It is not difficult to imagine how audiences in 1943 might have perceived and coded the 'African American' characters, from the bellboy to the Madison Square Garden audience, especially considering the negative characterization of black people state propaganda had been offering at least since the Ethiopian war.[30] The original cut film defines Italians as underdogs outnumbered by their black counterparts, placing one community in Brooklyn and one in Harlem, juxtaposing Amedeo's Italian theatre with the black jazz club, and allowing the screen cohabitation of both ethnic groups only in the elegant Commodore

Hotel, where the former are guests and the latter appear as low-ranking staff or musicians, and at Madison Square Garden. The postwar cut retains the racism of the original, but deploys it in a different way, mostly as highly offensive comic relief to an otherwise tense and dark story that involves the alarming possibility of straining, or even severing, family and national ties alike by choosing to assimilate into the American way of life.

The community of Italians living in New York, some of whom are American-born, exist in what Arjun Appadurai calls the 'diasporic public spheres', which to him are, ironically, 'the crucible of a postnational political order' (1996: 22). Contact and organization along ethnic lines is exhibited over several scenes that not only drive the narrative forward, but also provide positive and negative models of citizens living in the diaspora. If Appadurai imagines that 'the engines of their discourse are mass media (both interactive and expressive) and the movement of refugees, activists, students, and laborers' (1996: 22–3), in *Harlem* the sites for national solidarity are luxury hotels, dance halls, cabarets, nightclubs, and boxing gyms. Tommaso's trainer, for instance, declares he was born in Italy but migrated as a child: played by famed boxer-turned-actor Erminio Spalla, Frankie Battaglia exhibits his diasporic identity in his anglicized first name.

Among the positive models of diasporic citizenship is also the protagonist's love interest, Muriel, a first-generation Italian American who expresses her desire to visit Italy upon making Tommaso's acquaintance. The film's treatment of this character is more intricate than it might seem on the surface; her desire to be identified as Italian is fairly explicit in the ballroom scene, but at a later stage Pal ribs her for being too American: 'You cook like an American! You would even put jam on spaghetti!'[31] Muriel oscillates between love object of mitigated exoticness, a feature that entices Tommaso, and her Italian girl-next-door status, which makes her an ideal prospective spouse, and allows for the story to conclude on conciliatory tones – and even with the repatriation of her diasporic self. When Tommaso attempts to describe why he is acting according to the mores of his country of origin, he begins by saying, 'You see, Muriel, in my country we say that those who live on hope . . .' and she corrects him immediately: 'in *our* country', clarifying that in broader geopolitical terms, her loyalty lies with Italy.[32] The two first meet in the extravagant hotel ballroom, where Nazzari's character is also introduced. Clad in an impeccable tuxedo, Amedeo Rossi confidently strides to Tommaso's table and warmly greets his brother, apologizing for his tardiness, which was caused by some trouble with his aircraft.[33] Both the original cut and the *cineromanzo* contain some key lines regarding Tommaso's mobility that have been excised in the postwar print: when Joe asks about his plans for the younger sibling, Amedeo replies,

'He goes back to Italy in a few weeks! Lucky him! I'll stay in America, and that's enough!' 'America gave you money!' replies Joe; 'And troubles . . .', concludes Amedeo (*Harlem* 1943: 3).

While dancing with Muriel, Tommaso first suffers, and then reacts to, the provocations of the square-chinned Bob Bull. Bull's public knockout by the fist of an amateur boxer makes the front page of all the major newspapers. Consistent with the same stylizations utilized in *Luciano Serra pilota* and *Centomila dollari*, a classic print-reel montage provides (ideological) colour to the action:

Herald Tribune:	A Foreigner Knocks Out Bob Bull
The Observer-Star:	Bob Bull Knocked Out
Record Herald:	A Young Italian's Extraordinary Success
New York Chronicle:	*A Fellow Citizen* Knocks Out Bob Bull (my emphasis)

The meaningful progression of these titles should not go unnoticed. If, on the one hand, the *Herald Tribune* foregrounds the foreignness of Bob Bull's opponent and *The Observer-Star* does not mention him, on the other hand, the *Record Herald* highlights the man's nationality together with the extraordinary nature of his feat. But it is the headline of the *New York Chronicle* that truly captures the viewer's attention. The title aligns the journalist who wrote it and the paper's projected reader with Tommaso from a national point of view. Metonymically, such a headline would also connote the paper as an Italian paper, whose readership must be composed mostly of expatriates. Two more such montages appear in the film's original cut, with such titles as 'Italy vs. Ethiopia! Brooklyn vs. Harlem' and '"I Will Knock Out Negro Pride!" Says the Italian', providing Amedeo's jailers with an opportunity to taunt him, and worrying him about his younger sibling's safety.

While Tommaso's instant success prompts him to pursue the American dream via boxing, for which he shows a splendid talent, his series of victories trouble Amedeo, who tries to dissuade him from this dangerous but lucrative activity. During a conversation in Amedeo's office, the audience is also privy to the hardships and sufferings he has met on the long road to his success; in other words, the film quickly clarifies that Tommaso's swift rise to the top should not be taken for granted by any Italian harbouring a wish to migrate. Amedeo's slow and perilous ascent is the fruit of twenty years of hard work in a foreign land. Modesty and level-headedness are illustrated as the preferred qualities that lead to a successful life – and, we should note, one that should be pursued in the motherland. Moreover, not every Italian in New York City manages to achieve the Rossi brothers' status and wealth. As Amedeo tells us, two-thirds of the city's masons are, in fact, fellow countrymen. This small but significant piece of information, which on the surface denotes some national pride, reveals that the majority of unskilled labourers that start off as simple bricklayers remain just that, and even Amedeo's philanthropic work is directed at them. The Rossis are gifted with special talents, and not every immigrant should aspire to their greatness. The consonances between *Harlem*'s Amedeo and *Il gaucho*'s Maruchelli will become apparent in Chapter 5; at this stage, it should be noted that both are businessmen who built empires in the Americas, yet they are immobilized by their success, and they work strenuously to retain contact with their ethnic and cultural roots. In other words, Maruchelli is a commentary on Nazzari's overall career, and on these roles in particular. Robert Stam and colleagues call it celebrity intertextuality, or 'filmic situations where the presence of a film or television star or celebrity intellectual evokes a genre or cultural milieu' (Stam et al. 1992: 211). Of course, Maruchelli's 'mental illness' is also a direct jab at the cultural institutions and legacy of Fascist film, with its many im/mobile, yet extremely nationalistic, characters.

Harlem's rhetorical strategy shrouds itself in genre conventions, its 'abroadness' being a way to both appropriate and critique its American models. The film's bankrupt stance on race, gender, and class, as well as its scathing critique of an 'imagined' American society, are expressed through an appropriative practice based on the imitation of genre models and the integration of Fascist ideology, a characteristic that is still very much palpable in the purged postwar cut. Based on inclusion through national allegiance, this rhetoric targets Italian mobility by providing examples of how to navigate it properly: this is clearly shown in a variety of other instances, all corresponding to the main characters, who invariably demonstrate their loyalty to Italy, or at least their preference for Italian over American culture; for example, at the cabaret, where Muriel sings two Italian songs, one of which is 'Comme facette mammeta' ('As Your Mother Made You'), a Neapolitan standard set to a tarantella beat.[34] Later, when Pal is watching Tony, he croons 'Lacreme napulitane' ('Neapolitan Tears'), a 1925 song written by Libero Bovio and Francesco Buongiovanni in which a Neapolitan immigrant addresses his mother and describes the sacrifices and tears he must endure to earn America's 'bitter bread'.[35] Moreover, just before the boxing match with Grand Bullock, Joey informs Tommaso that the Italians of Brooklyn have bet a total of 50,000 dollars on him, furnishing the audience with another example of the 'correct' way to exist in the diaspora: by showing support for fellow countrymen. National solidarity ushers in the prestigious cameo of two boxing champions of the time, Primo Carnera and Enrico Venturi, who, unlike Erminio Spalla, play themselves – in particular, Venturi utters words of support and nationalism: 'Keep up the good name of Italian sport, ok?!'[36] In the original cut, the famed pugilists appear again, and Carnera even threatens violence against Black Eagle, a representative of the Ethiopian community, before the Madison Square Garden fight.

The danger of Tommaso's assimilation through his boxing career looms from the pages of newspapers, which dub him 'Tom Rossi' in the print-reel montage that visualizes his string of victories, to the very back of his robe, where his name is contracted into an even more English-sounding 'T. Ross'. Amedeo tries to redress this anglicization by reminding his friends that 'Once and for all, my brother's name is Tommaso!' It is in the course of the climactic fight, however, that Tommaso's true (tri)colours shine through: almost out for the count, the fighter gets up when he hears the cry 'Go Italy!' ring through the crowd, proceeding to defeat his opponent.[37] His victory is followed by another disembodied voice screaming 'Long live Italy!', extending Tommaso's triumph to that of the nation. The original cut tells an entirely different and much bleaker story, however, one that makes Americans openly hostile to the Italian pugilist, and that also appears in the *cineromanzo*: 'While he was down, he heard the cry "Down with Italy! Death to the Italians!"' (*Harlem* 1943: 25).

A further example of surviving nationalist rhetoric in the postwar edit comes to the fore during a conversation between the suave Amedeo and his nemesis, Chris Sherman, that is both in the film and in the *cineromanzo*. When asked why he is interested in purchasing Barney's cabaret, the older Rossi sibling replies that he plans to reclaim the whole neighbourhood ('bonificarlo') on behalf of his fellow Italian denizens, to whom he will provide decent housing for a dignified life. His word choice is tinged with Fascist overtones and recalls the language that was used to write the Pontine Marshes and the new cities narrative. But the significance of his plans reaches beyond the contingency of Fascist politics. Amedeo's (and the film's) aspirations cannot be understood as exclusively philanthropic, but colonial in nature. By stating his intentions to reclaim the neighbourhood and build a community of Italians *in* America,[38] the entrepreneur is clearly tapping into the long tradition of *La Grande Italia* (The Larger Italy), which dates back at least to the Liberal era. A philosophy of human mobility, La Grande Italia attempted to spin Italian emigration into voluntary colonization,[39] finding the silver lining of mass emigration in the opportunity to build Italy on foreign soil. This approach clearly clashed with the realities of integration and assimilation, especially in the United States where, as Donna Gabaccia notes, 'the history of modern migrations from Italy is in large part a history of state efforts to incorporate migrants into multi-ethnic nations' (2000: 10). The biopolitical nature of the film's rhetoric is even clearer in the original cut; on the night of Tommaso's fight with Grand Bullock ('The Bulldog From Cincinnati', as a newspaper article calls him), Amedeo elects to attend a fundraiser of the 'Nuova Italia Society' for the 'Opere Assistenziali Italiane' (Italian Charitable Organizations), where the conversations focus primarily on remittances and transatlantic family ties – and on Amedeo's value to the community. Of particular interest is the comment uttered by a character with a thick Veneto accent, who remarks that 'for us, Italy is the mother, and America the wife'. Here, Amedeo also delivers a nationalistic speech in which he bashes those who lack attachment to the motherland and promises to build a neighbourhood for Italians in the borough of Brooklyn because, as he puts it, he wants his fellow citizens 'to live like a great people, and not like negroes' [sic].

Ultimately, despite the bankrupt political agenda that the postwar excisions fail to conceal, *Harlem* remains tangible evidence of a widespread preoccupation with the well-being of the many mobile Italians in North America at a time of great suffering and strife; while its worldview is deeply flawed, it is *a* view of the world nonetheless.

Notes

1. 'Because of his vast body of work, his proclivity for the colossal and the popular, his smooth style, his cunning acquiescence to the audience's taste, his surprising longevity (his first film dates back to 1914), his instinct for the spectacular and his innate slapdash attitude, G. can be considered a sort of European DeMille' (*Film Lexicon* 1959: 911).
2. The list includes a number of films starring Aldo Fabrizi and/or Anna Magnani, such as *Avanti c'è posto* . . . (Mario Bonnard, 1942), *L'ultima carrozzella* (Mario Mattoli, 1943), and *Campo de' fiori* (Mario Bonnard, 1943). Vernon Jarratt reports that 'Blasetti, working in a field strange to him, that of sentimental comedy, directed in *Quattro Passi fra le Nuvole* (*A Stroll in the Clouds*) the only pre-war Italian film so far to have had any success, post-war, in England' (1951: 51). The film's palatability to audience members of a recent enemy nation is evidence of this shift from regime-friendly filmmaking to more challenging (and realistic) depictions of Italian living conditions and customs.
3. On this, see Zambenedetti (2017).
4. For evidence of *Harlem*'s sustained anachronism, one need look no further than the language employed by the characters. Valentina Ruffin and Patrizia D'Agostino note that the film consistently prefers Italian boxing terminology to English and French words, even when these appear in older films. The scholars conclude that 'it becomes clear, when comparing *Rubacuori* (1931) with *Harlem*

(1943), that during the autarchic period the technical Italian vocabulary, as it is emancipating and solidifying, finds in the cinema a powerful tool for repetition' (1997: 68). Since 1923, the Gentile school reform had emphasized a transition from the dialects to standard Italian, and by 1929, all the schools in the country adopted the same textbook. The advent of film sound also introduced a neutral, nimble, artificial language that resisted any regional inflections and often levelled class differences. See Raffaelli (1992); Rossi (2006, 2007). Conversely, historian Mark Choate reports that linguistic homogeneity was an impossibility amongst migrants, and that regional divisions proved comforting to the expatriate communities: 'Whether in Europe or in America, speaking dialect was the epitome of local tradition, unintelligible to foreigners and interlopers. The comfortable insularity of an intact local identity made transatlantic migration more liveable and successful. Regional expatriate units formed small economic niches and eased the uncertainties of return migration. By contrast, the study of written, standard Italian provided no immediate rewards and often appeared superfluous. [. . .] If an Italian emigrant learned to read and write a new language in the Americas, it was usually the local language – English, Spanish or Portuguese – rather than standard Italian' (2008: 107–8).
5. Of course, Pruzzo and Lancia are referring to the fall of the Fascist regime (25 July), and the public announcement of the signing of the armistice between Italy and the Allied forces (8 September). For more on this, see Morgan (2007).
6. According to Pruzzo and Lancia, *Apparizione/Apparition* (Jean de Limur, 1943) was shot in the spring of 1943 but was released in the winter of the same year (on 23 December), during the German occupation (1983: 91). The film's running time is only about seventy minutes.
7. Osvaldo Valenti and his partner Luisa Ferida were among the personnel that relocated to Venice when the Italian Social Republic (RSI) was established. Valenti eventually joined the X^a Flottiglia MAS, and was shot by the partisans in April 1945. In 2008, Marco Tullio Giordana directed *Sanguepazzo/ Wild Blood*, a film based on Valenti and Ferida's story.
8. My analysis of the film is based on a comparison of the postwar cut with the restored edition and the *cineromanzo*. The word 'negro' is used in both versions of films, as well as in the *cineromanzo*.
9. This is similar to a Photoplay, in which the film's plot is transformed into a short story accompanied by captioned stills from the film.
10. Of course, this also means that *Harlem*'s original cut was set in 1935, which explains why the surviving version strangely omits any reference to the armed conflict between Italy and the Allied forces, but focuses strictly on the high price paid by two upper-middle-class Italian brothers for their professional and personal success in New York.
11. On his second screen appearance, the young actor is billed in this picture as Gianni Glori.
12. The fictional boxer is probably modelled on real-life Italian American wrestler and actor Bull Montana (1887–1950).

13. Born Enrico Musy, the actor was Gianni (Glori) Musy's father.
14. Researcher Luca Martera, who is currently writing a book-length study of *Harlem*, has identified this actor as Ludovico Longo, an engineer, rugby player, and amateur boxer who studied at the University of Rome. Martera hypothesizes that Longo was the son of an Italian officer and an Eritrean woman. IMDb lists him as Abrata Batha Longo: see <https://www.imdb.com/name/nm1548074/> (last accessed 17 August 2020). I was unable to verify the credibility of this account.
15. La Direzione Generale per la Cinematografia was the film branch of the Ministero della Cultura Popolare (MinCulPop).
16. Raffaello Matarazzo's 1936 *L'anonima Roylott* is effectively an 'American' gangster film about the young chemist Giorgio Harris (Mino Doro), whose talents are exploited by his employers, the Roylott brothers (Italo Pirani and Carlo Lombardi). When the siblings are killed, their lawyer Giorgio Evans (Camillo Pilotto) takes the fall. Sentenced to the electric chair, Evans will be proven innocent at the eleventh hour, but the experience will leave him forever scarred. In the same fashion, Guglielmo Giannini's 1943 *Grattacieli* focuses on the investigation following a man's dubious fall to his death from a balcony. The American setting of these films is used to distance, physically and morally, the corrupt gangster lifestyle from Italy and its 'wholesome' citizenry.
17. Of course, given that the original ending focused on the fate of Nazzari's character, the postwar excision of his murder becomes particularly relevant to this discussion.
18. While working on his films, Fellini would also take residence in a small apartment located above the facility's storage rooms. Interestingly, Teatro 5 seems to have been used, time and again, to stand in for New York City. To this day, its facade is decorated with stencilled English-language signs, the residue of past productions.
19. Fondo Francesco Pasinetti, Archivio Carlo Montanaro. The Fondo Pasinetti is not inventoried and catalogued. I am therefore unable to produce more accurate bibliographic information.
20. Cecchi writes: 'The skyscraper is not a harmony of lines and masses, of empty and full, of forces and resistances. Rather, is it a multiplication, an arithmetical operation. Built solely around a vertical thrust, which has some affinities with the gothic, the skyscraper does not offer anything other than the matter of a mechanical problem, interested in pushing this thrust as high as possible. It does not live its weight, like classical buildings, with human poise. It is a ghost, an apparition, an explosion. An explosion that is frozen mid-sky. If we disregard old, sometimes half-demolished buildings, on Manhattan's short rocky shores we find, in a few years: the Chanin of 54 storeys, the Chrysler of 77 storeys and 314 meters, the Empire of 102 storeys and 410 metres. When the economic crisis arrived it put a stop to these architectural pyrotechnics' (1997: 1123).

21. Fondo Francesco Pasinetti, Archivio Carlo Montanaro.
22. The SS *Rex* was an ocean liner launched in 1931 that operated transatlantic crossings from Italy. The ship was laid up for safekeeping during the war, but it was sunk by Allied rockets in 1944. Federico Fellini famously captured the almost mythical allure of the Blue Riband winner in his 1973 *Amarcord*.
23. Now the Grand Hyatt New York, the hotel has a complicated history of distasteful renovations that have stripped it of its charm, and of litigious partnerships between hospitality juggernauts Hyatt Hotels and Trump Organization.
24. Of course, Cecchi was not the only intellectual to have published an account of his American journeys. In 1935, Mario Soldati released *America primo amore*, which contained, among other things, his reflections on his experience with the academic world: 'Soldati (1906–2000) arrived in America in 1929, during the Great Depression. He was only twenty-three years old and eager to start an academic career at Columbia University. His encounter with New York was ambivalent and fluctuated between passionate and depressed evaluations. Apart from the obvious lure of the city, Soldati was struck by the anonymity that marked everyone's life. In the suburbs, crowded by small houses and tiny annexed gardens, which reappeared with a monotonous regularity, Soldati perceived the desolating erasure of one's individuality. The loss of one's identity was for him particularly painful in the case of Italian Americans. No longer Italians and not yet Americans, these people lived in a liminal state, filled with the luminous dream of one day acquiring their green card, which would have sanctioned their final integration into the United States, that is to say, would have granted them citizenship' (Torriglia 2002: 84–5).
25. Including myself.
26. The original cut contains a long sequence detailing Tommaso's temporary fall from grace. With Amedeo in jail, his boxing career frozen by Chris Sherman, Tommaso must scramble to find work and joins the Great Depression breadlines.
27. The suggestion of corruption among immigration officers is also on display in *Anastasia mio fratello/My Brother Anastasia* (Stefano Vanzina, 1973), in which Alberto Sordi plays the brother of a powerful gangster who sends his henchmen to assure him a safe and expedited disembarkation from the ocean liner that brought him to New York. For more on this film, see Chapter 8.
28. In the original Italian, the lines are: 'Ho capito, tu sei di quelli che si offendono, eh?' And 'No, no, io non offendere mai, povero negro. Grazia, grazia signore!' Note the use of the infinitive, a racist screenwriting convention often indicating limited command of a language. All the black characters in the film, including the boxer Tommaso fights at Madison Square Garden, speak the same heavily accented Italian.
29. This account is problematic: in the author's note, Lenzi writes that 'As far as the film *Harlem* is concerned, the use of a large group of black Anglo-American POWs in the last boxing sequence is a historically proven fact'

(2009: 7). Film historian Noa Steimatsky (2020) offers a different explanation, whereby the black extras that appear in *Harlem* and in the German film *Germanin – Die Geschichte einer kolonialen Tat* (Max V. Kimmich, 1943) were South African POWs housed in 'Concentration Camp number 122', which was on Cinecittà grounds.

30. As we will see, echoes of such racism can be observed in films made long after the war.
31. Interestingly, the unpalatability of American cuisine is the source of one of Italian cinema's most iconic gags: in Steno's 1954 *Un americano a Roma/An American in Rome*, a comically xenophilic Alberto Sordi attempts to eat the foods he believes an American would, but in the end opts for an oversized bowl of pasta. The joke is reprised once more in Sordi's own *Un tassinaro a New York* (1987), when the American fiancée of the protagonist's son cooks an 'Italian dinner' in honour of her in-laws, who find her sugared spaghetti dish too revolting to eat.
32. Tommaso does not manage to utter the proverb's ending, which is indeed quite sobering: 'Those who live on hope, die in desperation.'
33. Of course, it is impossible not to read in this quick apology a cheeky reference to Nazzari's legendary role in *Luciano Serra pilota*.
34. This nod to immigrant music is also masking Harlem's African American cultural identity, and its place in the history of jazz music.
35. The same song will be featured in *Catene* (Raffaello Matarazzo, 1949), which I discuss in the next chapter.
36. Steven Ricci reports this exchange differently. He writes: 'Primo Carnera even makes a cameo in *Harlem*, warning the film's main character to be wary of the moral decay characteristic of contemporary America' (2008: 141). This warning does not appear in the prints I examined, nor is it printed in the *cineromanzo*, which does not mention Carnera and Venturi.
37. I should add that the 1946 cut I was able to examine displays an evident glitch in the sound precisely at this point. The anti-Italian chant is gone, and the words 'Forza' and 'Italia' have been clumsily edited together.
38. As opposed to Italian Americans, Italian-Americans, or Italoamericans. The most sophisticated discussion of 'the hyphen question' is still to be found in Anthony Julian Tamburri (1991), in which the author proposes that the slash (or the forty-five degree hyphen) be employed in defining American writers and cultural agents of Italian descent. According to the author, the hyphen creates an unnecessary and alienating distance between the national identities that, conversely, need to be understood in unison. On the issue of Italian Americans on-screen, see Bondanella (2006); Hostert and Tamburri (2002); D'Acierno (1999). In Italian, the volume by Paola Casella (1998) is the most comprehensive on the subject. Noteworthy also is the collection of essays edited by Cipolloni and De Rosa (2001).
39. See, for instance, Luigi Einaudi (1900). On the intricacies of nationalist and imperialist thought in Liberal and Fascist Italy, see Gentile (2009).

CHAPTER 4

Romancing: Postwar Im/mobilities in Raffaello Matarazzo's Melodramas

This chapter is devoted to the melodramas directed by Raffaello Matarazzo (1909–60) and starring Amedeo Nazzari opposite Greek-Italian actress Yvonne Sanson (1925–2003).[1] In the span of a decade (1949–58), the three collaborated on a series of commercially successful melodramas[2] that effectively redefined the notion of 'popular cinema' in the postwar period, a position that had been left vacant (or was only partially occupied by comedies) after the demise of Fascism. While leftist Neorealist cinema brought to the fore the material and spiritual needs of a country prostrated by over two decades of dictatorship and five years of war, Matarazzo's conservative weepies replaced the defunct *telefoni bianchi*, restoring popular cinema's focus on narratives centring on familial bonds, social mobility, the relationship between labour and capital, and the effects of religion. Because of their apparent concern with the repression, displacement, sublimation, and domestication of female desire, as well as their obvious pandering to the taste of their perceived target audience, in recent years Matarazzo's films have received the critical attention of scholars interested in gender (Günsberg 2005; Hipkins 2016; O'Rawe 2017), melodrama (Bayman 2015), and stardom (D'Amelio 2018). I will build on these scholars' important contributions by discussing how the construction of Nazzari's im/mobile on-screen persona, which solidified in the decade between the mid-1930s and the mid-1940s, informs the postwar Matarazzo films. Acting as a metaphorical (and chronological) bridge between Fascist-era cinema and the rise of iconoclastic Italian-style comedy, the melodramas tempered Nazzari's heroic qualities and expunged his characters of any youthful idiosyncrasy, transforming him into a righteous *pater familias* broadly constructed as 'a site of complex relationships between the private and the public, the domestic and the foreign, and pre-war and post-war gender roles' (D'Amelio 2018: 20). Of course, in examining the specific modification Nazzari's im/mobile character undergoes in the Matarazzo films, I am also mindful of Tim

Cresswell and Tanu Priya Uteng's observation that 'narratives of mobility and immobility play a central role in the constitution of gender as a social and cultural construct' (2008: 2).[3] While in the previous chapters I focused exclusively on Nazzari's male, cisgendered, and heterosexual im/mobility, in this chapter I take into account how patriarchy, religion, and the politics (and the policing) of female desire affect the im/mobility of the characters played by Sanson.

In his volume on Italian postwar melodrama, Louis Bayman notes that character im/mobility is at the root of the genre's dramatic tension:

> Scenarios of entrapment and disruption make personal emotions the source of shelter and isolation, while melodramatic style suggests, but cannot provide passage to, a higher realm. The world is then melodramatic, in that forceful emotion governs it, and emphasizes the weakness of its carriers. (Bayman 2015: 3)

Writing specifically about the Matarazzo films in her groundbreaking book on gender in Italian cinema, Maggie Günsberg argues that they are inherently concerned with narratives of human mobility across physical (geographic) and ideological (societal) borders:

> Centring on illegitimate and orphaned children, on single, abandoned mothers and absent fathers, Italian melodrama explores the heart-wringing dispersal of family members. The films often end with the reuniting of the family unit, with the final scene, as in many of the contemporary *fotoromanzi*, akin to a family photograph displaying reassuring membership and generational continuity of a social unit essential to both patriarchy and capitalism. (Günsberg 2005: 59)

In *Catene/Chains* (1949), the series' first film, the centrifugal force that drives the main characters apart is embodied by a returning lover, Emilio (Aldo Nicodemi). Marked as a villainous character from the outset of the film, the man is also a return migrant, a corrupt *americano* similar to his prewar predecessors: as he tells Rosa (Yvonne Sanson), 'I've been back for a while. I lived for a long time in Turin, then I went to France, then the war came, and now I'm here.' The ambiguity in Emilio's language regarding his position and activities during the war speaks of the possibility of desertion, a scenario that is alluded to later when the man tries to rekindle the flames of their long-forgotten love:

> Remember when you ran away from home to come see me in Salerno, where I was a soldier? And when you walked me to the ship because you didn't want me to leave? You held onto me, you were desperate. You cried. You were devastated. And I left. I travelled the world. I would do anything. I became a ship's boy, and I worked as a banker in Cuba. Funny stuff. I had troubles with the police all over the world. I've

had a hundred names and a hundred faces. But when I saw you, I became myself again.

Similarly, in *Torna!* (1953), the gambler Giacomo (Franco Fabrizi) returns to the family shipyard after two years spent travelling in the company of Viviana (Enrica Dyrell), a woman he meets in a casino: 'I've been here and I've been there, I travelled the world', he explains. Unable to forget his cousin Susanna (Yvonne Sanson), who turned him down and favoured the attentions of Roberto (Amedeo Nazzari), Giacomo resorts to blackmail, fabricating evidence of an affair. For his ability to destroy the lives of others because of an incontrollable desire that ultimately is the cause of his own demise, Günsberg describes this recurring character as an *homme fatale*, a variation on the *femme fatale* of American film noir. While the mechanics of the characters' actions and the nature of their desires and manipulations are undoubtedly similar, this regendering of the *fatale* character is not altogether unproblematic: as a woman in mid-century America, the *femme fatale* used her sex appeal for personal gain in (and often against) a society in which she was systematically disempowered.[4] Emilio, Giacomo, and the many *homme fatales* of Italian melodrama act from a position of power granted to them by patriarchy, their words often deemed more valuable (and believable) than those of their female counterparts – a fact that is frequently used as a plot device to 'entrap' the innocent woman.

In fact, as Günsberg also underscores, Rosa and Susanna are *matres dolorosae*, whose 'inability to speak signals the forced confinement of femininity in the pre-linguistic, essentialist language of the body, a disempowered language with no voice, speaking only in the psychosomatic terms of the sick, hysterical body' (2005: 39). Sanson's frequent silencing in the Matarazzo films is often accompanied by a corresponding (bodily and/or spiritual) confinement, either in a correctional facility (*Catene*, *Chi è senza peccato . . .*, *L'angelo bianco*), a convent or religious order (*I figli di nessuno*, *L'angelo bianco*), or in the home of a charitable woman (*I figli di nessuno*, *Torna!*). Alternatively, she is sent into a state of forced mobility, either by being cast away from the home (*Catene*, *Torna!*) or searching for employment following the loss of a (patriarchal) family unit (*Tormento*, *Chi è senza peccato . . .*).

In *Catene*, Emilio's extraordinary mobility is contrasted with Rosa's husband's immobility, which is grounded in humility and level-headedness. While geographically rooted, the mechanic Guglielmo Aniello (Nazzari) wishes to be socially mobile via venture capitalism, and he is initially deceived by Emilio's intentions to invest in the expansion of his garage. Of course, Emilio only wants to get close to Rosa, and eventually the family is broken apart when Guglielmo, blinded by jealousy, murders Emilio and escapes. Believing Rosa to have been unfaithful to her son, Guglielmo's mother Anna (Anna Franchini) enforces his desire for Rosa to be cast from their home and forbids any interaction with her two children. Günsberg notes that this is a recurrent action in Matarazzo's films, one that is often allocated to

> another woman, postmenopausal, asexual and older than the central female protagonist-victim against whom she acts on behalf of patriarchy, whose interests she represents. She is the classic bad phallic mother-figure, who in these melodramas derives her power from property and uses her economic autonomy against other women. (Günsberg 2005: 42)

While this is generally true, this character does not appear in all the films, and in some of the titles she does not victimize only other women, but also men and children through her opposition to interclass unions (*I figli di nessuno*, *Chi è senza peccato* . . .). *Torna!*, for instance, does not avail itself of this character. However, a similar dynamic is presented, with the dyad Sanson–Nazzari in the role of the (re)productive couple who climb the social ladder via hard work and level-headed investments, and the specular couple (in this case Fabrizi–Dyrell) driving a wedge between them. Interestingly, in *Torna!* Nazzari's ease with vehicular/mediating technology is scaled up from automobiles to ships.

As I have discussed in Chapter 2, in the prewar picture *Montevergine* Nazzari's character is wrongly accused of murder, and he escapes the law by migrating to South America, but in a twist of fate he is framed and imprisoned for smuggling drugs. The coupling of migration with immobility or imprisonment transfers onto the Matarazzo films almost wholesale: in *Catene*, Guglielmo is sent into exile by the murder of Emilio. He boards a ship with counterfeit documents and befriends a man carrying a guitar: 'Are you going to America to seek fortune as well?' the man asks Guglielmo, who responds affirmatively. He continues, 'Great land, America. I sing and play the guitar, but I'll adapt to any job.' The man is none other than Neapolitan singer-songwriter Roberto Murolo (1912–2003), whose musical abilities frame one of the film's most memorable sequences, which opens with a dissolve on this sign: 'American Railways. Ohio. Barrack 9.' At Christmas, a company of railway workers plays ring-a-ring o' roses around a decorated tree. One of them is dressed up as Santa Claus. An accordion can be heard providing a soundtrack to the dance. Guglielmo is in his bunk, and he receives a piece of mail from his mother with news of the children. The Italian workers begin reminiscing about Italy, regional foods (roasted chestnuts and doughnuts), wine (Barbera, which they prefer to local whiskey), and their children, whom they imagine gathered around nativity scenes. A shot of a bedraggled Nazzari, still clutching his mother's letter, dissolves into the nativity scene back in Naples, where his children, watched over by a pensive Anna Aniello, bemoan their parents' absence. When the sequence returns to a medium shot of Guglielmo, Murolo begins to sing 'Lacreme napulitane' ('Neapolitan Tears'), a song about a Neapolitan migrant writing to his mother at Christmas and lamenting his distance from his native city – a song that was also featured in *Harlem*, as I discussed in Chapter 3. The community of Italian migrants listens intently, breaking down into tears, one by one, and even the stoic Guglielmo is overcome with emotion.

Film historian Mario Franco comments on the 'almost paradoxical' screen encounter of the masculine Nazzari and the understated Murolo, arguing that 'if Matarazzo's plots were fundamentally at the service of Catholic ideology with regards to the family, piety, and Providence, Murolo underscored the artificiality of their perfect and mechanical construction, similar to a popular novel' (in Colasanti and Nicosia 2007: 96).[5] Murolo's appearance in *Catene* is a musical pause that shifts the film's accent from the narrational to the emotional; it is a moment of pure 'immigrant's nostalgia' which, according to Salman Akhtar, capitalizes upon the individual's 'libidinal experiences in the land of origin as well as upon his guilt in voluntarily leaving that land' (1999: 129). This is an especially woeful feeling whereby

> [p]ain is evoked by the awareness of separation from the now idealized object and joy by a fantasized reunion with it through maudlin reminiscences. Cultural artifacts from 'back home' and *pieces of native music* and poetry readily evoke tears of aching pride and affection. (Akhtar 1999: 125; my emphasis)

To underscore the poignancy of this moment, as soon as Murolo is done singing Guglielmo receives a visit from the authorities and is repatriated. He calmly gets dressed and complies, but just before leaving he walks over to Murolo's bunk and shakes his hand. His return journey aboard the ship *Esperia* is elided, but Matarazzo does include the moment of his disembarkation, which ends with a lengthy shot of Nazzari walking towards the camera on the dock. Echoes of *È sbarcato un marinaio* (see Chapter 2), but also of the equally moustachioed strongman George Bancroft in Joseph von Sternberg's 1928 *The Docks of New York*, reverberate through the scene. Günsberg argues that 'emigration songs lamenting loss of the motherland highlight the sense of isolation of the Italian in America in *Catene* and *Chi è senza colpa* [sic] or Canada in *Disonorata senza colpa*'

(2005: 23).⁶ While emigrant songs are associated with faraway fathers, absent mothers are evoked by references to motherhood and parentage in general, which are signalled by the appearance on the soundtrack of the song 'Mamma' by Cesare Andrea Bixio and lyricist Bixio Cherubini. In *Catene*, the melody remains extradiegetic, but in *I figli di nessuno*, the song is performed by the singer-songwriter Giorgio Consolini, who appears as a hitchhiking minstrel. As Peter Adey notes,

> Music carries considerable freight by transporting the baggage of different cultures. Ideas of 'home', 'locality' and 'bounded identity' are transmitted forth into the different environments music might come to occupy. This is not to say that music simply overwrites the cultural spaces it comes to occupy. Musical cultures have actually evolved because of the movement of people and music. (Adey 2017: 250)

Much of *Tormento* unfolds along the lines of *Catene*: the entrepreneurial Carlo Guarnieri (Nazzari) is framed and imprisoned for a murder he did not commit, and his pregnant fiancée Anna Ferrari (Sanson) is left to her own devices. Anna seeks her elderly father's help (Annibale Beltrone), but her letters are intercepted by her stepmother (Tina Lattanzi). Anna's undesired state of im/mobility lands her a job as dishwasher in the club where Enzo (Murolo) performs. In a specular sequence to the barrack serenade in *Catene*, Anna, in a medium full shot, is seen drying dishes with a towel. Murolo's voice carries into the kitchen, and Matarazzo cuts to a shot of the singer on the stage performing 'Reginella', a song about former lovers who, occasionally, reminisce of their past love. The narrative pauses until Murolo is finished; he then goes to the kitchen, recognizes Anna as a former fellow student in the music conservatory, exchanges a few words with her, and then returns to the stage, where he proceeds to sing 'Dicitencello vuje', a song about a man declaring his love to a woman. Matarazzo cross-cuts between Murolo and Sanson, documenting the woman's reaction to the song. Eventually, Enzo's intercession results in Anna's promotion to hatcheck girl, and the editing pattern is repeated a third time: Murolo sings 'Canzone appassiunata', a song about unrequited love, and Anna listens from her booth. While the intertext might lead the spectator to believe that the man is still romantically interested in Anna, as he was back at the conservatory, Enzo's affection remains brotherly and, unbeknownst to her, he becomes her benefactor.

As Mario Franco writes, Murolo's participation in the Matarazzo films does not affect them dramaturgically but emotionally: 'it's a kind of short-circuit that sends the plausibility of the image into a crisis, and enriches the tale with a musical counterpoint that does not comment on the action, but lets it unfold as event without a finality' (2007: 96). What Murolo brings, in fact, is cultural specificity: the use of Neapolitan language in his songs and his appeal as a rising musical icon endow the films with local flavour; as Günsberg notes, 'Italian cinematic melodrama is a genre exhibiting many features of *italianità*, or features distinctive to Italy' (2005: 26).

Similarly to *Catene*, *Tormento*, and *Torna!*, the diptych *I figli di nessuno/ Nobody's Children* (1951) and *L'angelo bianco/The White Angel* (1955) interrogates human im/mobility across gender, class, and religion. While the former two films focused primarily on how the actions of an *homme fatale*, or a postmenopausal woman could jeopardize the happiness of a married (or soon to be married) couple, the latter two complicate the notion of 'family romance' (Günsberg 2005: 46) by extending their analysis to intergenerational trauma. *I figli di nessuno*'s protagonist, quarry owner Count Guido Carani (Amedeo Nazzari), is in love with Luisa Fanti (Yvonne Sanson), the groundskeeper's daughter. His mother, Countess Carani (Françoise Rosay), opposes the interclass union so, to delay their marriage, she sends her son to London and Belgium to research new extraction equipment. While the young man is away, she enlists foreman Anselmo Vannini (Folco Lulli) to scheme against Luisa, and they succeed in chasing her away from the property and blocking her correspondence with Guido. Unbeknownst to them, the young woman is pregnant with Guido's son, whom she delivers at a nearby farm. When the Countess learns about the child, she tasks Anselmo with kidnapping him, which he does, but he also accidentally sets fire to the farmhouse, leading Luisa to believe that the boy has perished in the flames. The grieving mother takes the veil and retires to a convent. Years go by, and little Bruno (Enrico Olivieri) grows up in a boarding school, where he is frequently bullied. Guido marries Elena (Enrica Dyrell) and they have a daughter, Anna (Rosalia Randazzo). Wishing to discover who has been sponsoring his education, Bruno runs away from the school. He hitchhikes his way to the quarry, passing by the convent, where he runs into his mother, who does not recognize him. Eventually, he ends up working for Anselmo in the Carani quarry. On her deathbed, the Countess unloads her guilty conscience to her priest, and drafts a will in which she bequeaths much of her estate to Bruno. Elena overhears, learning that Bruno is, in fact, Guido's son, and later relays this information to her husband, but not before attempting to steal the will. Anselmo, slighted, decides to blow up the quarry; Bruno tries to stop him and he is gravely injured in the explosion. Guido and Luisa, now Sister Addolorata, meet at the boy's hospital bed, where he expires in his mother's arms.

As Louis Bayman has noted, Matarazzo's

> films hinge on returns and repetitions of situations, characters and memories within and among themselves. This is perhaps most evident in the way that they rely on the repetition of the two principal actors as the ill-fated couple in each of the four films. (Bayman 2015: 162–3)[7]

The relationship between *I figli di nessuno* and its sequel, *L'angelo bianco*, extends the mechanics of repetition and variation well beyond the level of plot and casting. More than a simple continuation of the events that doom the couple's happiness in *I figli di nessuno*, *L'angelo bianco* is a formal doubling of the original, a complex operation of homage and restructuring that expands its reflections on gendered mobilities. The film begins with Guido's and Luisa/Sister Addolorata's grief, which is conveyed in a series of flashbacks of Bruno's final moments that appear on-screen as ghostly superimpositions. Guido holds his wife Elena responsible for the child's death, and starts the legal process to formally separate from her and obtain custody of their daughter Anna. When the judge grants it, Elena does not accept the decision and attempts to escape with Anna on the family's elegant motorboat. However, the distraught woman is unable to properly operate the vessel in rough weather, which results in the drowning of both its occupants. Remorseful and bereft, Guido retires to a solitary life in the family seashore villa.

As this brief account demonstrates, the film's first act replicates the trauma experienced by the protagonists in its prequel's last, with the accidental death of a child being its central tragedy. But while Bruno's passing is caused by his heroic temperament, Anna's drowning is determined by her mother's reckless use of transportation technology. Her sudden burst into action is not accompanied by proper boating knowledge; her wealth gives her access to a speedboat, but she does not possess the skills to operate it safely. In many ways, Elena recalls the bourgeois characters in *Gli uomini, che mascalzoni!/Men, What Rascals!* (Mario Camerini, 1932) and *Due cuori felici* (Baldassarre Negroni, 1932) who relied on their young and talented chauffeurs (exempla of ideal Fascist men) to drive and maintain their expensive automobiles. If in the romantic comedies of the early 1930s this incompetence elicits laughter, in the 1950s melodramas the implications are much darker, and not simply because of the characters' fate. The regendering of this lack of skills speaks not of a nation that entrusted its destiny to the working class, albeit from an ideologically bankrupt standpoint, but of a society in which patriarchy and the enforcement of heteronormative gender roles are the necessary conditions that prevent the world from descending into chaos (Figure 1.10).

Figures 1.10 and 1.11 Gendered mediated mobilities: Elena and Lina.

Guido abandons his voluntary confinement at the request of his quarry foreman, Poldo (Alberto Farnese), who warns him that without his stewardship the company will soon go bankrupt and the workers will lose their jobs. With its owner back at the helm, the company is once again profitable. Guido goes on a work trip to scout for new equipment for the quarry, and from his train window, seated on a carriage moving in the opposite direction, he sees a woman who bears an uncanny resemblance to Luisa. Shocked, the man approaches her and learns that she is a nightclub dancer headed to Modena with her crew. From this moment on, the film takes a singular turn: the performer Lina Marcolin, also played by Yvonne Sanson, becomes Guido's romantic obsession. A doppelgänger of sorts, this character is associated with extreme im/mobility, sexual freedom, and crime. For a long stretch of its complicated narrative, *L'angelo bianco* anticipates Alfred Hitchcock's *Vertigo* (1958), in that its protagonist attempts to retrieve an emotional (and familial) plenitude by fashioning a mysterious woman into the memory of the one he has lost. The encounter is marked by Lina's ability to move freely and confidently through a variety of gendered spaces: she uses her body to flirt with Guido in the narrow space of the train compartment and from the window (Figure 1.11); she descends rapidly from the theatre stage to the orchestra when she learns that Guido is there to see her; she confidently shuttles between city streets, cafés, restaurants, nightclubs, and rented rooms. Unlike the cloistered Luisa/Sister Addolorata, her doppelgänger can be understood as a *flâneuse*, a figure who

> witnesses the architectural, social, and technological transformations caused by the phenomena of modernity and pre-modernity, which change her status in the city and her ways of circulating on streets and 'interior' spaces – galleries, malls, cafés, theatres, etc. –, of watching and studying urban objects and reacting to the new shocks. (Vargau 2016: 83)

When a suitcase of counterfeit money is found in her apartment, however, Lina is incarcerated and sentenced to serve four years and two months. Once more, the film changes its generic qualities, pivoting into a prison drama. It is in captivity that Lina's 'redemption' from dangerous *flânerie* to immobile motherhood begins: the woman finds out that she is pregnant, and she dies delivering the baby. As Danielle Hipkins notes, the policing of Lina's mobility reflects a societal anxiety regarding her sexuality:

> In the end, the 'bad' woman dies, and the 'good' woman rescues the male child that is a product of her union with their shared lover, remaining nonetheless in the convent. Here the emphasis on sacrificial (Virgin) motherhood and the expulsion of the sexual is central to the understanding of femininity as virtue. However the use of the same actress to play both figures betrays unease with the very possibility of a single, pure woman. (Hipkins 2016: 153)

In a narrative spiral (a symbol that acquires particular relevance in the comparison with Hitchcock's *Vertigo*), in *L'angelo bianco* Lina's reproductive body provides Guido with the child that was lost in *I figli di nessuno*. Guido therefore marries a frail Lina *in extremis*. The inmates take advantage of the ceremony to try to break out of the penitentiary, using the baby as a human shield. Luisa/Sister Addolorata intercedes with the rioting prisoners and delivers the newborn into Guido's arms, pleading with him that the baby be (re)named Bruno.

In the last two films in this chapter, *Chi è senza peccato* ... (1952) and *Malinconico autunno/Melancholic Autumn* (1958), the focus returns primarily (but not exclusively) to Nazzari's mobility, both as character and as actor. The latter is a Spanish and Italian co-production that was partly shot in Spain, while the former is a loose adaptation of the novel *Geneviève, histoire d'une servante* by French romanticist Alphonse de Lamartine (1851). Set between Italy and Canada, *Chi è senza peccato* ... was made entirely in Italy, Valle D'Aosta's Val Ferret providing the spectacular alpine backdrop. The protagonists are lumberjack Stefano Brunot (Nazzari) and shopgirl Maria Dermoz (Sanson), whose romance unfolds against a pastoral mountain setting that recalls, among many of Nazzari's 'rustic' titles, *Montevergine* and *Il brigante Musolino/Cowboy Girl* (Mario Camerini, 1950). The star-crossed lovers find themselves intermittently in states of im/mobility that jeopardize their union throughout the narrative, until at the very end of the film they are able to form a family unit. First, when Stefano works in a sawmill in Winnipeg (a location erroneously signified by a mountainous background and by the presence of Royal Canadian Mounted Police officers) and wishes to send for his fiancée, but cannot leave the country or he will lose his visa; second, when Maria is unjustly accused of child abandonment and is sentenced to serve one year and six months in prison. While the first bureaucratic obstacle is overcome by a proxy wedding, the second proves insurmountable and drives an emotional and temporal wedge between the characters. Similarly to *I figli di nessuno*'s Countess Carani, Countess Lamieri (Françoise Rosay) wishes to prevent the interclass union between her nephew Dario (*Harlem*'s Gianni Musy) and Maria's sister Lisetta (Anna Maria Sandri), who is pregnant with their son Nino (Enrico Olivieri). In a series of actions that send characters into various states of im/mobility, the Countess ships Dario to Argentina, abducts Lisetta's child, frames Maria for the crime, and finally intercepts the distant lovers' correspondence, causing Stefano to nullify the marriage and to seek fortune in the dangerous lands of Northern Canada – 'beyond the Great Lakes', as he puts it. Twelve years pass, and Stefano returns to Italy a rich man, his only wish being to see Maria again. After another series of vicissitudes, Maria, Stefano, and Nino are reunited as a nuclear family.

Penned by long-time Matarazzo collaborator Aldo De Benedetti, the screenplay of *Chi è senza peccato* . . . interrogates national anxieties about human mobility by creating an intricate web of overlapping juridical hurdles, linguistic barriers (at the outset of the film, Stefano is unable to read English-language official correspondence directed to him), and temporal disjunctures typical of diasporic lives. In fact, as Ranajit Guha writes, the migrant is perpetually

> in a temporal dilemma. He must win recognition from his fellows in the host community by participating in the now of their everyday life. But such participation is made difficult by the fact that whatever is anticipatory and futural about it is liable to make him appear as an alien, and whatever is past will perhaps be mistaken for nostalgia. (Guha 2011: 9)

As we have seen, many Matarazzo films reify this interior dilemma into a series of outward complications that result in the disconnection of characters for long stretches of time. Similarly to what happens in *Montevergine* and *Catene*, in *Chi è senza peccato* . . . Stefano and Maria are 'out of synch' for much of the film's narrative. Financially motivated, their disconnection is precipitated by Stefano's mobility, which inadvertently raises the bureaucratic, communicative, and temporal barriers exploited by the Countess to prevent the lower classes from contaminating her aristocratic bloodline.

Conversely, in *Malinconico autunno*, it is precisely Nazzari's character's extraordinary mobility that allows for the 'family romance' to take root. Shot at Madrid's Chamartin studios, Barcelona's Orphea studios, and on location in Catalonia's capital city, the film stands apart from its predecessors precisely for its remarkable use of physical spaces, most notably in the outdoor scenes at the harbour. The captain of a commercial ship docked in Barcelona, the handsome Andrea (Nazzari) romances the jealous nightclub singer Lola (Mercedes Monterrey) – who also replaces Roberto Murolo in the customary musical number. Lola's suspicion of Andrea's infidelity is not misplaced, of course, since we later learn that the seaman does indeed have 'a girl in every port', including Olga (María Rivas) in Genoa, but he is unwilling to talk marriage with either. His rather liberal approach to sexuality harks back to a younger Nazzari in *È sbarcato un marinaio*, but while the maritime profession is similar, the 1958 film adjusts his rank to a more age-appropriate one (from sailor to captain), and reframes his overall trajectory.

A womanizer at the film's inception, Andrea will complete his arc as *pater familias*, a figure that, as Maria Elena D'Amelio writes, 'embodies a traditional masculinity that belongs primarily to a rural world, in which the *pater familias* bears the responsibility for his family's survival and protection against external threats and changing times' (2018: 29). When the captain befriends the little Luca Martinez (Miguel Gil) and his rambunctious dog, his redemption begins. He poses as the boy's father at his school, paying for the damages caused by the mutt, and eventually courts Luca's single mother, Maria Martinez (Yvonne Sanson). Andrea is also begrudgingly involved in a smuggling operation facilitated by Giacomo (José Guardiola), his second in command, but the boy's friendship convinces him to abandon these criminal activities and to propose to his mother. Luca, in fact, even embarks clandestinely on the ship to bond with Andrea, the ship emerging (as it did in *Harlem* and *Montevergine*) as a particularly productive site for the generation of viapolitical affects. The child is almost killed in the course of the various complications required by the melodramatic form, but Andrea saves his life and the new family unit is eventually created.

Andrea's mobility is as *routed* as it is *drifting*. By virtue of his profession, the sea captain moves across highly sophisticated and regimented geographical and juridical networks that include routine border crossings and cargomobilities (Birtchnell et al. 2015: 1). However, at the outset of the film, his personal life and affective sphere are drifting: as Kimberley Peters notes, 'The sailor, a global nomad without a fixed abode, spent time drifting – from one tavern to the next, from one brothel to the next – engaged in a life of vice that came with their mobility ashore' (2015: 265). Once again, Nazzari's character moves from a state of (physical and sexual) mobility to one of immobility: in settling down with Maria, Andrea repudiates his drifting lifestyle for one of middle-class social (and sexual) stability and respectability. Yet, while the heteronormative 'family romance' effectively neuters the subversive[8] potential embedded in the idea and practice of drifting, *Malinconico autunno*'s ending introduces a highly modern iteration of this formula: a multicultural, multilingual, international family whose coming together is facilitated rather than obstructed by mobilities.

Notes

1. The 1955 film *L'intrusa*, which stars Lea Padovani instead of Sanson opposite Nazzari, is not included in this analysis, nor is *L'ultimo incontro* (Gianni Franciolini, 1951), in which Nazzari plays an Alfa Romeo mechanic opposite Alida Valli.
2. With the notable exception of the last film in the series, *Malinconico autunno / Melancholic Autumn* (1958), all the Sanson–Nazzari pictures produced high box office returns. See Cavallo (2010).

3. As I describe in Chapter 2, I use the undecidable formulation 'im/mobile' to indicate that Nazzari's characters shuttle between states of mobility and immobility. He oscillates between technologically enhanced auto- and aeromobility (that is generally proper to the Fascist-era pictures) and stasis, captivity, and imprisonment (in his postwar work). These temporal and industrial boundaries, however, remain porous throughout his career.
4. On the empowering effects of being *fatale*, see Cowie (1993).
5. Mario Franco also shares an anecdote he learned from Murolo himself. According to the singer, in the course of their friendship Nazzari would occasionally ask him to sing 'Lacreme napulitane' ('Neapolitan Tears') and he would be moved every time (2007: 94).
6. Günsberg is referring to *Chi è senza peccato* . . . .
7. Bayman does not extend his analysis to *Chi è senza peccato* . . ., *Torna!*, and *Malinconico autunno*.
8. Peters underscores that 'The meaning encompassed in acts of drifting often makes evident societal processes of power and of the construction of normative landscapes. In many accounts of the drifter, the style of their motion – aimless, purposeless wandering – is deemed transgressive. Such figures challenge or deviate from the norm; the "ordinary track" that is expected to be followed; the purposeful life good citizens are meant to lead. Such accounts of drifters alert us to the political contestation bound up with drifting' (2015: 264).

CHAPTER 5

Migrating:
The Pathology of Im/mobility

At the midpoint of Dino Risi's 1964 *Il gaucho*, Ing. Maruchelli (Amedeo Nazzari) invites the inconstant impresario Marco Ravicchio (Vittorio Gassman) to join him for a nightcap on the rooftop terrace of the luxury hotel where the latter is staying. Flown to Argentina by a rich producer (clearly modelled on media mogul Angelo Rizzoli) to promote an 'arthouse' film starring ageing diva Luciana (Silvana Pampanini) at the Mar del Plata International Film Festival, the ebullient publicist Ravicchio is immediately befriended by the eccentric millionaire Maruchelli, whose obsession with the distant motherland is satirized throughout Risi's feature. The city waking up behind them, the two make their way to an upholstered swinging bench, slowly walking in a circular motion around the camera, which keeps them in the frame by gently panning right, thereby revealing the vastness of the urban landscape behind them. As they sit down facing the camera, the frame gradually tightens to an intimate two-shot. Indifferent to Ravicchio's pronounced yawns, Maruchelli confesses that his longing for the city of Rome, which he compares to a past lover, is in fact pathological: 'complesso della bandiera', the tearful expatriate diagnoses it, or 'psicosi della patria lontana' (flag complex; faraway motherland psychosis).

The film sets up a variety of gags based on Maruchelli's fixation, skewering both the peculiarities of the Italian community living in Argentina and the film troupe's snobbism – their apparent reticence to associate with the expatriates is a clear mark of the asynchronicity between the two groups. Salman Akhtar argues that this condition is in fact distinctive of the immigrant experience, which the eminent psychoanalyst disentangles from that of refugees and exiles who, because of the traumatic circumstances that pushed them to leave their places of origin, do not need to 'resort to hypercathexis of the objects' (1999: 125) which they have lost with their relocation. Conversely, 'the immigrant employing this mechanism comes to live in the past. His most powerful affects become associated with his recall of the houses, cafes, street corners, hills, and countryside of his homeland' (Akhtar 1999: 125). As I mentioned in Chapter 2, Akhtar describes this temporal dissonance as 'immigrant's nostalgia'.

In the course of the film, the affluent gentleman chaperones the ragtag Italian troupe across an Argentine landscape upon which he built his fortune: they visit cattle farms, slaughterhouses, nightclubs, sandy Atlantic beaches, and Italian restaurants teeming with raucous émigrés. Preoccupied with the artists' well-being, Maruchelli takes care of every detail, throwing lavish parties in their honour, and arranging motorcades to their every destination: at the cry of 'Viva Agnelli', he proudly announces that the delegation will travel in Fiat automobiles from the airport to their hotel (a fleet of 1963 Fiat 1500s, to be precise); later on, he lends Ravicchio his wife's luxurious 1958 Alfa Romeo 2000 Spider Touring, and he sits behind the wheel of his elegant 1962 Cadillac Coupe DeVille Hardtop.[1] In other words, Maruchelli's troubled success manifests itself in a paradoxical state of im/mobility: on the one hand, the film underscores that his wealth grants him extraordinary automobility, able as he is to purchase multiple vehicles of international renown and from a variety of automakers;[2] on the other hand, his affairs also keep him away from Italy, a state of (ethnic) immobility that amplifies his immigrant's nostalgia to the pathological degree described by Akhtar.

On several occasions, Ravicchio responds to Maruchelli's unhealthy attachment to the memory of his faraway motherland with caustic wit, trying to make him aware of the fact that he views Italy through rose-coloured glasses. On this point, Susan Stewart writes:

> Nostalgia is a sadness without an object, a sadness which creates a longing that of necessity is inauthentic because it does not take part in lived experience. Rather, it remains behind and before that experience. Nostalgia, like any form of narrative, is always ideological: the past it seeks has never existed except as narrative, and hence, always absent, that part continually threatens to reproduce itself as felt lack. Hostile to history and its invisible origins, and yet longing for an impossibly pure context of lived experience at a place of origin, nostalgia wears a distinctly utopian face, a face that turns toward a future-past, a past which has only ideological reality. This point of desire which the nostalgic seeks is in fact the absence that is the very generating mechanism of desire. (Stewart 1984: 23)

Maruchelli's reiterated idealization of an Italy that, as Stewart puts it, has never existed except as narrative,[3] is contrasted with the financial difficulties experienced by Stefano Liberati (Nino Manfredi), whose social status forces him to live with his wife in a modest apartment by the harbour, a place of transience par excellence, and to walk everywhere, unable as he is to even afford to take a taxicab. Liberati's destitution provides a counter-narrative to Maruchelli's wealth, which insulates him from the much humbler experiences of his fellow expatriates and affords him a (pathologically) nostalgic affective dimension. Conversely, Liberati's hardships keep him well grounded in reality, to the point that he is unable to forget his troubles even when he is invited to one of the many parties in honour of the Italian artists, and he sees right through Maruchelli's empty promise to give him employment.[4]

In his perceptive analysis of what he terms 'Italian Post-Neorealist Cinema', Luca Barattoni writes that '*Il gaucho* is a reactive comedy that destabilizes the notion of Italian identity, and ridicules committed cinema for good measure, reducing it to a means to get by' (2014: 20). The scholar underscores Dino Risi's interest in investigating Italian identity from abroad, connecting the elite experience of cinema executives travelling to a film festival with the variety of vantage points offered by the community living in the diaspora, and ultimately lampooning both. Appropriately to the film's genre, in which *Il gaucho* is only one of the director's many towering achievements, Risi's technique is not shorn of self-referentiality and irony. On the level of plot, the film is loaded with small gags and inside jokes, such as Ravicchio's run-in with a Roman motorist whose car horn is identical to Gassman's in Risi's own *Il sorpasso/The Easy Life* (1962). But most importantly, the film is also a comment on Italy's evolving star system and contemporary culture at large: for instance, the capricious Luciana, whose best professional years are behind her and who in the course of the festival romances a wealthy Argentinian in the hope of orchestrating a dignified retirement, is modelled on stories from Silvana Pampanini's own public and private life. In fact, by 1964 the star of the former Miss Italia contestant had lost much of its shine, and Risi would be one of the last directors to employ her – a career turn she will reference in her cameo in Alberto Sordi's *Il tassinaro* (1983). Moreover, the casting of Amedeo Nazzari in the role of the emotionally troubled Ing. Maruchelli capitalized on the three decades the Sardinian actor had spent playing a variety of characters whose im/mobility reflected the shifts in Italian identity (and gender) politics, from Fascism to the postwar, from the economic boom to the ensuing downturn (which Ettore Scola satirized in his 1965 *La congiuntura/Hard Times for Princes*). As Flavio De Bernardinis notes,

> Risi himself declared that *Il gaucho*'s central idea was the portrait of a migrant millionaire suffering from nostalgia, as the focal point of the contradictions of a certain Italian ethos. Well, contradiction within a contradiction, Nazzari's performance goes *beyond* the character. An actor who grounds his screen presence on his iconic dimension (the factor that distinguishes the player from the divo), exceeds the personality of the character he plays. (2007: 104; emphasis in the original)

Nazzari's own mobility brought him to shoot three films in Spain,[5] and his fame in the Spanish-speaking world led him to Argentina in 1948, where he publicly refused to play the villainous protagonist of the film he was offered, claiming that the screenplay slandered the character of his compatriots.[6] Eva Perón's intervention managed to keep Nazzari in Argentina to work with director Carlos F. Borcosque on *Volver a la vida/ Return to Life*,[7] which was shot in 1948 and distributed in 1951, although it never reached Italy. Pruzzo and Lancia report that during this stay the actor actively engaged with the Italian community in Argentina, even facilitating return migrations: 'Nazzari stayed in Buenos Aires approximately for one year, during which he travelled the country and helped many emigrants return to Italy' (1983: 23). Interestingly, the plot of *Volver a la vida* also capitalizes on Nazzari's long experience with im/mobile characters. According to the review published on 12 January 1951 in the morning edition of the Argentine newspaper *La Prensa*,

> What can be highlighted in this work is the intervention of the Italian actor Amedeo Nazzari, widely known for his performance in films of European origin. The result is picturesque and at the same time appropriate to the character of the production, his Spanish language, with a strong Italian accent, serves to aptly characterise the character and the environment in which he acts. Nazzari interprets an Italian captain recently arrived in Buenos Aires, after having suffered the tragedy of the war. According to his own expression, he is a man who lives but who carries death inside. That situation, however, suffers a change after a crisis that endangers his life, when the hope of a new existence is reborn in him, for the love inspired by a woman of his new land. This is how Argentina appears as a generous land of well-being for those who seek human solidarity. This is the instructive end of the film, which proclaims the always possible restoration of man through understanding and faith. (*La Prensa* 1951: 8)

In the March 1951 issue of the magazine *Primer Plano*, the reviewer praises the film's director, shifting the focus from the international stardom of its male lead to the film's stance on human mobility and nationalism, arguing that 'We should not take for granted the words of praise for Borcosque, who with this film sings the virtues of our people and *the hospitality never denied on our soil*' (my emphasis). In this case, Nazzari's character's nationality provides an opportunity to reflect on Argentine identity politics and immigration policies in the aftermath of the Second World War, at a time when Juan Domingo Perón's government was offering protection to escaped Nazi war criminals. This problematic history is satirized in at least two films dealing with Italians in Argentina: *Come scopersi l'America/How I Discovered America* (Carlo Borghesio, 1949), starring Erminio Macario, and *Il gaucho*. In the latter, Maruchelli's gardener bears an uncanny resemblance to an appropriately aged Adolph Hitler. Ravicchio notices the man and, partly in jest, he invites him to hold his right hand up in a salute. Without flinching, Maruchelli confesses that he was asked by a Jewish family to give him up, but that he refuses to do so on account of the gardener's abilities. While the joke could be interpreted as another reference to Maruchelli's latent Fascism, I would like to suggest that it should be understood in relation to Nazzari's complicated relationship with Fascist cinema, which I have attempted to elucidate in the first three chapters of Part One.

Notes

1. In her pioneering study, Natalie Fullwood discusses the gendering of automobility in Italian-style comedy, noting that in this film genre, [s]tereotyped representations of bad female driving appear', such as Ines Maruchelli's reckless overtaking in *Il gaucho*, but there are also 'rare examples of female characters who are constructed with economic as well as sexual identities. [. . .] Although much more limited than the attention given to men's relationship to the car, a range of female attitudes and experiences related to driving are represented' (2015: 153–4).
2. John Urry reminds us that 'cars provide status to their owners through their various sign-values that include speed, home, safety, sexual success, career achievement, freedom, family, masculinity and even genetic breeding' (2007: 116).
3. Flavio De Bernardinis underscores the temporal cleavage suffered by the emigrant: 'Ing. Maruchelli, as emigrant, has an asynchronous view of Italy, dating back to the time of his melancholic departure for South America. Marco Ravicchio, the publicist played by Vittorio Gassman, is quick at reassuring him: "Don't worry, Engineer. Nothing has changed in Rome, except for the brothels!"' (2007: 102).
4. According to Dino Risi and Ettore Scola, who contributed to the film's screenplay, this subplot was added at the last minute – which might account for the difference in lighting and sound quality of the apartment scene. Manfredi was touring in Argentina with *Rugantino*, the musical comedy by Pietro Garinei and Sandro Giovannini, and the filmmakers approached him with the idea of writing a character for him. See the video interviews with Risi and Scola in the DVD extras for *Il gaucho*, Cecchi Gori Home Video, 2006.
5. *Cuando los ángeles duermen* (Ricardo Gascón, 1947), *Conflicto inesperado* (Ricardo Gascón, 1948), and *Don Juan de Serralonga* (Ricardo Gascón, 1949). Nazzari would continue to star in Spanish films such as *La puerta abierta / The Open Door* (César Fernández Ardavín, 1957) throughout the next decade.
6. Nazzari's account of this episode is chronicled in his daughter Maria Evelina Buffa's collection of memories of her father *Amedeo Buffa in Arte Nazzari*

(2008: 136–9). Gubitosi interprets Nazzari's foreign adventures differently, alleging political reasons for his departure from Italy: 'At that time, since the cinema became the fighting ground for the two political coalitions – spearheaded respectively by the Christian Democrats and the Communist Party – that in years around 1948 clashed head on, Nazzari was even forced to look for work in Spanish and Argentine cinema' (1998: 128).

7. According to the script for the original opening credits, which is housed in the library of the Museo del Cine Pablos Ducrón Hicken, the film's working title was *Calle Arriba*. Nazzari's rejection of the roles offered to him in Argentina is a testament to his ability to craft his public persona through his careful casting choices. Ernesto Nicosia notes that 'Amedeo Nazzari's success is attributed, in good measure, to his ability to choose his roles, to the attentive selection he made of the characters that would have embodied the audience's expectations. He did not interpret these expectations, he represented them, and he rejected the roles that were not aligned with his sensibility' (Nicosia 2007: 6).

Conclusion to Part One: Driving the *Flâneuse*: *Le notti di Cabiria*

In the 1943 film *Apparizione/Apparition*, a soaking wet Amedeo Nazzari walks into the lobby of Albergo delle Terme, where Andreina (Alida Valli), dressed prematurely in her wedding gown, is expecting her fiancé Franco (*Harlem*'s Massimo Girotti) to arrive at any moment. Forced to stop at the closed hotel during a rainstorm by a mechanical issue with his luxurious two-seater 1938 Lancia Aprilia Pinin Farina cabriolet (a notably *domestic* vehicle; Figure 1.12), the ascot tie-wearing movie star (playing himself) makes quite an impression on the crowd of friends gathered to celebrate the couple's engagement. A big fan of the actor, Andreina takes a picture with Nazzari while still wearing the gown, a transgression that unleashes Franco's jealousy, who in a fit of anger slaps his fiancée across the face. The woman reacts by asking Nazzari to take her away with him, and the gentleman complies, his intentions still unclear. In contrast with the country hotel's rustic charm, the star's elegant Rome apartment is modern and functional, but Andreina is clearly ill at ease when Nazzari has the butler serve them dinner in his opulent bedroom. Frightened by the actor's suddenly predatory courtship, the young woman pleads with him, but his manners become even more brutish and she finally storms off in tears. Nazzari, of course, is in cahoots with Andreina's family, and his coarse behaviour was meant to scare her back into Franco's arms.

Produced by Giuseppe Amato, 'The film was directed smoothly by the Frenchman [Jean] de Limur. It exemplifies, so to speak, the excesses that the infatuation for a star can cause, but without even remotely anticipating a satire or critique of society. It is only a light romantic plot' (Pruzzo and Lancia 1983: 91). It is undoubtedly true that *Apparizione* returns to the same binaries upon which much of Fascist-era comedies were predicated: country dwelling versus city life; proletariat versus bourgeoisie; blue-collar, manual labour versus white-collar, clerical professions; wholesomeness versus (pretend) corruption. However, its metalinguistic strategies are certainly worth noting, since Nazzari's reflexive appearance

Figures 1.12 and 1.13 Amedeo Nazzari's pre- and postwar vehicular stardom.

as 'Nazzari' hinges on some features that are typical of his characters, such as his temporary im/mobility, his elegance, and his confident masculinity, yet others seem closer to his private persona, such as the impeccable wardrobe and the extravagant luxury of his apartment. In fact, according to Fellini's biographer Tullio Kezich,

> We can be almost certain that Federico worked on the screenplay for *Apparizione* (*Apparition*). [. . .] Shot in the summer of 1943, it's released early in the dark year 1944 – when practically no one is going to the movies because of the bomb scares. A typical romantic comedy, *Apparizione*, which was officially written by Amato, Tellini, and Lucio De Caro, rides the mood of a smug society anticipating crisis – early signs of a new reality. Fellini's participation in the film is strongly suggested by the casting of Amedeo Nazzari, who plays himself, as he'll do a decade later for Fellini in *Le notti di Cabiria* (*The Nights of Cabiria*). (Kezich 2006: 69)

In Chapter 4, I sought to demonstrate how Matarazzo's melodramas appropriated the stoic masculinity Nazzari embodied in his early heroic (Fascist) roles and retooled it for a postwar popular cinema that found expression in the traditional values championed by the Catholic Church and espoused by a society that was all too comfortable with patriarchal rule. In other words, by the mid 1950s, Nazzari's on-screen persona had morphed into the *pater familias* so aptly described by Maria Elena D'Amelio (2018). However, when Federico Fellini cast him to play the thinly veiled character of Alberto Lazzari in *Le notti di Cabiria*, the resulting commentary contained both the pastness of Nazzari's youthful exploits and the futurity of Italy's evolving star system, a reflection the director was poised to famously perfect in *La dolce vita* (1960). Although divergent from a sociopolitical standpoint, both periods represented pivotal moments in Italian film history and, relevant to this analysis, were singularly predicated on vehicular mobilities – unlike Neorealism, which was a cinema largely populated by peripatetic characters. It is hardly coincidental, therefore, that in both *Apparizione* and *Le notti di Cabiria* Nazzari's stardom be associated with luxury automobiles as well as with extravagant abodes, and that either could successfully anchor the preoccupations of their respective cinematic moments.

In Fellini's masterpiece, the nocturnal perambulation of the titular prostitute played by Giulietta Masina[1] brings her to Rome's Via Veneto, where she happens to witness a quarrel between famed actor Alberto Lazzari (Amedeo Nazzari) and his fur-clad, capricious girlfriend Jessy (Dorian Gray) outside the Kit Kat nightclub. The fight escalates to physical violence, with the lovers exchanging slaps in the middle of the street. When the two finally separate, Lazzari gets behind the wheel of his two-tone 1956 De Soto Fireflite convertible, an extravagantly large *American* car whose bouncy suspensions are challenged by the Roman cobblestone streets (Figure 1.13). Looking to get even, Lazzari signals Cabiria to get into the car, promoting her from *flâneuse* to passenger of an ostentatious, imported automobile. The scene continues at the Piccadilly, another hot-spot for the elite, where the wiry Cabiria launches into an unbridled mambo. Eventually, the unlikely duo ends at Lazzari's suburban residence. Here, the humble prostitute is first offered a dinner of champagne, caviar, and lobster (which she has seen in the movies, she remarks) and then she is hastily locked into the bathroom upon Jessy's untimely return. Trapped until morning, Cabiria must watch the lovers' subsequent reconciliation through the door's keyhole. Gianfranco Angelucci recalls that

> Fellini shared with me that the sequence in the film (*Le notti di Cabiria*, 1957) came to him when he visited Nazzari to tell him about the story in which he wanted him to get involved. When visiting his home he was struck by this extraordinary parade of elegance that amused and fascinated him. It was the exact connotation that he was looking for in order to depict the fabulous dimension of a being turned into a divinity by his audience. (2007: 110)

Kezich also expounds on the singular similarities between Lazzari's and Nazzari's lifestyles:

> Amedeo Nazzari, a natural choice for the part of the big movie star, at first had 'some justifiable hesitation' (to quote Federico) about the role. The most popular celebrity in Italy isn't entirely mistaken in this, as many of his personal habits, already well known to readers of gossip magazines, are on display here: his attraction to *La dolce vita* nightclubs, the stormy love affairs, *a passion for sports cars*, his massive wardrobe, his butler, the many rooms and white telephones in his mansion (on via Cassia rather than on via Appia, as in the film) where he lives alone – just like in real life. In short, Amedeo senses that he's being mocked. What's more, the director doesn't dare suggest that they use his real name, like they did for *Apparizione*. In the screenplay the character is simply named 'Actor,' though once they start shooting he's baptised Alberto Lazzari, for practical reasons. Once Nazzari actually comes on board, however, he displays a good sense of humour and isn't at all opposed to being mocked. (Kezich 2006: 182; my emphasis)[2]

As Kezich notes, in *Le notti di Cabiria* the boundaries between the actor and his character are left purposely very porous; but while the syntagm N/L-azzari is legible to the external observer, the diegetic Cabiria can only appreciate his cinematic persona through the viewing device of the key/peep-hole, which, as Frank Burke writes, is a metaphor for the medium itself – and, I would argue, for its apparatus: 'Through Lazzari, Cabiria refines four different ways of getting beyond herself: role-playing, vision, projection, and make-believe. All of these are obviously associated with movies' (1996: 87).

Fellini's famous lack of commitment to genre conventions, narrative strictures, or other filmmaking dogmatisms comes into full relief in the encounter between Cabiria and Lazzari: if the former could be understood as the director's own reinterpretation of the many Neorealist urban wanderers – from *Ladri di biciclette/Bicycle Thieves*' Antonio Ricci (Vittorio De Sica, 1948) to *Umberto D.* (Vittorio De Sica, 1952), from *Germania anno zero/Germany Year Zero*'s Edmund (Roberto Rossellini, 1948) to *Viaggio in Italia*'s Katherine (Roberto Rossellini, 1954) – the latter embodies Fellini's critique of melodrama, delivered *through* the physical presence of Italy's foremost melodramatic star.[3] What Cabiria witnesses from the darkness of her sequestered 'viewing room', then, is not only a private moment between two squabbling lovers, expressed in the heightened sentiments proper to melodrama; she watches a synthesis of *the whole genre*, one specifically conceived for a female audience, unfold before her eyes. The explanation for this dramatic compression, so to speak, is to be found in *Apparizione*, where 'Nazzari', back at the hotel, unrequitedly interceding on Franco's behalf, explains to Andreina that her jealous fiancé's behaviour is following a script that he himself, as an actor, has memorized and acted out many times before: 'Creative as they may be, screenwriters almost always make their characters say the same words, which are more or less the ones we utter in real life.'[4]

Allow me to conclude this book's first part with the cinephile's equivalent to a thought experiment, a hypothetical 'game' that vaults over Neorealism entirely: what would happen if *Le notti di Cabiria*'s bedroom exchange between Lazzari and Jessy, whose earlier public outburst was motivated by jealousy, were to be swapped with *Apparizione*'s predatory seduction of Andreina by a 'Nazzari' who is only *pretending* to be interested in her – or shall we say he's acting? I would argue that Cabiria would hardly notice the substitution; in fact, while she is able to correctly identify the star, she places him in the wrong movie: 'I didn't act in that one', comments an amused N/L-azzari.

Notes

1. For an enlightening discussion of Cabiria's singular status of *flâneuse*, on which these closing observations are based, see Marina Vargau's essay 'La figura della flâneuse nel film *Le notti di Cabiria* di Federico Fellini' (2016).
2. Nazzari's daughter, Maria Evelina Buffa, recalls that 'He liked cars. He would tell me that he would drive down via del Corso at 100Km/H on his MG . . .

With the Ford convertible, which he bought in the 1960s when I was a child, the three of us would take long drives. This one time, in order to help my mother overcome her fear of driving, he made her follow him from Sabaudia to Rome. And he made her promise to follow him no matter what. My mother agreed, staying close to him the entire way, emulating his speed and overtaking other cars like him! When she arrived she was white as a ghost, and naturally she refused to drive for many years. No, at times he was not exactly a fine psychologist . . .' (2008: 100).
3. 'Cabiria, the little prostitute whose simple soul is rooted in hope, is not a character out of melodrama', notes André Bazin, adding that 'Fellini's realism, though social in origin, is not social in intent' (2011: 197–9).
4. Interestingly, just before the actor enters the scene to deliver this speech, Andreina sneaks into the barn where Nazzari's Lancia is sheltered, climbs behind the steering wheel (not without some hesitation due to the curious push-button door handle, which disappears into the vehicle's sleek body), and drifts into reverie.

Part Two
Alberto Sordi

Introduction to Part Two: Alberto Sordi's Mobile Comedies

A photograph dated 5 April 1956 and housed in the Black Star Collection at the Ryerson Image Centre in Toronto, Canada, depicts an elated Alberto Sordi (1920–2003), wrapped in a stylish trench coat and wearing sunglasses, being carried in triumph by a cheering crowd (Figure 2.1). Two years prior, famed automaker Alfa Romeo launched the Giulietta model, the marque's most successful automobile to date. Designed by Franco Scaglione, it was first introduced as a 2+2 coupe, and a four-door saloon Berlina was added to the line-up in 1955. Much like Piaggo's iconic Vespa, which was also built utilizing a smooth unibody construction, and the contemporaneous Fiat 600 and 500 models, the Giulietta became one of the main symbols of Italy's postwar modernization. It was behind the wheel of a custom 1956 Alfa Romeo Giulietta Berlina that the Roman actor won the third edition of the Rallye del Cinema jointly with Sophia Loren, who drove a much sportier luxury coupe, the iconic Mercedes-Benz 300 SL Gullwing.

As this press photograph demonstrates, the rise of car culture and mid-century Italian stardom are inextricably linked. Moreover, Italy's storied relationship with automobility is often interwoven with motorsports and its heroes, from legendary makers Enzo Ferrari (1898–1988) and Ferruccio Lamborghini (1916–93), to entrepreneurial families like the Maserati Brothers and the Agnelli dynasty, who founded and still control much of Fiat. Writing about automobilities in North America, Freund and Martin explain that 'Working on and maintaining cars as well as racing them is for many a form of pleasure, in which traditionally masculine skills are displayed' (1993: 90). While this may be true with regards to the geographical area they discuss in their discipline-defining study, the case of Italy complicates this gendered assumption, and the national cinema is an especially useful archive to probe for more nuanced and culturally appropriate observations. In the words of Natalie Fullwood:

Figure 2.1 Celebrity automobility: unknown photographer, [The triumph of Alberto Sordi at the third 'Rallye del Cinema'], 5 April 1956, gelatin silver print. The Black Star Collection, Ryerson Image Centre (BS.2005.209410).

Personal mobility and stasis in Italian society (and western culture more widely) have traditionally been gendered along a male/female binary. [. . .] Yet, in Comedy, Italian-Style, although the representation of the car as commodity is predominantly associated with male status and identity, the act of driving is far from represented as an all-male activity. (Fullwood 2015: 153)

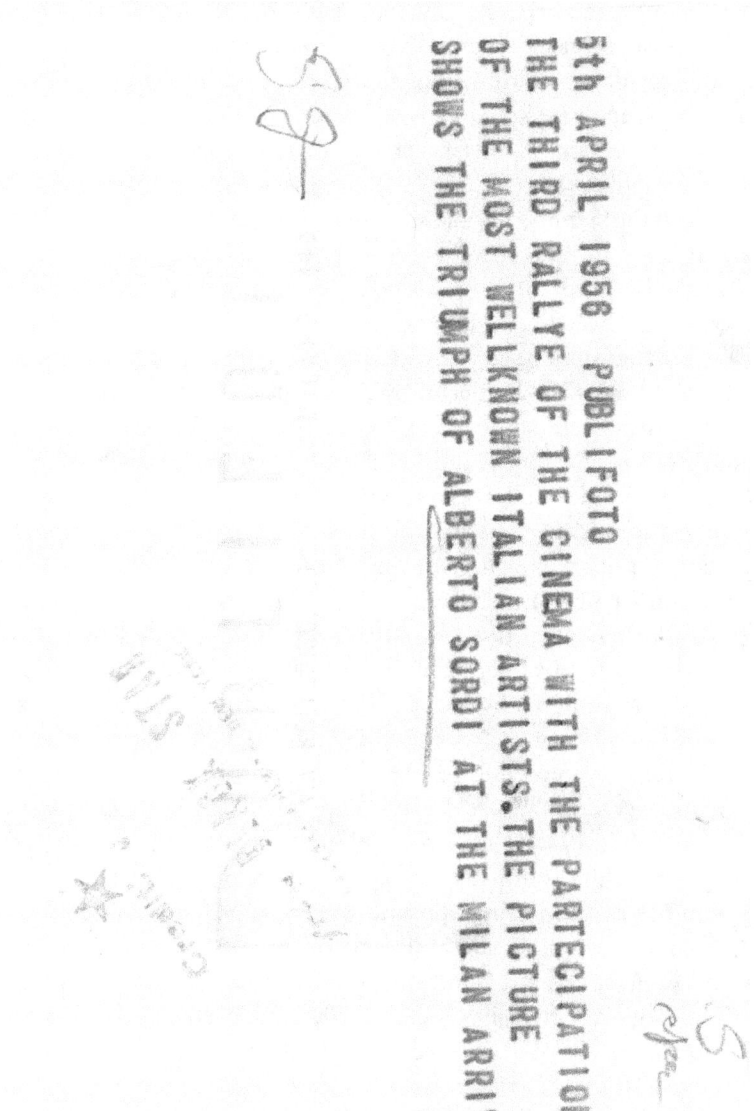

Figure 2.2 Celebrity automobility: unknown photographer, [The triumph of Alberto Sordi at the third 'Rallye del Cinema'], 5 April 1956, gelatin silver print. The Black Star Collection, Ryerson Image Centre (BS.2005.209410).

On the eve of the genre's explosion, the Rallye del Cinema, a yearly race organized by television mogul Ezio Radaelli, anticipated the radical shift in gender politics instigated by Italy's newfangled consumer automobilities. Celebrities competed against each other on a four-day timed drive from

Rome to Sanremo, passing by Siena and stopping first in Montecatini and then in Varese, near Milan. With the number 44 painted on its driver and passenger doors, Sordi's Giulietta carried him to victory, delivering the ambitious actor into the hands of his adoring fans.[1] Snapped upon Sordi's arrival in Milan, at least according to the caption that appears on the photograph's verso (Figure 2.2), the image exemplifies the unique bond between the star and his audience, which sustained him, both literally and figuratively, for the second half of the twentieth century.

In 1954, Sordi appeared in no fewer than fourteen films, and the following year he acted in nine more.[2] Milanese publisher Sedit released the first monographic study devoted to the Roman actor in 1955, in which film historian Tino Ranieri prophesied that 'If it put some order, finally, in the innermost identity of its lucrative son, Italian cinema could shortly find itself – and this would be healthy indeed – brutally facing its own image' (1955: 45–6). In essence, the equation of Alberto Sordi with Italian (cinematic) identity – which would accompany the actor throughout his career and define much of the scholarship devoted to him – was already beginning to take shape.[3] The small volume was part of a series of *tascabili* (pocket-size books) edited by noted critics Giuseppe Calzolari and Tullio Kezich. It is hardly a coincidence that the series' first issue, also published in 1955 and authored by Aldo Paladini, be devoted to Amedeo Nazzari, the actor who had been synonymous with Italian identity, at home and abroad, for at least two decades – as I discussed in this book's first part.

Unlike Nazzari, whose debut lead performance in *Cavalleria* (Goffredo Alessandrini, 1936) had defined the rest of his long career, Sordi had been struggling to hit his stride since the late 1930s, stringing together a number of supporting appearances and small roles, often uncredited, to complement his steady radio and voice work. A basso with a knack for vocal impersonations, Sordi dubbed several international actors, including and most famously Oliver Hardy, and participated in a variety of radio shows. The audience response to his first leading roles in the self-produced feature *Mamma mia, che impressione!* (Roberto Savarese, 1951), which he co-scripted with Cesare Zavattini and Vittorio De Sica, and *Lo sceicco bianco / The White Sheik* (Federico Fellini, 1952) was lukewarm at best, if not outright hostile. Fellini famously lobbied to cast the actor in his ensemble follow-up *I vitelloni* (1953),[4] accepting the producers' condition that Sordi's name would not appear on the film's promotional materials for fear that his presence would sink the picture.[5] Instead, Sordi seized the opportunity with both hands, turning in an acerbic performance that not only defined his future relationship with the audience, but eclipsed his co-stars.[6] The definitive affirmation of his talent arrived in 1954, when he appeared as wannabe American (but dyed-in-the-wool Roman) Nando Moriconi in a segment of *Un giorno in pretura/A Day in Court* (Steno, 1954), acting opposite comedy giant Peppino De Filippo. Sporting jeans and a coonskin cap, Nando parrots gestures and voices from his beloved American films, singing 'Yankee Doodle' with gibberish lyrics at every opportunity. So beloved was this character that Steno devoted the 1954 feature *Un americano a Roma/An American in Rome* to him, propelling Sordi into the pantheon of mid-century Italian film stardom.[7]

As I discussed in Part One of this book, Amedeo Nazzari's on-screen persona was aspirational. Heroic in his Fascist youth, paternal in his postwar melodramatic middle-age, Nazzari represented an idea of Italian masculinity that was articulated largely in positive terms: tall, elegant, handsome, refined, moral, and strong. Conversely, Sordi's persona was petty, self-serving, simultaneously haughty and weaselly. As Stephen Gundle writes, summarizing Goffredo Fofi's observations, 'he was moved only by personal interest and had no political or civil convictions. He was obsequious toward the powerful and arrogant toward the weak. He had few thoughts, no real capacity for love, and no morality' (2017: 203). His persona presented a radically different idea of *italianità*, one that did not purport to offer any particular behavioural or societal model. It was based on observation rather than aspiration, holding up a distorting mirror to a country that was rapidly turning away from the political commitment that had inspired Neorealism to embrace the frivolities of consumer culture – its small-minded rewards compensating for the population's moral shortcomings.[8] As Andrea Bini writes, 'Sordi's characters live in a society in which modernity means that the old religious, political, and moral virtues, regardless of their value, have lost their significance, without being replaced by others' (2011: 136). Sordi moulded his immense comedic talent and his sudden dramatic turns onto this pre- and post-boom Italy, becoming its unapologetic cinematic embodiment, warts and all. According to director Ettore Scola, who had a long-standing relationship with the comedy genius, Sordi did not represent the *italiano medio* (average Italian citizen):

> his Italian 'citizen' was all but average. He was extreme, paradigmatic, exaggerated, crazy. The average Italian in his films was the protagonist's victim. He had this great mission: when we talked about his future roles, if the character was not negative enough, or was not an expression of one of humankind's evils, he wasn't interested. (Scola 2010: 93)[9]

These sharply contrasting frameworks come into full relief in Guy Hamilton's *The Best of Enemies* (1961), a comedy set during the 1941 war in Abyssinia starring David Niven as Major Richardson, a sarcastic

British officer who trades barbs with both Italian actors (see cover image). In a role that conjures up memories of his colonial films of the 1930s and 1940s, Nazzari plays Major Fornari, the principled commander of a retreating Italian battalion, and Sordi his craven subordinate, Captain Blasi – a character reminiscent of Sordi's magisterial performance as self-professed coward Oreste Jacovacci in Mario Monicelli's *La grande guerra/The Great War* (1959). When the righteous Fornari is killed in action, Blasi's rank catapults him into the lead position, a responsibility he is both reluctant and ill-equipped to assume.[10] Soon enough, the heated exchanges between the moustachioed English actor and the round-faced Italian star turn into commentaries on national stereotypes. For instance, when Major Richardson orders Captain Blasi and his men, who are prisoners of the British military, to build a pointless latrine in the desert, Blasi replies: 'You English have so much self-respect that you have none left for other people. You think there's only one way of doing things, your way! Well, I'm an Italian! I do things the Italian way!' And then he proceeds to build a fully functioning outhouse complete with a decorative pinwheel and flags, displaying a degree of engineering ability and resourcefulness that leaves Richardson speechless. While the Italians are often treated with contempt by the enemy soldiers, the film does manage to create situations of collaboration and compassion, and even to include some decidedly anti-colonial rhetoric (flying in the face of historical accuracy). When the Europeans are ambushed and overpowered by a native army, their leader proclaims, 'Gentlemen, down with the King of England! Down with the King of Italy! And now may I suggest that you fight in your own countries and leave us to fight in ours, and all will be well. Now, kindly, leave.'

A fantasy of gentlemanly warfare written by Suso Cecchi d'Amico, Age-Scarpelli, and Jack Pulman, *The Best of Enemy*'s narrative is built on the empathy developing between enemies in the course of a long journey of retreat across the desert, during which they gradually lose their armaments, their prejudice, and their will to fight. As Rachel Woodward and K. Neil Jenkings note,

> The soldier is always mobile. From Gilgamesh onward, the warrior lifestyle has been associated with the vagaries of a mobile occupation and the self-discovery this offers. The Odyssey is synonymous with the travails of the travelling soldier, and the traveller in general. (Woodward and Jenkings 2014: 358)[11]

It is precisely this storytelling device, which hinges on the troops' mobility, that allows for the soldiers' camaraderie to develop. In the end, the Italians are captured and shipped to a POW camp on a train. As they board their wagon, the English salute them, recognizing their military stature as well as their humanity.

In the context of my argument about mobility and Italian identity on-screen, it is plain to see how *The Best of Enemies* functions as a symbolic passing of the torch between Nazzari and Sordi as the movie star that best reflected the taste of a society that transitioned from dictatorship to consumerism, having lived through almost two decades of national reconstruction and international rehabilitation, actively reshaping its identity via print media, the cinema, and television. However, Sordi's acting career also began during the *ventennio* and his first efforts were aligned with regime cinema, as were Nazzari's. Such is the case of *I tre aquilotti* (Mario Mattoli, 1942), in which Sordi plays an aviation cadet, sharing the screen with Leonardo Cortese (1916–84) and Carlo Minello (1918–47). A love song to the Accademia Aeronautica (Aviation Academy), its fresh-faced pilots, and their romantic adventures, the film takes a turn in the third act, when the young aviators are sent into battle – documentary footage of the Aeronautica Militare (Italian Air Force) providing some of the remarkable combat and action sequences.

Sordi's nervous physicality and sardonic intonation are a far cry from Nazzari's gravitas and granite jawline in *Luciano Serra pilota* (1938); in his review published in the 30 August 1942 issue of the newspaper *L'eco di Venezia*, critic Gaetano Garancini described Sordi as a 'promising new signing of our cinema, a handsome and confident young man, gifted with a mobile and expressive face' (qtd in Fava 2003: 46). The aerial antics that shaped Nazzari's heroic persona, and that were aligned with the regime's heavy investment in military aviation, do not leave any permanent traces on Sordi, who will come to embody an altogether different kind of Italian masculinity.

Sordi's minor turn as an armoured soldier in Goffredo Alessandrini's *Giarabub* (1942), an outright propagandist film about the Siege of Jaghbub (a four-month-long military engagement between Commonwealth and Italian forces in Libya), did not define his career either. The only military role[12] that comes close to his pre-boom comic success is *I quattro bersaglieri* (aka *Tripoli, bel suol d'amore*, 1954), a period piece set in the early twentieth century and loosely based on Alexandre Dumas's feuilleton *Les trois mousquetaires* (1844). The film was the last effort by director Ferruccio Cerio, who had debuted with *Il cavaliere senza nome* (1941), starring Amedeo Nazzari, and who decided to relocate to Venice in 1943, hoping to continue working during the short-lived, Mussolini-led, and unrepentantly Fascist Repubblica Sociale Italiana (September 1943–May 1945). Sordi plays one of the titular *bersaglieri* (marksmen), Alberto Ruotolo, a peasant who leaves his family farm on horseback to enlist in the high-mobility (they run instead of marching), light infantry unit of the then-named Regio Esercito Italiano (Royal Italian Army). The farcical tone of Cerio's picture is better suited than *I tre aquilotti* and *Giarabub* to Sordi's comic timing, and the actor is given plentiful opportunities to display his vocal and physical abilities. He sings, masters the parallel bars, waltzes with Maria Carocci (Lyla Rocco), and engages in a fistfight that ends up as an all-out brawl on the stage of the theatre where Nadia (Fulvia Franco), donning a tricoloured dress, performs 'A Tripoli'. The film borrows its title from the song's first verse, which was written by Giovanni Corvetto (lyrics) and Colombino Arona (music) in 1911, on the eve of the Italo-Turkish War (29 September 1911–18 October 1912) that resulted in the creation of Italian Libya. Ironically, while *I quattro bersaglieri* anachronistically celebrates a colonial war, the aforementioned *The Best of Enemies* chronicles the demise of Italian colonialism, and in both films Sordi emerges as embodying an idea of the Italian soldier that was grounded in fiction (nationalist in the former, cowardly in the latter), rather than in historical record.

Unlike his contemporary Marcello Mastroianni, Sordi was never able to capitalize on his domestic success to become an internationally recognized movie star. His other roles in major foreign productions are the level-headed Father Galli in *A Farewell to Arms* (Charles Vidor, 1957), alongside an irresistible Vittorio De Sica,[13] and the buffoonish Count Emilio Ponticelli in Ken Annakin's *Those Magnificent Men in Their Flying Machines; Or, How I Flew from London to Paris in 25 Hours 11 Minutes* (1965), an ensemble comedy about an air race from London to Paris in the early age of aviation (again, unlike Nazzari, when piloting an aircraft the Roman actor never cuts a heroic figure).

As the following chapters will demonstrate, even when set abroad and perpetually on the move, Sordi's films remained culturally Italian, interested in commenting on the rapidly evolving society and the challenges facing it decade after decade. With a handful of exceptions, his career was marked by a desire to reveal Italians to themselves, rather than to outsiders. This book's second part is thus divided into five chapters loosely describing actions that motivate a journey or occur during an instance of mobility in a wide array of films featuring Alberto Sordi in a leading or supporting role.

Chapter 6 is devoted to vacationing, and focuses on a sample of Sordi's many travel comedies in the late 1950s, a sub-genre in which the Roman actor thrived. Chapter 7, which borrows its title from Article 1 of the Fundamental Principles of the 1947 Constitution of the Italian Republic, surveys films dealing with issues of labour mobility. Chapter 8 looks at lawbreaking in its various forms, at home and abroad, examining how infrastructure and transportation technology participate in crime's ability to cross national boundaries on screen. Chapter 9 introduces the figure of the actor-cum-explorer via the cinematic medium, reaching farther and farther into the travel imaginary of domestic audiences. The final chapter, Chapter 10, focuses on the rise of global petrocultures, looping back to Italy's peculiar relationship with celebrity, automobilities, and the diaspora.

Notes

1. In his biography of the famed actor, Giancarlo Governi notes that Sordi privileged small and utilitarian cars over more luxurious models: 'Alberto never owned a boat and his automobile was always an average one, for an average Italian person. His last car was a Fiat Punto' (2010: 10).
2. Twelve, according to Ranieri (1955: 24).
3. Many of my sources underscore the association of the Roman actor with Italian identity. To list just a few, Giancarlo Governi's volume is titled *Alberto Sordi, l'italiano* (2010); Enrico Giacovelli's book is *Un italiano a Roma: La vita, i successi, le passioni di Alberto Sordi* (2003); Silvana Giacobini's biography is *Albertone: Alberto Sordi, una leggenda italiana* (2018); *L'Italia in bianco e nero* is the subtitle of Goffredo Fofi's lengthy study of Sordi (2004); Vincenzo Mollica and Alessandro Nicosia's edited volume opts for *Sordi Segreto: Un italiano a Roma* (2004).
4. Kezich writes that 'Against the advice of everyone, Fellini wants Alberto Sordi, who is very unavailable. He's on tour with Wanda Osiris in the variety show *Gran Baraonda* (Big Ruckus), and the crew has to chase him from one stop to the next, following him to places like Viterbo and Florence, in order to film him. [. . .] Smuggled into the cast by Fellini against the producer's most ardent wishes, Sordi is now considered box-office poison in the movie world. So much so that the distributors demand a clause in the contract that his name won't appear on the posters. But it will be *I vitelloni* that will launch Sordi's career, and after this appearance he'll be like parsley instead of poison on the Italian screen.' Interestingly, it is a scene about automobility that stands out: 'The *vitelloni* [layabouts] are driving back from a day in the country and pass by some workers repairing the road. Sordi's character, Alberto, can't resist the temptation to taunt them. Leering out the car window he cries, "*Lavoratori!*" (Workers!), and then flips them the bird and gives them a raspberry. "Hard labor!" He persists and then their car breaks down – right there. Terrified, the coward runs off, the workers in hot pursuit, and the *vitelloni* are all caught and soundly beaten' (2006: 133–4).
5. According to Kezich, in Alberto Lattuada's *Il delitto di Giovanni Episcopo/Flesh Will Surrender* (1947), 'Alberto Sordi plays a shady part in the movie and, assisted by his friend Fellini's screenplay, begins developing what will

become his signature role: the insolent troublemaker. Fabrizi had harboured reservations about Sordi ever since he'd seen him impersonating a Roman soldier in a variety show, and Fellini recalls how irritated Fabrizi was at his co-actor's brash efforts to get noticed. During the shooting of *Episcopo*, he complains that Sordi is trying to steal his scenes' (2006: 64).

6. On Sordi's irreverence towards (if not contempt for) his audience, see Anile (2018).
7. In 1955, the actor was invited to Kansas City, where he received the keys to the city. He also scouted for locations for a sequel to *Un americano a Roma*, which was to be titled *Un romano in America*. The film was never made. On the contested genesis and tragic fate of this character, see Anile (2020). Marcia Landy rightly notes that 'A most important ingredient of Sordi's star persona, similarly to other Italian comedians, is his identification with a particular landscape, in his case the Roman, largely urban milieu' (2008: 145). While this is undoubtedly true, it is also worth considering that Sordi carried his Romanness in his voice, wherever he went – and as I show in this book, he travelled to many disparate places while remaining singularly Roman.
8. 'During the 1950s, and in particular during the years of the economic miracle, Italy saw a radical increase in the sociological importance of mass consumption. While the country remained poor by European standards, a modern consumer culture diffused by the media managed to establish itself as an overall referent for discourses on modernization' (Arvidsson 2003: 89).
9. I agree with Sergio Rigoletto when he writes that the expression *italiano medio* is often used rather imprecisely, and with him 'I refer to l'*italiano medio* as a discourse, as a term that is made intelligible and culturally meaningful by reference to its ability to reflect some of the putative attitudes and shortcomings of average Italians' (2010: 33). Of course, what exactly constitutes an 'average Italian' remains to be determined, since the very notion of shared commonalities is predicated on systemic exclusions.
10. It should be noted that in the English-language edition of this film, Sordi used his own voice, while Nazzari was dubbed. Sordi was nominated for a Bafta (1962) and a Golden Globe (1962) for his performance, but won neither.
11. For more on military mobilities and masculinity, see Higate (2003).
12. Of course, Sordi's most memorable war film is Mario Monicelli's masterful *La grande guerra* (1959), in which the actor gives one of his career-defining performances. Also of note is Sordi's turn as Lieutenant Alberto Innocenti in Luigi Comencini's *Tutti a casa* (1960), which chronicles the troubled journey home of military personnel after the armistice of 8 September 1943.
13. In her 31 March 1958 review of *A Farewell to Arms* in *La Gazzetta del lunedì*, Gugliemina Setti noted that 'in the role of the chaplain, Alberto Sordi proves that he could finally break out of the type to which our producers have thus far confined him' (qtd in Fava 2003: 113).

CHAPTER 6

Vacationing: The Rise of the Travelling Comedian

Through the figure of Alberto Sordi, this chapter considers the rise of travel comedies in the 1950s, a popular sub-genre that helps illuminate the complex interrelation between leisure travel, internal and external migration, capitalism, and infrastructure. In the Italian case, this kind of cinema allows us to interrogate issues such as the country's emerging position as industrial superpower vis-à-vis its varied development and changing demographics. When studying issues of mid-century Italian human mobility, we must consider several simultaneous phenomena, ranging from the beginning of international tourism to the opening of new routes for the ongoing diaspora; from economic chain migration from the South to the North of the peninsula to the slow decline in agricultural seasonal labour. Moreover, because of Italy's long history of deracination and displacement, the national film industry has been particularly active in liaising with Italian communities abroad, enlisting stars for international tours and nurturing diasporic organizations that regularly consumed its products.[1] Finally, while official rhetoric downplayed the country's involvement in colonialism, a repression that impacted scholarship and public discourse for half a century, Italian cinematic travel in the 1950s was still tied to the memory of recent military mobilities: for instance, in Michelangelo Antonioni's 1950 *Cronaca di un amore/Story of a Love Affair*, when the star-crossed lovers leave the planetarium where they had furtively met, Guido (Massimo Girotti) declares, 'It was like being in Africa. I spent whole nights gazing at the stars.' This sort of colonial recall is not a privilege afforded only to lofty existential melodramas. One of the films I discuss in this chapter, Camillo Mastrocinque's *Vacanze d'inverno* (1959), is set in the posh winter resort of Cortina d'Ampezzo; in this film, accountant (Rag.) Alberto Moretti (Alberto Sordi) explains to his adolescent daughter that men prey on women her age. He argues that his knowledge comes from his experience abroad: 'Your dad has lived, your dad knows the world, he's well travelled! I've been to Africa, Albania,

Greece, Yugoslavia, Montenegro . . .' Attempting to assuage his fears, his daughter replies, 'But you were there as a soldier! You know the barracks, life in the trenches, you didn't stay in Grand Hotels . . .' Similarly, Sordi's character in *Il diavolo / To Bed or Not to Bed* (Gianni Polidori, 1963), which I will discuss in the next chapter, confesses that he killed a Greek man when he was deployed in Albania.

In this chapter, I will consider *Vacanze d'inverno*, *Racconti d'estate / Love on the Riviera* (Gianni Franciolini, 1958), *Oh! Qué mambo* (John Berry, 1959), *Costa Azzurra* (Vittorio Sala, 1959), and *Brevi amori a Palma di Maiorca* (Giorgio Bianchi, 1959), a representative sample of travel comedies all featuring Alberto Sordi in one of their many vignettes, or storylines. This relatively new type of film often featured a large ensemble cast and episodic narratives, and showcased picturesque locations at home and abroad; these 'translocalities', as Arjun Appadurai terms them, are communities where

> the logic of movement is provided by the leisure industries, which create tourist sites and locations around the world [. . .] in which ties of marriage, work, business, and leisure weave together various circulating populations with kinds of locals to create neighborhoods that belong in one sense to particular nation-states. (Appadurai 1996: 192)

The success of these titles and their rapid serialization can be explained by the transformations in Italy's socioeconomic structure brought about in the mid-1950s and early 1960s by a set of favourable factors, including the financial upturn generally described as the 'boom' or the 'miracle'.[2] The boom created a class of citizens for whom the notion of leisure travel coexisted alongside migration, diaspora, economic displacement, and seasonal labour, historically the more traditional forms of Italian human mobility. In general terms, the development of Italy's tourism industry corresponds to the timeline developed by sociologist Adrian S. Franklin, who identifies two principal eras of tourism mobilities in the west: Mobilities I (1850–1960), which was characterized by the railway expansion and establishment of tourist hubs; and Mobilities II (1960–present), which was occasioned by the mass ownership of automobiles and the advent of commercial airlines (Franklin 2014). As cultural historian Anna Maria Torriglia comments, 'the journey became, around the fifties and well into that decade, a major icon to represent the changing sociocultural landscape of Italy' (2002: 119). For the first time in the history of the country, average Italians enjoyed some degree of mobility inside and outside the country, and even relocation to a place that would have been considered exotic before the boom became more of a choice and less of a necessity for many.

In his book on the history of Italian film comedy, Enrico Giacovelli argues that

> now even travelling becomes a status symbol, at times even a mass phenomenon, since it is a direct heir of the boom and of the energies it needed to unleash. After having explored Italy and its surroundings, we explored the world. But the world is just a way to better understand Italy. (Giacovelli 2002: 112)

In other words, travel comedies were a kind of cinema that lent itself to the articulation of national concerns, particularly in their depiction of encounters and clashes between Italians and 'others' as the former endeavoured to cross cultural, sexual, economic, ethnic, class, and racial boundaries. Moreover, as Valerio Coladonato and Paolo Noto observe, these pictures also selected 'landscape as the privileged means by which Italian cinema both defined itself as national and participated in the process of national identity building' (2017: 111). In travel comedies, they continue,

> the national landscape is to some extent 'feminized' as a space of contemplation, an object of the gaze (and a product thereof); but it is also – and perhaps even more significantly – the space where an updated set of competences emerge for male characters, thus making tourism one of the activities that mould the complicated relationship between consumer culture, the modernization of the nation, and the new (or at least updated) gender roles of this decade. (Coladonato and Noto 2017: 113)

In fact, as we will soon discover, it is not uncommon for travel comedies to feature examples of sexual tourism (predominantly, but not exclusively male and heterosexual) that range from the romantic to the outright predatory.

In the pre-credit sequence of the Italian-language version of John Berry's *Oh! Qué mambo* (1959), Alberto Sordi, his back to the camera, walks towards the sea on a windy beach. He begins to chuckle when, peeking over his shoulder, he realizes that he is being followed by the invisible cinematic eye. He turns, rests his elbow on the side of a fishing boat, and addresses the intruder: 'What do you want? You recognized me . . .', he says looking straight into the lens, coquettishly running his hand through his hair. 'Yes, I'm in the movie too. In truth, I shouldn't be in this story, because it takes place entirely on the French Riviera, and I'm a Roman . . . Allow me to introduce myself: I'm Nando, a lifeguard.' And then he proceeds to reveal how his character, Nando, ended up on the Riviera, where he runs a fitness programme for elderly (rich) women – the obvious implication being that in order to enjoy their wealth, he must suffer their companionship. He confesses that his life became more complicated upon the arrival of the beautiful Liliana (Magali Noël), but before giving away the movie's plot, he runs off saying, 'I'll see you later! I'm in the movie too! Mambo!'

By 1959, Sordi had long overcome his early-career box office troubles. In fact, he had accumulated a long list of credits, some of which were in leading roles, and most in scores of light-hearted ensemble cast comedies. Clearly, this highly reflexive prologue was an attempt to anchor the film to the actor's rising star, which in Italy far outshone even that of Magali Noël, who would go on to appear in a variety of Italian films, including Luciano Emmer's *La ragazza in vetrina/Woman in the Window* (1961), and Federico Fellini's *La dolce vita* (1960), *Satyricon* (1969), and *Amarcord* (1973).

Oh! Qué mambo is a French–Italian co-production primarily centred on the conjugal troubles of Liliana (Noël) and her husband Miguel, who is played by the multitalented Darío Moreno (1921–68), the polyglot Turkish singer and songwriter who enjoyed enormous success in the 1950s and 1960s with his Latin-inspired club music. Noël receives first billing, Moreno second, and Sordi is a distant fifth, his name introduced by a qualifying 'and with'. Nonetheless, the actor appears fairly prominently in the film, often stationed on the beach or the adjacent boardwalk (liminal spaces that befit his foreign masculinity), as he despotically subjects his army of elderly admirers to a fitness regime as rigorous as it is silly. While the prologue's reflexivity is not sustained throughout, the film does contain a small nod to the character of Nando Moriconi, Sordi's breakout role in *Un americano a Roma*. The boardwalk features a large poster for Edward Dmytryk's *The Young Lions* (1958), a Second World War drama starring Marlon Brando, Montgomery Clift, and Dean Martin; when Liliana rejects Nando's advances, she compares him unfavourably with Brando, whom she deems 'a truly handsome man'. After the woman walks away, Nando gazes wistfully at the poster and admits, 'Brando, of course ... He's an American!' – implying that his nationality, which was Nando Moricone's envy, somehow gives him an advantageous position in matters of the heart. The lifeguard then returns to the beach, enters a changing booth, and resurfaces as a poor-man's Brando, mannerisms and all: shirt unbuttoned, hair combed forward, jaw protruding outward. Certainly not by coincidence, *Oh! Qué mambo*'s Italian title is *Il giovane leone* ('the young lion'), a clear marketing effort to capitalize on Brando's appeal via Sordi's caricature, and to shift the spotlight from Moreno onto the Italian star.

This rebranding can also be observed in the film's ending, in which the wayward married couple is finally reunited. The last scene takes place in a nightclub where Miguel, donning a sombrero, performs the film's final musical number. Nando, who struck out with Liliana, resumes his previous occupation as trainer (and private companion) of elderly ladies, but is now facing the tough competition of 'Mister Costa Azzurra '58' (Mr French Riviera '58), a bodybuilder who crushes Nando's fingers when shaking his hand. However, the film's Italian edition closes with an incongruous epilogue entirely devoted to the lifeguard (and quite possibly shot on the very same day and location as the equally independent prologue): wearing the outfit he dons in the opening, but styled differently, Nando addresses the camera from behind a fence, confessing that he has since left the posh French Riviera and returned to humble Ostia, where he is employed in a Catholic seaside colony for children. There, his efforts to sweet-talk an attractive foreign bather are neutered by an officious nun.[3]

As this brief account shows, much of the travel comedies' appeal was tied to fantasies of sexual conquests and extramarital affairs that often remained unfulfilled. One of the sub-genre's first examples was Luciano Emmer's *Parigi è sempre Parigi/Paris is Always Paris* (1951), which established the tropes that would reappear in Sordi's many travelling romps. In this film, the event occasioning the railway travel of a group of Italians to the French capital is a football match between the respective national teams. The film's structure is simple: it utilizes an exotic and chic location as a backdrop against which many vignettes are set. A large ensemble cast of actors with different characteristics and acting styles allows for the greatest degree of identification and empathy on the audience's part.[4] If in *Parigi* the *Italiano all'estero* (Italian abroad) tropes were still very much incubating, it is possible to detect a certain typification that is most evident in the secondary characters, which include a swindler, a 'Latin lover', a die-hard Francophile, and some LGBTQ personages whose sexuality is sensationalized for (cheap) comedic purposes. One of the film's many narrative strands is concerned with the romance between the handsome Franco (Franco Interlenghi) and a French girl who works in a newsstand, Christine (Hélène Rémy). The short-lived affair, whose touching sweetness is made possible by its intrinsic brevity, contains the possibility of deracination and migration for either lover, which is ultimately curtailed by the group's narrative trajectory. Franco must return to Italy and leave Christine behind for their fling to have memorable status; it is the very fact that their union remains only potential that makes it so compelling.

Parigi è sempre Parigi is not a film about migration; it is a comedy about Italy's fast-growing economy, which for the first time allows its citizens to visit locations for leisure, and not only while searching for employment and social mobility, freely taking advantage of the rail infrastructure the regime had kept hostage for two decades. Migration remains an unexplored avenue for the young international lovers in order for the film to project the image of a changed Italy; no longer that of Neorealism and the immediate postwar as in *Il cammino della speranza/The Path of Hope* (Pietro Germi, 1950), a film about the harrowing journey from Sicily to the French Alps of a group of destitute migrants, but the more optimistic one ushered in by reconstruction and economic recovery. Emmer recalls that this storyline was added to the film after the others were completed:

> I wanted to finish the film, but the producers deserted it, because they did not want a story like this one. I went to the distributor, a Greek who owned Minerva Films. I told him that this was criminal, that without this story the film did not exist. He gave me a cheque, I went to Paris with one operator, a camera and the two actors, and I shot the episode. It was a beautiful moment. (Emmer qtd in Francia di Celle and Ghezzi 2004: 215)

As we shall see, the last film in this chapter, *Brevi amori a Palma di Maiorca*, includes two variations on this delicate theme and, in a strictly evaluative sense, botches both. In fact, many of Sordi's travel comedies, especially the episodic ones, reprise this familiar scenario by virtue of their formulaic nature: characters travel to an exotic destination (by rail, car, ship, or more rarely air) where they experience a sexual awakening which gives way to self-discovery, often made explicit during (or immediately before) their return voyage.

Released only weeks after *Oh! Qué mambo*, Vittorio Sala's *Costa Azzurra* (1959) is similarly set in the French Riviera and chronicles summer flings and the conjugal troubles of vacationing Italians. Sordi's storyline begins aboard a train, his character delivering much of the expository dialogue, which was written by Rodolfo Sonego: Alberto (Sordi), a Roman greengrocer, is travelling with his wife Giovanna (Giovanna Ralli) to France for a screen test with the famed film director Maestri (Luciano Mondolfo). Despite her obvious beauty, Giovanna's suitability for acting is immediately questioned. However, Maestri takes an interest in Alberto, inviting him to his villa for a private chat. The film clearly codes Maestri and his assistants as gay in stereotypical and homophobic ways, but the Roman couple remains unaware. When Alberto meets with Maestri poolside, the director breaks the news that he will not employ Giovanna in his next film; however, he also compliments Alberto's 'natural' behaviour (a quality that comes across in Sordi's scene-stealing reaction to Maestri's decision), and one of his assistants compares him to a young Jean Gabin. Similarly to what happens in *Oh! Qué mambo*, the comparison furnishes Sordi with the chance to launch into an impression of the iconic French actor. Interestingly, when he presents his new persona to Giovanna, the woman compares him not to Gabin, but to Alberto's emigrant grandfather who, she says, donned the same plaid ivy cap, a clear indication that, at this stage of Italy's socioeconomic transformation, leisure mobility and migration were still entangled within the Italian subconscious.

Also of note is Alberto's choice to hum the song 'C'est si bon' at every opportunity; written in 1947 by Henri Betti (music) and André Hornez (lyrics), the tune was popularized not by Gabin, but by the Italian-born French *chanteur* and actor Yves Montand, who also made a cameo appearance in *Parigi è sempre Parigi* to sing the equally popular 'Les feuilles mortes'. When the film returns to this vignette, Alberto has slipped further into character, reciting lines (scrambling French and Italian) from the classic *Pépé le Moko* (Julien Duvivier, 1937), in which Jean Gabin plays a gentleman bandit who has taken refuge from the police in Algiers's casbah – another highly heterocultural Mediterranean location. Still wearing the cap, Alberto is fully immersed in the role when Giovanna interrupts him, demanding an explanation for his strange behaviour. His shirt unbuttoned, Alberto explains to his puzzled wife that he secretly harboured a desire to be 'discovered', and expresses his admiration for Marlon Brando and other notable American actors – which he shares with *Oh! Qué mambo*'s histrionic lifeguard. In the following scene, Alberto's impression has morphed into a stylized James Dean: his hair is combed into a pomaded pompadour, and he wears a bright red shirt, collar upturned, a look that apes Dean's signature get-up in *Rebel Without a Cause* (Nicholas Ray, 1955); but unlike Dean's denim-clad lower limbs, Sordi's knock-kneed legs remain bare.

The synchronicity of travel and migration comes into full view when Alberto is invited for a 'prova decisiva' (final test) at Maestri's villa, where he learns that the butler is also a Roman who's been plucked out of a pedestrian job (he shares that he used to be a bartender on cruise ships) to live beside the famous director, a destiny that has filled him with 'malinconia' (melancholy) – likely his own definition of immigrant's nostalgia. In the end, Giovanna interrupts this final test, which consists of a candlelight dinner followed by a poolside tango with Maestri. Alberto, still under the spell of promised stardom, does not realise that the man expected him to succumb to his advances. The vignette ends the way it began, with the Roman greengrocer recounting his adventures to a fellow passenger in a train compartment, presumably on the way home. However, something has changed in Alberto: he still wears his hair in a pompadour, his shirt collar is turned up, and he cools himself with a handheld fan. In other words, Alberto's demeanour has acquired a softness and coquettishness that he did not possess at the outset of the film. His awareness of what the director's final test might have entailed is unclear, as is his willingness to take it. While the train leaves the Riviera and enters a tunnel, Alberto gazes wistfully out the window, humming 'C'est si bon'.

It is hard to imagine that, to a mid-century audience accustomed to mainstream cinema's heteronormativity, this vignette read as anything other than a homophobic joke at the expense of a community that, significantly, is depicted as residing abroad, outside of the biopolitical boundaries of both the country and the nation. However, when scrutinized with a twenty-first-century sensibility, Maestri's predatory behaviour also prompts Alberto to confess his innermost desires of being moulded (as he puts it) into a star, and perhaps helps him learn something about himself. In fact, in his 18 September 1959 review for *La Stampa*, the perceptive Leo Pestelli panned the film, nevertheless noting that 'the film's least worst episode is the rather courageous one featuring the couple Alberto Sordi–Giovanna Ralli' (qtd in Fava 2003: 135). Of course, the implications of Alberto's discovery, as well as the film's overall stance towards homosexuality, are well beyond the scope of my analysis. Nevertheless, a cursory look at the history of Italian cinema set abroad reveals that *Costa Azzurra* might be, in this respect, surprisingly progressive. For instance, in Luciano Emmer's aforementioned *La ragazza in vetrina*, when brawny miner Federico (Lino Ventura) realizes that he has erroneously patronized a gay club in Amsterdam's red light district, he reacts with extreme violence, throwing punches left and right until he is unceremoniously kicked to the kerb. While the text itself condemns Federico's behaviour and overall machismo, it does not contemplate the notion that he might learn something from the exchange, nor does it depict gay characters in a shared, open urban environment, instead relegating them to a space that is inherently transgressive. Conversely, *Costa Azzurra* envisions a scenario in which power relations are reversed, the gay characters holding all the metaphorical cards. Wealth, education, and status are theirs to dole out to Roman greengrocers, Swedish models, and any other aspiring stars to whom they give audience in their sun-drenched seaside court.

The trajectory of Alberto's subplot in Camillo Mastrocinque's *Vacanze d'inverno* is not too dissimilar from that of his namesake in *Costa Azzurra*, but it is shared with (and partially displaced onto) his teenage daughter Titti (Christine Kaufmann), and articulated across two transportation technologies: the automobile and the railway (Figures 2.3 and 2.4). It is behind the wheel of his modest Fiat 600 (a brilliant flash of inspiration of co-screenwriter Rodolfo Sonego) that Rag. Alberto Moretti and Titti reach picturesque Cortina D'Ampezzo, limbs frozen after a twenty-hour drive from Rome. Nicknamed 'la Perla delle Dolomiti' (Pearl of the

Figures 2.3 and 2.4 Families in transit: social mobility via transportation technology.

Dolomites), Cortina is home to the Grand Hotel, an upscale establishment frequented by international aristocrats and businesspeople – echoes of Edmund Goulding's 1932 *Grand Hotel* reverberate through the picture. Alberto and Titti, who are of middle-class background, have won an almost all-inclusive stay in the extravagant ski resort on a TV game show, and they struggle to keep up with the costly lifestyle of the upper crust. To be more precise, Titti manages to navigate the situation with poise, quickly making friends and attracting the attention of Prince Franco (Geronimo Meynier), while Alberto overspends in an attempt to compensate for his lack of social graces and status. The man's inability to fit in with the posh environment is clear from the very beginning: while Titti and Alberto are being checked into their rooms by none other than Vittorio De Sica, who plays the hotel's dignified concierge, a bellboy asks the piqued accountant to move his vehicle, claiming that he has parked it in the way of the hotel's entrance. Over the course of the film, Alberto develops a taste for luxury, and proceeds to splurge on expensive drinks, dinners, and gifts for the distinguished patrons. He also flirts conspicuously and clumsily with Countess Paola Parioli (Eleonora Rossi Drago), who receives his attention with grace, but remains faithful to her husband. In the meantime, level-headed Titti coyly romances the young prince, who genuinely falls for the girl. In the end, Alberto must leave his car behind as collateral for the 300,000 lire he owes the Grand Hotel, an arrangement he comes to with the sympathetic concierge. The accountant and his daughter leave on the *Ferrovia delle Dolomiti*, a line operated by Società Ferrovia delle Dolomiti (SFD), whose trains used to connect downtown Cortina with Dobbiaco and Calalzo di Cadore (in the province of Belluno), where the duo will catch the express train to Rome. Leaning from the window of the characteristic white-and-blue car, Alberto listens to an embarrassed Franco confess his love for Titti, who reciprocates his affection. After setting some boundaries, Alberto invites the young man to call him 'papà' (Dad).

At the film's beginning, ownership of an automobile constitutes a point of pride for the Roman family – although their Fiat 600 is a far cry from the red Alfa Romeo Giulietta coupe parked outside the hotel in the establishing shot. The idea of driving from the capital to the Alps belongs to Alberto's wife, whose concern with appearances forces her husband and daughter to endure an uncomfortable and lengthy journey across half the country. Conversely, the rational Titti makes a point of telling her father that she would have preferred the comfort of a train. In the end, for the family's social status to actually improve, which happens by way of courtship and a possible marriage, private automobility must be surrendered. Replaced by mass transit, albeit in the form of the exquisitely wood-trimmed cabins of the electric SFD train, the humble Fiat 600 stays behind in Cortina. Similarly to *Costa Azzurra*'s ending, the train (or in this case, the platform) becomes the site for public confessions of emotional growth, self-discovery, and (possibly) sexual awareness.

In Gianni Franciolini's 1958 *Racconti d'estate*, the social status of Sordi's character is analogously tied to automobility, as is the outcome of his cinematic journey to the picturesque Tigullio Gulf. Shot in lush Eastmancolor and wide Totalscope format, the Italian–French co-production makes the most of the upscale facilities and the breathtaking vistas of the Ligurian coast. All but one of the film's episodes are based on sketches by Alberto Moravia; the one featuring Sordi was written by his trusted collaborator Rodolfo Sonego, and was shot quickly, since at the time the actor was in Hamburg working on *I magliari*/*The Swindlers* (Francesco Rosi, 1959) (Sanguineti 2015: 173).

Aristarco Battistini (Alberto Sordi) arrives at the Excelsior Palace Hotel in Rapallo behind the wheel of a luxurious 1958 Plymouth Belvedere convertible belonging to Miss Ada Gallotti (Anita Allan), a corpulent soprano he showers with constant attention. Aristarco lives off the wealthy artist, fulfilling the duties of private secretary and reluctant lover. The seaside location is replete with temptations for the man's wandering eye, and he even launches into a dance through a crowd of sunbathing girls. Sordi never missed a chance to improvise a few steps, and in this case the dance is consonant with the backstory of his character, who claims to have left professional ballet to look after Ada and support her career. Crossing paths with his old flame Jacqueline (Dany Carrel, who first appears in a much smaller 1958 Fiat 1100 alongside five friends) throws Aristarco into a tailspin, and he begins to meet his lover in private – interestingly, these short scenes take place primarily on boats. Aristarco lies to Jacqueline about his finances and begins to plan an escape with the young Frenchwoman. At the same time, he intends to defraud Ada of her Tuscan villa, a scam he engineers with the complicity of her lawyer. However, the scheme backfires, and Aristarco is forced to marry Ada to share in her wealth: in the episode's closing beats, the newlyweds climb into the Plymouth before an incredulous Jaqueline. A tearful Aristarco turns his head to gaze at her one last time, and then drives off. On the way out of town in their outsized American car, the couple aptly performs 'Là ci darem la mano', the duettino between Don Giovanni and Zerlina in Wolfgang Amadeus Mozart's comic opera chronicling the indiscretions of the fictional Lothario.

Social status and romantic bliss appear to be mutually exclusive to Aristarco and to Sordi's other travelling characters in *Oh! Qué mambo*, *Costa Azzurra*, and *Vacanze d'inverno*. In other words, their ability to move (up the social ladder or across an especially beautiful landscape) is inversely proportional to their happiness, a characteristic that these pedestrian travel comedies share with the more hallowed titles in the *commedia all'italiana* (Italian-style comedy) canon.[5] In fact, as Marcia Landy writes,

> The *commedia all'italiana*, like the *commedia dell'arte*, was dependent on three significant elements integrally linked to Sordi's star persona: first, a versatile range of comic social figures; second, an emphasis on energetic physical comedy, on clowning, gags, tricks, and verbal play; and third, an episodic, in some instances improvisational, form of narration. (Landy 2008: 146–7)

This chapter's last film, however, might constitute the only outlier in this string of bittersweet endings. Sordi is first billed in the opening credits of Giorgio Bianchi's 1959 *Brevi amori a Palma di Maiorca*. In broken Spanish, the comedy genius sings an upbeat song that accompanies these first shots, creating the impression that he is actually the film's protagonist. However, even if the picture was sold entirely on his back (as the trailer suggests), his screen time in *Brevi amori* is quite limited, amounting to a handful of scenes that he shares with English actress Belinda Lee, who also co-stars in Francesco Rosi's *I magliari*, a contemporary title I will discuss in the next chapter. Similarly to *Racconti d'estate*, Sordi's episode was written by Rodolfo Sonego.

True to form, the travel romp employs the choral structure pioneered by *Parigi è sempre Parigi*, intercutting between the romantic adventures of two vacationing handsome young men, Ernesto (Antonio Cifariello) and Gianni (Vicente Parra), and the stalking of famed American actress Mary Moore (Lee) by the clubfooted Anselmo Pandolfini (Sordi). The title credits are superimposed on footage of a cruise ship gliding into Palma's harbour in fair weather, and the closing shots reverse the trajectory, depicting the characters as they board the vessel that will return them to Italy, end credits rolling while it gets underway.

Transportation technology is front and centre in most travel comedies, speaking volumes about notions of class, social status, and mobilities, and *Brevi amori* is no exception. Moreover, Peter Adey reminds us that maritime mobilities are particularly rich sites for the interrogation of the relationship between private and public spaces, since ships 'provide secessionary islands of privacy and prosperity for the rich', and that 'cruise ship mobilities move along with, and are supported by, a range of other infrastructures and investments that tie up global capital with exotic locations, while untying local economies and the population from the benefits' (2017: 140). By replacing auto and rail with maritime mobilities of the cruise ship variety, *Brevi amori* both circumvents the issue of Italy's modernization and gets right to its core: with wealth still being the primary engine of tourism (which will not necessarily be true with the advent of low-cost airlines and study-abroad programmes), cinematic fantasies of international travel are tied to class mobility and romance.

In addition, what changes from the titles discussed above is the fact that Sordi gives Anselmo a limb difference, a peculiarity that was absent in his other 'vacationing' roles.[6] Kim Sawchuk contends that while impairment is a biomechanical fact related to the condition of one's physical body, disability is a social construction inherent to space (which is generally designed and articulated for 'normal' bodies) and culture (which is governed by multifarious and stratified relations of power) (Sawchuk 2014: 411). According to Sawchuk, impairment and disability must be understood within the framework of 'differential mobilities', since our bodies are both unique to each of us and in constant transition (from young to old, across different conditions of im/mobility), an understanding that yields a 'perspective on impairment as an ontogenetic process' that 'is intended to dismantle the binary system of normal/abnormal, impaired/healthy, abled/disabled' (2014: 410).

Through his raucous performance as the limping, yet athletically gifted Anselmo, Sordi punctures these binaries with confidence, his hand steady at the wheel of a characterization that never veers into the pathetic or the offensive. If anything, the vitality of his storyline, propelled by his physical verve as well as by Lee's impeccable timing as the comedian's straightwoman, reveals the flatness of the principal ones. In fact, Ernesto and Gianni begin their vacation as young wannabe Casanovas (as one of the Spanish characters dubs them), and they court sexually liberated older women; but in the end they return to Italy engaged to a wholesome Italian and a demure Spaniard, respectively. Conversely, Anselmo perseveres in his pursuit of Mary, weaselling himself into her life: he slides notes under her cabin door before they disembark; he shows up at the bullfight, where the actress is enjoying some local folklore; he manages to get invited to her poker night (and proceeds to sweep up all the winnings); and eventually he convinces her to go to a club together, where he displays his dancing abilities and becomes the life of the party. His limb difference, in other words, is not a disability. His love rival, the fair-haired and square-jawed John (Manuel Gil), underestimates Anselmo's charm, and on the fateful night he drinks too much and ends up being carted out of Mary's room by the enterprising Italian, who wins her over in the end.

We can turn to Jacqueline Reich's *Beyond the Latin Lover: Marcello Mastroianni, Masculinity, and Italian Cinema* (2004) for a framework that can help us analyse *Brevi amori*'s gender politics. In her book the film historian surveys the actor's career in relation to the public's perception of his on-screen and off-screen personas; she argues that, despite the widespread understanding of Mastroianni as the quintessential Latin lover of Italian film, his trajectory was a far more complicated and interesting one. Through a detailed analysis of the most important roles of his career, Reich questions the assumption that Mastroianni always portrayed the incorrigible *tombeur de femmes*; in particular, she notes that Marcello Rubini, his character in Federico Fellini's *La dolce vita* (1960),

> is a classic *inetto*. Mired in mediocrity as a tabloid journalist and emotionally impotent in his relationships with women, he actively chooses passivity and alienation as a way of life as he joins a world of aristocratic decadence at the end of the film. (Reich 2004: xiv)[7]

A quick comparison of Marcello and Anselmo reveals interesting parallels: both men are, in a sense, 'impaired'. Marcello is emotionally unable to connect with other human beings, and his inability to care about other people's feelings results in compulsive lying and philandering. Anselmo's 'impairment' is physical, but he compensates for it with an exuberant personality that borders on grating arrogance. Both men pursue Nordic-looking women who, in their respective films, are big movie stars with prominently public lives and jealous drunk boyfriends;[8] but if Marcello comes to blows with his rival and has to take it in his stride, Anselmo emasculates the handsome American man by showing Mary that the latter is unable to hold his liquor, which makes him an unsuitable sexual partner. Finally, both men are susceptible to *gallismo*, or to 'feeling or imagining oneself as talented in matters of love' (Reich 2004: 54);[9] but if Marcello's sexual voracity leads him to emotional apathy, Anselmo's exploits are to him a veritable mission that motivates his life choices, and that commands a great deal of admiration from his fellow men.

Most relevantly to this analysis, the underlying difference between Marcello and Anselmo is, ultimately, their location. While *La dolce vita* is a film about the rise of a certain culture in Italy that coincided with a crisis in Italian masculinity, *Brevi amori* is a phallocentric fantasy of conquest in which Italian men both consume the exotic location and seduce all the viable partners it harbours. In a sense, *Brevi amori* postulates a masculinity that is antithetical to the diseased ineptitude of many other films of the same period, but as the films in the next chapter will demonstrate, the notion of Italian *gallismo* is not always uncomplicated, even when the stage for its performative aspects is, in fact, a foreign country.[10]

Notes

1. For more on this, see the ongoing projects International Circulation of Italian Cinema, available at <https://www.italiancinema.it>; and Italian Cinema Audiences, available at <https://www.italiancinemaaudiences.org> (both last accessed 17 August 2020).
2. For more on the economic boom, see Leonardi et al. (1997).
3. Sordi did not appreciate the Italian marketing strategy that sought to capitalize on his persona, and wrote a scathing letter to film critic Maurizio Liverani explaining that he had no part in the ploy. According to Claudio G. Fava, the letter was published in the newspaper *Paese Sera* (2003: 127).
4. A stalwart champion of Italian postwar cinema, André Bazin lamented Emmer's turn away from hallowed Neorealism to commercial cinema in his review of the 1952–3 season, writing that 'It would be better for Luciano Emmer's reputation if he were to forget as soon as possible his second feature film, which is the disastrous result of an impossible co-production. On the theme of the "Italians in Paris," Emmer tries in vain to depict for the benefit of these two nations the material and psychological aspects of superficial

tourism. But how could he possibly have survived the handicap of a ridiculous and monstrous dubbing, which makes the French speak Italian in the Italian version and the Italians speak French (with a Marseilles accent!) in the French version? The failure of Emmer's *Paris Is Always Paris* (1951) on the French market will, I hope, serve as a lesson for producers who would still be attracted by such two-headed monsters' (2011: 139).
5. See, for instance, the fate of murderer Ferdinando Cefalù (Marcello Mastroianni) in *Divorzio all'italiana* (Pietro Germi, 1961), or that of the ragtag burglars in *I soliti ignoti / Big Deal on Madonna Street* (Mario Monicelli, 1958).
6. Rodolfo Sonego, the film's screenwriter, claims to be responsible for Aristarco's limb difference. He recalls, 'I harnessed Alberto's passion for deformities and I created for him the figure of a nosy clubfooted man' (qtd in Sanguineti 2015: 174).
7. A recurring character in early twentieth-century Italian literature, the 'Italian inetto (the inept man), [is] a man at odds with and out of place in a rapidly changing political, social, and sexual environment' (Reich 2004: xii). Mired in self-doubt and alienated from his own feelings, the *inetto* is often unble to experience great passion or to navigate the world with panache.
8. The famous episode in *La dolce vita* was based on a 1958 real-life scuffle between paparazzo Tazio Secchiaroli and Anita Ekberg's British husband Anthony Steel.
9. 'The pleasures of gallismo, which consist in believing oneself furnished with an abnormal ardour, flood the ears of Italian men with blood', writes Brancati in *Il borghese e l'immensità. Scritti 1930–1954* (1973: 13).
10. For a detailed discussion of how Mastroianni came to play the *inetto* in many Italian-style comedies, see Reich (2004: 49–77, 105–93).

CHAPTER 7

Working: 'L'Italia è una Repubblica Democratica, fondata sul lavoro'

In this chapter, I will outline how *I magliari/The Swindlers* (Francesco Rosi, 1959), *Il diavolo/To Bed or Not to Bed* (Gianni Polidori, 1963), and *Bello, onesto, emigrato Australia sposerebbe compaesana illibata/A Girl in Australia* (Luigi Zampa, 1971) help us frame Italian labour mobilities during and after the economic boom. While vastly different in scope and ambition, these films were all largely shot abroad, featured Alberto Sordi in a prominent role, and connected (un)employment with a variety of social discourses that gained traction during the 1960s and 1970s, including gender and sexuality.

The first film in this section was directed by the Neapolitan Francesco Rosi, who in the 1960s and 1970s became the frontrunner of Italy's *cinema impegnato* (engaged cinema), a brand of filmmaking that sought to denounce social and political injustices, often taking on controversial issues and hot-button topics. A disciple of Luchino Visconti, Rosi was assistant director on three of his films – *La terra trema* (1948), *Bellissima* (1950), and *Senso* (1954) – and worked on many other titles before debuting in 1956 with his own *Kean: genio e sregolatezza*, a biopic of the histrionic British actor Edmund Kean, played by Vittorio Gassman.

After this exotic first feature, Rosi began to focus on Italy's many sociopolitical issues, beginning in 1958 with *La sfida*, a *Camorra* story set in his hometown of Naples. This film, which is often considered his real debut, earned him great critical acclaim and won a special jury prize at the XIX Mostra Internazionale d'Arte Cinematografica di Venezia. The following year, Rosi wrote the treatment to *I magliari* with Suso Cecchi d'Amico, also a veteran Visconti collaborator. The two then teamed up with Giuseppe Patroni Griffi to write the screenplay for Rosi's second *cinema impegnato* project.

In his book on the Italian director, film critic Francesco Bolzoni writes that '1959 is a revival year of "grand themes" for Italian cinema: the resistance and the Second World War. [. . .] Rosi, in his turn, does not look back. He wants to shed light on a difficult situation: emigration' (1986: 54). Bolzoni rightly identifies a trend that involved many filmmakers who felt that the national cinema had strayed too far from the lesson of Neorealism's 'heroic' days, during which film had become the privileged site for critiquing the various ailments of contemporary society and the failures of its recent past. If the immediate postwar period was concerned with chronicling the effects of the conflict on communities, the 1950s turned their gaze to individuals, and human mobility emerged as particularly appropriate for cinematic inquiry. In fact, the years following the Second World War witnessed the resurgence of a phenomenon that Fascism had long struggled to suppress: internal migration. At least temporarily, the Fascists successfully stymied the exodus from the country's rural to its urban areas with the promulgation of a 1939 law. Historian Paul Ginsborg explains that this absurd measure, which was

> designed specifically to prevent internal migrations and urbanization, trapped the would-be migrant in a Catch 22 situation: in order to change residence to a town of more than 25,000 inhabitants, the migrant had to show evidence of employment at the new place of abode; however, in order to gain such employment the migrant had first to produce a new residence certificate. (Ginsborg 1990: 218)

This bureaucratic roadblock was not officially repealed until 1961, but 'by then it was being even more widely ignored than most Italian laws' (Ginsborg 1990: 218), and it only contributed to making the migrant an even weaker negotiating party in the search for lodgings or employment.

In 1950, the Christian Democrats tried to boost the economy of the Southern rural areas by passing a series of agrarian reforms that were meant to redistribute the land and break

> the power of centuries-old southern elites; but only a small proportion of peasant families ended up as beneficiaries, and those that did become smallholders were rarely able to make a decent living from the few hectares of poor quality soil that they acquired. (Duggan 2007: 356)

For many, migration became the inevitable solution to their poverty. In this context, Rosi's *I magliari* was a film about the present and, more specifically, about the state of Italian migration to Northern European countries in 1959. But it was also a reflection on the past, inasmuch as it updated the figure of the postwar labour migrant as it had been articulated in films such as *Emigrantes* (Aldo Fabrizi, 1948),[1] *Il cammino della speranza* (Pietro Germi, 1950), and even the comedy *Napoletani a Milano/Neapolitans in Milan* (Eduardo de Filippo, 1953). These films had attempted to redress the historical inaccuracies and ideological manipulations spread by the propagandist fare of the Fascist period, such as *Passaporto rosso* (Guido Brignone, 1935) and its ilk, which had misrepresented migration by problematically wrapping it in the tricoloured flag. Conversely, Rosi takes stock of the subtleties of Italian labour mobility during a period in which the forces of modernization were widening the cleavage between the ruling class and communities, polarizing demand for unskilled workers around northern – Italian or European – metropolitan areas, hence pushing more and more people to find a solution in economic migration. Finally, as we shall see, through the prescient figure of Alberto Sordi, *I magliari* forecasts Italians' future mobilities, which will know no bounds, taking them to increasingly exotic destinations and faraway lands.

Mario Balducci (Renato Salvatori) is a factory worker from Grosseto who is defeated in his aspirations of building a life in Hanover, Germany. About to board a train to Italy, he makes the acquaintance of Ferdinando 'Totonno' Magliulo (Alberto Sordi), who instead keeps him in Germany and brings him into an organization of *magliari*, Italian travelling textile salesmen. Totonno is a cunning swindler who plans to move farther north to Hamburg, take over the local market and ditch his boss, Don Raffaele (Carmine Ippolito). Mario follows his mentor to Hamburg, where he has an affair with the beautiful and bored Paula (Belinda Lee), who is married to Mr Mayer (Joseph Dahmen), Totonno's primary supplier. However, Totonno's plan proves more difficult to implement than he thought, and his organization clashes with the local gang of Poles who control Hamburg's criminal activities. His last resort is to extort money from Paula by coercing Mario into blackmailing her, and then pay off the Poles. But Mario, who is genuinely in love with the woman, cannot move forward with this plan, and betrays him instead. Don Raffaele, with his powerful connections, is called in to resolve this power struggle; he chases Totonno out of town and becomes Mayer's partner, expanding his control from Hanover to Hamburg. Mario decides to abandon the organization and return to legality, and he asks Paula to follow him, but she turns down his offer.

Much of Italian cinema about migration focuses on individuals existing on the margins of society. The commonest narrative trajectory is one that depicts the efforts undertaken by the characters in order to move from such margins to the centre, often crossing borders that are both physical and invisible – travelling, relocating, settling, climbing the social ladder, acquiring respectability and eventually even wealth. Because of the illegal nature of their activities, Rosi's characters must remain on the fringes of society, even when they are financially successful. The sly Totonno is the epitome of this marginality: as film historian Sandro Zambetti puts it, 'Totonno is [. . .] suspended between the margins of legality, which he does not respect, and the margins of illegality, which he walks without taking too many risks' (1976: 26).

The relative affluence enjoyed by the fraudulent travelling salesmen in Germany is not an unproblematic narrative of dynastic success, as *Passaporto rosso* portrayed the rise of the Italian diasporic community in Argentina, nor is it the fruit of hard and honest labour and national solidarity abroad, as it is in *Emigrantes*. Rather, *I magliari* investigates the unholy commixture of organized crime and chain migration, the international setting accentuating the stereotypical regional differences already present at home. In her study of Italian criminal mobilities, Felia Allum explains the historical connection between the *Camorra* and the *magliari* networks, organizations that originated in the Campania region and became fully integrated in the 1980s:

> there were groups of travelling magliari and sometimes an Italian-Neapolitan immigrant who acted as the interface between the clan and the magliari network. But the already existing magliari were extensively recruited in Naples among the unemployed and sent abroad. Abroad, they were not recruited but violently forced to work for the alliance. They returned to Naples to replenish their stock, and would transport their goods to their different markets. Violence was used with the magliari when they did not respect orders, but it was rarely used with local citizens. Money made in Germany was regularly returned to Naples to the common fund as well as to pay Neapolitan manufacturers. (Allum 2014: 591)

Although the film's critical reception was rather mixed, it is worth noting that Rosi's approach to the material was original in that it sought to combine what was essentially a social issue (emigration and the sense of bereavement felt by the workers abroad) with the naturally cinematic qualities of the crime genre. What makes this melange possible is the encounter of the naive but principled Mario with the duplicitous Totonno; imbued with different moral values, these characters also epitomize different genre conventions that, to some degree, have trouble congealing into a coherent whole. On this point, Alberto Cattini writes:

> Deliberately, the plot traces a hard line between the Italian who relies on cunning and scams people, and the Italian who tries to live with integrity and solidarity. The first one does not evolve, he is identical from beginning to end, even when he is defeated by the boss he does not give up, and tries to affirm his own originality. The second learns from the degrading experience he has lived, and is convinced that he needs to get out of such corruption. He must stay with the beautiful woman who embodies Germany during the economic miracle, and he must recompose the torn social fabric. (Cattini 2001: 8)

Cattini elaborates on this observation by maintaining that Mario is associated with melodrama and *populismo*,[2] whereas Totonno's scenes alternate between comedy and motifs commonly found in crime fiction.

While Sordi is first billed in the opening credit, Totonno is technically not the film's protagonist. *I magliari* is focalized through the gentle Mario, and it begins with a nod to the sentimentalism that characterizes him. The scene opens with a shot of his feet as he walks over a work of public art that maps out Hanover's distance to other major European cities. When he reaches Rome ('Rom', which is 1,200 kilometres away) he kneels down and caresses the metal letters inlaid in the pavement. Suitcase in hand, Mario wanders through the streets of the German city absentmindedly, his disconnection from the environment made palpable by his solitude. He stops at a food stand, orders a *Würstel*, and then retreats, disgusted, at the smell and sight of the traditional sausage. Across the street is La Bella Napoli, an Italian restaurant where he is welcomed with hostility by the staff. Totonno intervenes, inviting Mario to his table, where he is enjoying spaghetti and wine in the company of other Italian men. The *magliari* are not all Neapolitan: when Mario tells his dinner companions that he is from Tuscany, Vincenzo (Nino Vingelli), shoulders to the camera, remarks: 'Italy is well represented here! The Roman, the Tuscan, and the Neapolitan!' Totonno shows the poor factory worker sympathy, but also uses sleight of hand to steal his passport from his coat pocket when the police enter the restaurant looking for him. Since Mario cannot prove his identity, he is taken into custody instead.

In this lengthy opening scene, Rosi establishes the film's power relations; Mario's naivety will cause him to be manipulated by Totonno, who later offers him an apology and a job: he is to take part in the *magliari* network. Don Raffaele also dines at La Bella Napoli, and his presence is noted by the Italians, who treat him with deference and respect. His ascendancy over Totonno and his men is unquestionable. From this moment on, the film's narration proceeds by juxtaposing these two discourses: Mario's innocence versus Totonno's cunning, the honest migrant versus the fraudster expatriate, legality versus illegality, melodrama versus comedy, *populismo* versus crime. But this initial dichotomy is progressively complicated: Mario starts off as a defeated man holding onto his principles, but the longer he associates with the *magliari*, the more he abandons his lofty ideals. In the end, only the grand gesture of quitting the gang and breaking up with Paula can ultimately redeem him.

This dualism is present in the film's editing pattern, which in a handful of scenes pits the two worldviews against each other, coming into full relief when Mario follows Totonno on two sales in order to learn the ropes. One pitch takes them to the factory where the worker used to be employed. While Totonno is busy scamming the German woman who owns the tavern near the factory, Mario visits his former co-workers in their barracks, which are as crowded as they are depressing. The meek but honest workers, their faces unshaven, chain-smoke and compliment Mario on his quick social climb, but also question the legality of the travelling salesman's dealings. The juxtaposition between the two locales highlights the main characters' inherent difference: Mario tries to instil hope in his friends, whereas Totonno takes advantage of everyone. During the sales pitches, Totonno practises a sort of instrumental self-stereotyping; he taps into the narrative of the Italian emigrant and reappropriates its markers, using them at his convenience. When he sells rugs to the German tavern owner, he pretends to slip and fall; he elicits the woman's sympathy by crying and moaning, and by draping himself in the stereotype: 'I am alone and abandoned in this foreign land!', he laments. In the previous pitch, he scams a recently widowed woman;[3] pretending to learn about the death of the woman's husband for the first time, he delivers a tearjerking pitch that ends with a gratuitous 'mandolino e maccaroni' (mandolin and macaroni). This ending has the sole function of depicting him as an innocuous serenading and pasta-eating Italian, a simpleton who just happened to stumble into a hairy situation.

Totonno's awareness and reappropriation of the Italian stereotype is also what makes his Neapolitan co-workers so insufferable to him. He constantly harps on at them with cruel jokes about their ways and their attachment to all things Neapolitan. In *Emigrantes*, Aldo Fabrizi joked about the Neapolitans' *campanilismo* (parochialism) even when they are abroad; in *I magliari*, this seemingly harmless joke becomes a way to draw a line between the Italians who, in a way, create the stereotype (the Neapolitans, but also Mario for his bleeding-heart honesty) and the Italians (namely, Totonno) who reappropriate the stereotype and use it to their advantage, flying in the face of adversity. In this light, Totonno's sales pitches are more than comic set-pieces; they illuminate the transition between the generations of Italian migrants.[4]

Mario's wake-up call comes in the scene after Totonno's histrionic rug sale. When the two drive away in Totonno's stylish two-door 1954 Borgward Isabella saloon, two policemen on 1955 BMW R60 motorcycles appear in the rearview mirror. Totonno believes that the cops are after them and begins to panic. Mario realizes that the *magliaro* activity is an outright fraudulent one, and he calls Totonno out on it:

Mario:	I am right, then! What you do is a fraud!
Totonno:	And?
Mario:	I was never chased by the police.
Totonno:	And I was.
Mario:	I was looking for a job! If I'd wanted to be a swindler I'd have stayed home!

Mario's worldview is based on ideals of lawfulness and morality that, as he reveals, are as binary as they are geographically bound: if the Italy he left behind represents illegality, swindling, and unemployment, surely Germany must be legality and honest work. This realization throws a wrench into this dichotomous system: the *magliaro* casts a dark shadow on Mario's idea that migrating to Germany represents the opportunity for him to earn his living without having to step out of the legal bounds of a society that, in the postwar period, has acquired a European dimension.

Before meeting Totonno, Mario had already failed in his project of moving from the margin to the centre of society. He was a righteous worker who lost his job and must return home. From a storytelling point of view, Totonno's function is to hijack Mario's character arc: he does not allow him to be sanctimonious and to write for himself a narrative of martyrdom according to which he left Italy and endured terrible suffering and deprivation in order to make an honest living. Conversely, Totonno does not have a moral compass, which makes him a linear character: he stays true to himself and his values throughout the film. Totonno's function is evident when the two first break bread at La Bella Napoli: Mario, seeking his fellow countrymen's solidarity, begins to tell his story of hardship and sacrifice, but Totonno cuts him short: 'Oh, no! Troubles, nix! We don't want to hear them. Besides, why tell them, you have them written all over your face! Let's eat, now!' As far as migration is concerned, Totonno is the evolution of the species; he rejects the narrative of the poor Italian emigrant who is underpaid and exploited, but uses his seemingly underprivileged position to his own advantage: he turns the rules of migration upside down, and gets ahead by scamming the local population, by outsmarting the host culture.

These two worlds begin to overlap when Mario is introduced to mercenary sex; his weakness for beautiful women, rather than Totonno's promise of easy riches, is what causes his fall. Rosi spends some time illustrating the *magliari*'s position in German society, focusing in particular on the seedy underbelly (the margin) in which they operate. The extended sequence that shows Mario's first concrete step into corruption begins in a fancy nightclub (the New York City) where the protagonist watches, almost in a trance, a semi-nude dancer perform. Here, the Italians, expert swindlers, refuse the requests of the club's blonde entertainers to buy them drinks and are singled out as cheap patrons. Irritated by the situation, the men decide to leave the club, and as they pick up their coats they become the object of the girls' laughter. They take the party to the Copacabana, a less ritzy establishment, where Mario is introduced to Frida (Lina Vandhal), his girlfriend for the night. When the woman asks his name, Mario replies with his full name, last name first: 'Balducci Mario.' Frida repeats, 'Ah, Balduccio.' Frida's mistaking of the man's name (possibly for that of the medieval sculptor Giovanni di Balduccio), signals the interchangeability of her Italian johns, no matter their ethical principles: in the eyes of the prostitute, Mario is a *magliaro*, nothing more, nothing less. As Cattini puts it, 'Mario's chapter, marked by the first work experiences that produce moral scruples, ends in sex, which silences them. It also foreshadows the much more complex chapter of the relationship with Paula' (2001: 30).

In simpler terms, Frida is a gateway to Paula, but sex is not the only means by which Rosi narrates Mario's involvement with Totonno's affairs. When Don Raffaele realizes that the sleazy *magliaro* wants to break free of his control and bring his Neapolitan salesmen to Mayer, he sends some cronies to rough him up. Mario intervenes, taking the beating in his stead; a sacrificial lamb, he operates by the misguided principle that friends (and fellow Italians) must stick together. In addition, by getting into a street fight at night, he crosses the line of genre conventions: he steps outside the boundary of melodrama to participate in a gangster motif, and he loses. In Hamburg, Mario becomes a pawn in Totonno's hands; he is sent to seduce Paula, who must intercede with her husband on Totonno's behalf. But what is originally a relationship borne out of business soon becomes pleasure, and prevents Mario from understanding that his role in the exchange is that of the offering; Paula is a stunningly beautiful woman who is unfaithful to her husband, and Mario is a handsome young man who becomes her prey, not the other way around. In other words, Mario proceeds down the path of corruption by temporarily embracing Totonno's manipulation, but not without pleasure for himself.

Initially depicted as a man-eater, Paula grows fond of Mario as their affair progresses. An indication of her interest in the man is in one of their first conversations, in which she takes him to a low-class bar by the harbour (where she arrives in her luxurious 1958 Mercedes-Benz 220 S Cabriolet) and confesses her humble origins to him, sharing a scandalous detail of her past:

Paula: Think about how strange it is. You came to Germany seeking fortune. And I went to work in Italy. I wanted to eat, and be less cold. I didn't have this. [Caressing her fur coat]
Mario: In Italy, where?
Paula: Sad times.

Paula has experienced migrant status, and by telling Mario she seems to level with him. But unlike the tormented factory worker reluctantly turned *magliaro*, she does not have lofty ideals of honesty and integrity. Her refusal to add any detail regarding her past mobility, and to answer any questions about it, suggests that she used sex as a means to get ahead, eventually trading her independence for a better life beside a wealthy older man, Mayer. In other words, at this stage in the story, her trajectory mirrors his: poor and hungry at home, these characters must accept the 'corruption' that (the film seems to argue) comes with the migrant narrative; to Totonno, Mario's obstinate refusal to do so is as hypocritical as it is childish.[5]

Totonno's position as the boss of the *magliari* fringe that followed him to Hamburg comes with new responsibilities: not only must he furnish capital, he must also arrange protection. Therefore, when the Poles who control the Hamburg market become openly hostile to the new gang of Italian swindlers who moved into their territory, Totonno must intervene. Interestingly, the first intimidation attempt comes in the form of tire-slashing, temporarily crippling the travelling salesmen's mobility. Totonno's reluctant response is inadequately weak, showing that he is unfit to guide and protect his salespeople. In the sequence that depicts the face-off between the Italians and the Poles, Rosi deploys the conventions of the gangster movie: first, Totonno seeks parley with the gang's mysterious boss, and he is also unable to detect a Pole who spies on the Italians all night. Second, he disappears into a whorehouse and his men are ambushed by the gang, who engage the Italians in a street brawl at dawn. Third, Totonno tries to blackmail Paula, in order to obtain the money he needs to pay off the Poles and allow his men to return to work in Hamburg. But even this plan – his last resort – goes awry, because Mario eludes his control and tells Paula, who prepares a counterattack: the *magliari* are told to meet Mr Mayer at their storage room the next day, and Mr Mayer appears with Don Raffaele, who resumes control of the fringe and promises to pay off the Poles. He then confronts Totonno and chases him away. The gangster storyline comes to a close with the standoff between Don Raffaele and Totonno, in which the elderly boss offers him a gun and dares him to shoot him. Incapable of performing such an action, Totonno flees the scene instead. Mario runs after him, offering him an apology for the betrayal. But Totonno is unwilling to listen, and storms off in his automobile. In a very melodramatic fashion, Mario holds on to his window and Totonno drags him for a few yards, until he finally lets go of the car and finishes face down in a pool of mud. During this grotesque and implausible parting scene, Totonno exposes Mario's hypocrisy: 'How naive! My young friend! The honest worker! I believed in you, and you tricked me.'

From a tonal point of view, *I magliari* ends in the same way it begins: with sentimentalism. Mario's migrant narrative, with its melodrama conventions, frames the gangster storyline. It begins with his nostalgia and ends with his last meeting with Paula, in which he asks her to leave everything and follow him. Paula tries to dissuade him by offering to literally buy his affection:

> Paula: Think how happy I would be to take Mayer's money and give it to you.
> Mario: But I always earned my money with my hands. I always lived among people who only see it that way.

Film critic Sandro Zambetti underlines the artificiality of Mario's character in commenting on his choice to leave Hamburg and Paula before his corruption becomes permanent:

> his final decision, therefore, seems quite tacked on from without, as it does not have any other premise if not some sort of inner goodness, of instinctive moral rectitude. That is, it belongs to the stereotype of the honest worker, and certainly does not foreground a conscious choice, the indication of a struggle. (Zambetti 1976: 27)

But this double goodbye (to Totonno and to Paula) is not Mario's only action to ring hollow. His loyalty to Totonno as well as his insistence on legality are out of place at best in the story. Francesco Bolzoni points his finger at the didactic function of this character's storyline and writes: 'Salvatori-Balducci's honest face is that of the "good" worker, which was a creation of certain intellectuals of Neorealism who knew little about the people and talked a great deal about them' (1986: 56).

At the time of its release, Rosi's film did not receive universal critical acclaim: reviewers tended to underscore the disconnect between the film's different plot lines, and the heavy-handedness with which Mario's tale of fall and redemption is brought full circle.[6] What most critics agreed upon was the quality of Alberto Sordi's scene-stealing performance, as he completely overshadowed the wooden Renato Salvatori. In particular, both Alberto Moravia and Angelo Solmi point to Totonno's final minutes on-screen as one of the film's highlights (qtd in Fava 2003:

Figure 2.5 Moving forward, driving east.

132). Framed in profile, Totonno drives off from Don Raffaele and his *magliari*; in order to overcome his fright, he gives himself a long pep talk that displays a wide range of emotions, from the initial fear to his determination to pull himself up and start over, from relief at having survived his face-off with the dangerous Don to mocking his opponent (Figure 2.5). This powerful scene, which is entirely absent from the published screenplay, must be credited to Sordi's comic genius. As Goffredo Fofi writes,

> in the last scene Rosi lets go of a different idea for the finale and follows him in his long soliloquy in the car, after his defeat. It's one of those formidable dialogues Sordi had with himself, all questions and answers, like the ones we are accustomed to seeing in his comedies. Rhetorical questions and obvious answers, confirming the amorality and vitality of his character, but also his despicable reasons, as befits comic roles. Sordi becomes perfectly Sordi, and only Sordi, to the point that the great and lengthy scene could appear in some other preceding film. It's a 1950s Sordi beginning to face the 1960s. (Fofi 2004: 150)

This bravura set-piece does not bring closure to the character, nor is it a simple rehashing of the trope of self-commiserating Italian (Bolzoni 1986: 56), which Totonno had forcefully dismissed when Mario first sat at his table at La Bella Napoli. Conversely, it is thrust towards the future, delivered as it is by an utterly mobile character at the wheel of his speeding automobile. It is an elegy of single-minded entrepreneurship, forecasting new destinations and future business ideas for the ebullient Italian.

Totonno's imagined labour trajectory extends to Japan, a faraway market for an 'adventurer' like himself, for whom Europe has already become too stagnant.

In 2015, Italian film scholar Tatti Sanguineti published a massive study entitled *Il cervello di Alberto Sordi: Rodolfo Sonego e il suo cinema* (*Alberto Sordi's Brain: Rodolfo Sonego and His Cinema*) with the prestigious publisher Adelphi. The volume positions Rodolfo Sonego (1921–2000) firmly within the pantheon of Italian screenwriting legends. If Suso Cecchi d'Amico was arguably the most important and prolific screenwriter of the second half of the twentieth century, and Cesare Zavattini certainly the most radical and influential, Sonego was the one whose oeuvre is the most relevant in the context of Italian cinematic mobilities, especially when these are studied through the prism of Alberto Sordi's career. The many international cinematic travels of the Bolzano-born screenwriter include, but are not limited to, his collaborations with Sordi; Sanguineti devotes a section of his monograph to his journeys, which took him to the Belgian mining town of Marcinelle (*La ragazza in vetrina*), the French Riviera (*Costa Azzurra* and *Crimen*), Sweden (*Le svedesi* and *Il diavolo*), the United States (*Una moglie americana*), Australia (*Bello, onesto, emigrato Australia sposerebbe compaesana illibata*), Norway (*Sottozero*), and a number of other destinations for films that were never made.[7]

According to Sanguineti, Sordi met Sonego in 1954 when working on *Il seduttore* (Franco Rossi), striking up a friendship and partnership that defined the careers of both: 'Sonego became Alberto Sordi's first choice and last resort' (2015: 573), he argues, noting that 'in a span of 46 years, between 1954 and 2000, the two made 53 films together; features, shorts, credited and uncredited. [. . .] These films contributed to the success of their locations, their resorts, their vacations, this boom' (2015: 38). The critic maintains that there is a direct relationship (be that of correlation or causation) between Sordi and Sonego's cinema and the rise of leisure travel in and out of Italy, anticipating the phenomenon of cinematic tourism as theorized by Rodanthi Tzanelli (2007). In her pioneering volume on the effects of location shooting on the tourist industry, the sociologist investigates the various effects following the establishment of physical places as cinematic 'signs' by featuring them in the cinema: on the one hand, seeing a place on the screen generates the desire to visit it (a psychological effect imparted by the medium onto the spectator); on the other, by becoming a tourist site the place in question might undergo significant physical and financial transformations (new revenue might be extracted from the location, but increased usage might also cause it to suffer deterioration or to be permanently damaged).[8]

Directed by Gian Luigi Polidoro from a story and screenplay by Rodolfo Sonego, much of *Il diavolo* (1963) was improvised on location, a filmmaking style that agreed with Sordi's acting talent, and that would influence his own directorial method. According to Sonego, 'I edited *Il diavolo* because it was a travel film, mostly improvised, that I wrote bit by bit each night. No one could have been able to find their bearings in the footage' (qtd in Sanguineti 2015: 224). As the extraordinary monologue he delivers at the end of *I magliari* shows, the actor was extremely comfortable in front of the camera, working with a very loose script (if any) that put his character, Amedeo Ferretti, an Italian fur merchant travelling to Sweden, into various situations in which he tries to seduce the Scandinavian women that surround him: 'imagined and failed adventures, marked by the obligatory *gallismo* that, in the end, prescribes a comfortable homecoming' (Fava 2003: 169; my emphasis). In fact, the role earned Sordi a Golden Globe for Best Actor in a Comedy or a Musical in 1964, and the film won the Golden Bear at the Berlin International Film Festival the previous year. A symbolic new chapter in the life of the travelling comedian, now a serious businessman stuck in a marital rut, the film begins where *Racconti d'estate* and *Vacanze d'inverno* ended: on a train. Peter Thomas reminds us that 'railways created new socialites and transformed people's senses of self', noting that 'different cultures move and press up against each other in the space of the train – relations that are as much affective as they are ideological' (2014: 215). Railway travel, in other words, is both material and symbolic, a physical conduit for people and goods as much as it is an imagined vehicle for experiences and encounters, a mobile locale where a temporary reshaping of a passenger's identity takes place.

It is in his cabin berth that the ponderous businessman delivers the film's first voice-over monologue: 'I enjoyed the noise of the train that was taking me far away. Away from my old provincial town, my office, my friends. Toward northern lands. Toward Sweden. It was the first time I left the country, and the first I time I left my wife for a long voyage.' While these sentences initially position Ferretti in the mental space of the railway voyager who wishes for knowledge and experience to arise from his travels, the film quickly reframes his exploration as one motivated by sexual desire for Scandinavian women. In other words, if fur trading is the official purpose of Amedeo's trip to Sweden, his *gallismo* – and his failure to deploy it successfully – is what drives most of his actions and informs his ideas of what northern women are like. But as Jacqueline Reich observes, 'the irony of *gallismo* and the discourse which is at its base' is that 'exotic sexuality goes hand in hand with Italy's status as a less civilized and restrained culture in comparison to other Western nations' (2004:

76). Therefore, Amedeo's status of *gallo* manqué does not necessarily imply that he devolves into an *inetto*, because his failure is informed by constructs that operate on a level of macrostructures, such as national affiliation and ethnic stereotyping. This level of sophistication, which is completely missing in the travel comedies, is the reason for *Il diavolo*'s ultimate success; as Alberto Pesce put it in his 1963 review,

> Polidoro's film is not an erotic romp in Swedish lands, nor is it a carousel of the adventures of a provincial gigolo; *Il diavolo* is an unforgiving, melancholy documentary on northern femininity, illuminated in each instance by a mystified Latin man. (qtd in Fava 2003: 171)

Nonetheless, voyaging is a culturally enriching experience for Amedeo, furnishing him with the opportunity to connect with people from diverse backgrounds. For instance, when his ferry cruises past Kronborg castle in Denmark, the man takes a cue from a fellow passenger, who is reciting Hamlet's monologue, to offer it in its Italian translation. Shakespeare's celebrated words about the pain of existence reverberate in the air in multiple languages while the boat glides on the water and the two gaze at the castle through binoculars, creating a moment of intercultural communion via their shared love of literature. Amedeo is not an uncultured man; he navigates this environment mixing German, French, English, and Italian words. In the course of the film, he entertains conversations about life, religion, cultural differences, and most prominently about northern women and their sexuality with a number of characters he encounters along the way: a Jewish physicist, a Swedish Lutheran pastor (Ulf Palme), a young woman he takes back to his hotel room, and so forth. What hinders his ability to fully comprehend the host environment is not ignorance or prejudice, but the default conservatism of his own background.

Il diavolo's loose narrative is tied together by Sordi's voice-over narration, which accompanies most of the film and exposes the character's motivations. In one particular instance, Amedeo visits a nightclub in the hope of meeting Swedish girls. The narration that introduces the scene explains that Cafe Triumf is patronized by Southern Italian migrants and local women. As he stands in front of the entrance, Amedeo sees a tall blonde leave the club arm in arm with a very short, dark-haired man who tells her, in Italian, 'Mamma wrote.' The mismatched appearance of the couple, which reinforces both Italian and Swedish stereotypes, inspires admiration and envy in Amedeo. The comedy seems to hinge on the man's infantile desire to talk about his mother to his date. But what on the surface may seem like a crude visual rendition of the inferiority complex of the 'Latin man' (as Fava puts it) towards Nordic cultures and peoples, is in fact a melancholic nod to the hardships of the diasporic condition; although the diminutive Italian man should be happy at having found such a desirable mate, his thoughts are focused on his faraway mother. In this scene, tourism and migration converge, since Amedeo's goal unites him to the club's Southern Italian patrons. Inside the club, Amedeo watches silently while dark, moustachioed men approach fair-haired girls; seen through his eyes, these men are animalized, voracious sexual predators, and initially he is uncomfortable at the idea of imitating their behaviour. But eventually he does, and he manages to leave the club with a girl; but the scene ends with a joke at Amedeo's expense, since the girl turns out to be only thirteen. Shocked by this information, the man has no other choice but to run away like a thief in the night – but in the voice-over, he admits regretting his decision, a troubling confession of his illicit desire.[9]

Amedeo's inability to understand the sexual and spiritual mores of the Swedes is compensated by his efficiency and competence at the pelts auction, where he leverages a Russian acquaintance to seal a particularly advantageous deal for his company. In many ways, *Il diavolo* reverses the *gallo* archetype, making the Mediterranean man especially competent at work and, conversely, inefficient in matters of the heart. He even manages to attend the Nobel Prize ceremony (a remarkable feat of guerrilla filmmaking accomplished by the crew, who snuck into the gala by pretending to be affiliated with Italian television), where his visible boredom attracts the attention of an age-appropriate companion who introduces the narrow-minded Italian to her open marriage. Welcomed within her group of friends, Amedeo continues to explore Swedish customs: he takes a sauna and then rolls in the snow (which causes him to faint), and he participates in a car demolition derby on ice. This example of culturally specific automobility (a bravura sequence that amounts to a motorized waltz) is especially taxing for the man, whose thoughts go to his wife back home when the ice cracks and his car begins to sink into the lake.

After the helicopter rescue, Amedeo returns to Italy on a train, his voice-over narration reversing the trajectory of the opening lines: 'I enjoyed the noise of the train that was taking me back to my old town, my office, my friends, my wife.' Bookending the film is a slideshow of the women he encountered on his journey, their faces superimposed onto the train car window, where Amedeo's reflection also gleams. Ghostly apparitions on an evanescent screen made of cigarette smoke, these memories are compared to angels, while the businessman likens himself to the titular devil. Amedeo is an im/mobile spectator of his own recollections: travelling at railway speed, yet stationary in his cabin berth, the man watches this carousel of female characters with latent desire. More importantly, this textbook Mulvey-esque ending gives way to a card in which 'Alberto Sordi thanks the women who collaborated in this film by kindly revealing all the secrets of their sweet and mysterious personalities. Viva women!'

As critic Giuseppe Marotta noted in his 23 April 1963 review of the film on the pages of the magazine *L'Europeo*, 'in this *Il diavolo*, it is not the plot that makes the actor, but the actor who makes the plot. Without Alberto Sordi, this film would amount to half a documentary, albeit of good quality' (qtd in Fava 2003: 171). Due to its unusual production circumstances, the film's authorship was highly contested, leading to a public falling out between Sordi and director Polidoro, who never worked together again. Conversely, Sordi and Sonego would collaborate on many more titles, including the last film in this chapter, Luigi Zampa's *Bello, onesto, emigrato Australia sposerebbe compaesana illibata* (1971), which, similarly to *Il diavolo*, investigates the intricate relationship between labour and sexual mobilities.

Zampa's career began during Fascism, when he penned the screenplays of romantic comedies such as *Mille lire al mese* (Max Neufeld, 1939), *Dora Nelson* (Mario Soldati, 1939), and the Amedeo Nazzari vehicle *Centomila dollari* (Mario Camerini, 1940), which I discussed in Part One. In the postwar period he directed powerful indictments of Italy's present condition and recent foibles, such as *L'onorevole Angelina* (1947) and *Anni difficili* (1948). In the context of Italian cinematic mobilities, his *Signori, in carrozza!/Rome-Paris-Rome* (1951) is especially significant, as it is the tale of a polygamous railway conductor shuttling between Rome and Paris, where he maintains two different families. Zampa, Sordi, and Sonego's first collaboration was the 1960 comedy *Il vigile*, in which the Roman actor, astride a 1959 Moto Guzzi Falcone, creates another signature character. His motorized traffic policeman is as fastidious as he is petty, wearing his squeaky-clean leather uniform proudly, but also wielding his limited power to take revenge on the people who used to bully him. He is a perfect example of the postwar aspiring bourgeois to whom, as Andrea Bini writes, Sordi lent voice and body: 'childish, conformist, cowardly, irresponsible, and sly, although usually so inept in his short-sighted *furbizia* [malicious cunning] that he was frustrated in his attempt to get what he wanted' (2011: 136).

Bello, onesto, emigrato Australia sposerebbe compaesana illibata (1971)[10] reunites Sordi and Sonego with their *Il diavolo* collaborators, composer Piero Piccioni and cinematographer Aldo Tonti. The film is a further investigation of mobility and identity, but one that uses road movie conventions to portray, in comedic tone, the perils of Italian emigrants in Australia, to where 138,000 people migrated between 1946 and 1957, as historian Paul Ginsborg reports (1990: 211). Amedeo Battipaglia (Alberto

Sordi), lives in the tiny fictional village of Bun Bun Ga, New South Wales, where he works for the local phone company installing and fixing lines. On the eve on his fiftieth birthday, Amedeo feels the need to find a spouse and turns to his handsome friend Giuseppe (Riccardo Garrone) for advice. Giuseppe allows Amedeo to use his picture to entice an attractive mail-order bride to come to Australia to marry him. The stratagem works, and Carmela (Claudia Cardinale) flies to Brisbane to meet Giuseppe. However, the woman fails to disclose an important detail about herself; she is not the demure Calabrian shepherdess she claimed to be in her letters, but a city-dwelling prostitute who wants out of the lifestyle. Ashamed of his own lie, Amedeo conceals his real identity, and pretends to be just a friend Giuseppe has sent to collect Carmela at the airport. Unaware of being mutually lied to, the two hit the road to Bun Bun Ga. During the four-day journey, which in Amedeo's plan was supposed to be their honeymoon, the couple has a series of misadventures. When the truth is finally revealed, Amedeo and Carmela have a falling out, but eventually decide to stay together and make a life in the remote Australian village.

A bittersweet satire that celebrates and lampoons one of the last frontiers of Italian mobility, *Bello* is perhaps both the end point of travel comedies, with which it shares some generic characteristics, and a film embodying the transitional period within the longer arc of *commedia all'italiana* (1958–79), which in its second phase, the 1970s, would become increasingly more cynical and lugubrious.[11] As did *I magliari* and *Il diavolo*, the film interrogates the relationship between labour mobilities and sexuality, the bewilderment that is intrinsic to diasporic existence, and the issues of identity underpinning both. For instance, *Bello* turns the conventions of Italian *gallismo* upside down; while Giuseppe embodies the stereotype of the Latin lover, Amedeo is unable to find a suitable life partner in Australia, and he enlists the help of the local Italian priest to find a match by mail. His actions are motivated not by ineptitude (the flip side of *gallismo*), but by the cruel logic of numbers; there simply are not enough Italian women in his community to meet the demand of the numerous eligible bachelors. This emotional isolation in a foreign land is underscored when Amedeo goes dancing at the 'Italian Club – casa dell'emigrante'[12] in the hope of meeting a potential mate. In his nicest blue suit, Amedeo lines up with other suitors – all caricatures of Italian 'types', much like the Southern men crowding *Il diavolo*'s Cafe Triumf – to ask the few available emigrant women if they would like to dance with him, and his request is turned down by all the bachelorettes.[13] Shot as a comic vignette, this scene acquires a deeper meaning when, towards the end of their journey, Carmela asks Amedeo why he never considered marrying an Australian woman. He replies:

Amedeo:	Me? I can't.
Carmela:	Why?
Amedeo:	Well, first of all because they are not my type. And then because they drink, they smoke. Almost all of them have a degree. They come home at 2AM and if you dare ask 'where have you been?' they get mad and reply meanly: 'This is my business!'
Carmela:	What does it mean?
Amedeo:	It means 'it's my business!'
Carmela:	No kidding!
Amedeo:	That's right! You see, Carmela, we emigrants want to marry Italian women because they are obedient, pretty, nice, affectionate.

Amedeo's understanding of gender roles is not only out of place in Australia, it is also outdated by 1971 Italian standards; of course, the emigrant's vision is deeply anachronistic: educated and independent women intimidate him to the point that he would rather take a chance on a mail-order bride than try to assimilate and embrace Australian culture. Amedeo's incompatibility with the host culture also signals his inability to integrate into society, and consequently to remain an exploited labourer whose social status is stationary. As he reveals in another conversation with Carmela, many emigrants were able to make fortunes rapidly by investing in the gold-mining business like Giuseppe. Unfortunately, the hard and dangerous work made Amedeo ill with silicosis, and he had to resort to other jobs, thus losing the ability to get ahead in life.[14]

When Giuseppe learns that Amedeo did not have the courage to reveal his identity to Carmela, he tries to take advantage of the situation and to keep the gorgeous bride to himself. He is willing to betray Amedeo (and with him, any vestige of national solidarity) for sex, showing that he is guided only by self-interest, not by the anachronistic system of values that informs Amedeo's moral compass. Nonetheless, Zampa plants many clues to Amedeo and Carmela's kindredness of spirit throughout the film; the most notable is in the beginning, when their relationship is still only epistolary. In a masterful shot, Zampa frames him in close-up, sitting on the ground, his back against a telephone pole. Slowly the camera pulls back, lifting off the ground, into a very long helicopter shot that reveals the barren, deserted landscape in which Amedeo works. In voice-over, Amedeo's words to Carmela describe his feelings for her and his happiness at her upcoming visit. Zampa then cuts to a still shot of the Colosseum, travelling thousands of miles in a single splice, to introduce the audience to Carmela's working environment: the streets. In a revealing dress and a blonde wig, the woman is seen trying to procure johns in Rome. The camera then pulls back from her and zooms back to Amedeo, as if delivering Carmela's next letter (which her voice-over is reading) straight into his hands. While the film plays up the unlikeliness of Sordi and Cardinale as romantic partners for comedic purposes (Sordi was eighteen years Cardinale's senior), it also relies on their chemistry as road buddies. Zampa uses the paper-thin premise of the mail-order bride to showcase 'a world coloured with absurdity by the nostalgia for the faraway fatherland, the landscape's unreality, and the strangeness of its mores; and where, therefore, everything is possible' (qtd in Fava 2003: 234) – even a happy marriage between a sickly emigrant and a former prostitute.

If *Bello* is a film about the migrant condition, it is also a documentary of infrastructure, communication technology, and intercontinental motorized mobility. Through the figure of Carmela, the film travels across Rome on the back of the motorcycle that takes her to the airport where she climbs aboard a Quantas flight, underscoring the differences between the wealthy multicultural passengers in first class and the salami-eating migrants crowding the economy cabin. In his turn, Amedeo takes us on a railroad track aboard a pump handcart, a device akin to the camera dolly used to frame him in the tracking shot that accompanies him, crossing the open Australian landscape *with* and *for* the cinema (Figure 2.6). The couple's journey begins in the parking lot of Brisbane airport, where Carmela overestimates her prospective spouse's means and takes her seat behind the wheel of a black 1955 Rolls-Royce Silver Cloud I, while Amedeo is stowing away her luggage in the back seat of a much more modest 1954 Morris Minor Series II Convertible – she will be much more impressed by Giuseppe's two-tone 1967 Pontiac Tempest Custom. The emblem topped by an Italian flag, the light blue Morris takes them on a road

Figure 2.6 Italian cinema on Australian (dolly) tracks.

through the jungle; driving with the top down, Amedeo explains that he and his friends took part in the construction of the 600 kilometre-long slash through the dense vegetation, reminding us that, as Peter Merriman writes:

> roads and motorways are not simply products of political decision-making, planning or engineering, for a large number of actors are required to bring about such socio-technological achievements: from human actors such as planners, politician, engineers, lobbyists, labourers and landscape architects, to distinctive arrangements of concrete, tarmac, and steel. (Merriman 2014: 201)

Returning as a user to the road he helped build, the inherently mobile Amedeo is now able to enjoy the view from his motorized vehicle: 'Road, car and driver set the speed and rhythm with which the passenger moves through and embodies the landscape. Landscape, movement and sensation become entwined' (Merriman 2014: 201).

When Carmela finally resigns herself to staying with Amedeo, the mobile eye of the camera attaches itself to a new migrant who, travelling on the train that the film's protagonists have just left, gazes wistfully at a photograph of Carmela's friend Rosalba. Just as in *Costa Azzurra* and *Vacanze d'inverno*, the train becomes a conduit for deep emotional connections, a special place where feelings are revealed and truths discovered in a film that is *in* motion as much as it is *about* motion. As the man, in voice-over, writes Rosalba his first love letter, the camera pans across the train's dusty window, focusing on the figure of Amedeo who, in the distance, carries his spouse across the threshold of his lonely country home.

Notes

1. Tullio Kezich writes that '[Federico] Fellini was offered the opportunity to codirect a new film in Argentina, *Emigrantes* (*Immigrants*), with Fabrizi. But he turned it down because he'd already made other commitments and wasn't entirely convinced about the project and because he was beginning to cultivate a reluctance to leave Rome (an attitude that over time became second nature). In the summer of 1948, Fabrizi set off alone for South America' (2006: 62).
2. Cattini uses this word in a narratological sense. He refers to a particular set of clichés employed in the Mario storyline, such as Paula's backstory (the woman of humble origins who is corrupted by her association with an older, wealthy partner), but also Mario's own trajectory of righteous man who momentarily strays from the straight and narrow path but ultimately returns to it. As I have illustrated in Chapter 4, Raffaello Matarazzo's many postwar melodramas unfolded according to this model.

3. This pitch is replicated beat by beat by Peter Bogdanovich in his *Paper Moon* (1973), in which Ryan O'Neal plays a trickster who sells Bibles.
4. Lina Wertmüller's fifth feature film, *Mimì metallurgico ferito nell'onore* (1972), is a story of internal migration and organized crime told from the point of view of the titular character. The director utilized a high degree of formal opacity, capitalizing on the experience of Francesco Rosi's *I magliari*, which deals with a similar subject. The protagonist is Carmelo 'Mimì' Mardocheo (Giancarlo Giannini), a Sicilian worker who relocates to Turin after he refuses to bow his head to the Mafia and become an accomplice in their attempt to buy a local election. As Wertmüller monographer Claudia Cascone writes, 'Mimì represents the *stereotype* of a Southerner and, in the story's context, he does not simply embody the figure of a worker on the run, but more importantly that of a rebel that fights Sicilian tradition, Mafia power, and Southern social conventions' (2006: 64; my emphasis). Wertmüller's conscious and reflexive use of stereotypes is not restricted to the character of Mimì; in fact, the director creates a whole world that is predicated on the exaggeration of regional customs, political convictions, climate, even of fashion choices. Everything, from the actors' performances to their clothing, is determined by their local affiliation in a display of hyperbolical dichotomies: Sicily is as torrid as Turin is inhospitably cold and damp, the Southerners are as traditional as the Northerners are progressive, Mimì is as dark and hairy as Fiore (his Northern mistress played by Mariangela Melato) is blonde and fair skinned. This prickly sociopolitical satire exposes Italy's corruption and the hypocrisy of both the Southerners, who bury their heads in the sand and stick to the *omertà* code of silence, and the Northerners, who hide behind the leftist parties to absolve themselves of their political inaction. The society Wertmüller describes is one that is plagued by its own indolence, one that finds comfort in the perpetuation of patriarchal gender roles, social mores, even labour inequality. At the film's inception, Mimì's apparent discomfort with the order of things forces him to migrate North, but his journey ends with a return not only to his native Sicily, but to the political lethargy from which he was just temporarily awakened. *Mimì metallurgico*, possibly Wertmüller's finest achievement, extends to the level of the whole narrative the same self-stereotyping process Alberto Sordi created for the character of Ferdinando 'Totonno' Magliulo. This time, however, it is not a ploy developed by a single Italian to take advantage of the German customers, but a caricature of all Italians with which an uncomfortable audience is made to contend.
5. My use of terms such as 'corruption' should not be understood as a moral condemnation of the behaviour the characters exhibit in this or other films. I am simply reporting how these narratives frame their protagonists' choices.
6. For a selection of reviews, see Bolzoni (1986: 57–9).
7. On the most documented of the Sordi–Sonego unmade travels films, see Sanguineti (2018).

8. It is worth reproducing here Tzanelli's discipline-defining passage in its entirety: 'the cinematic tourist is a Hollywood myth, a construct that emerges out of a decontextualization of the actual touring experience. The Hollywood model of the tourist exists within cinematic texts, in the movies that we watch: it suggests ways of consuming places, enjoying and "investing in" (for educational purposes) our holiday time. At the same time, touring through cinematic images produces a second type of tourist who uses the power of imagination to explore the world. This version of the tourist corresponds to the movie viewer, who "reads" and consumes film. The surplus meaning of a film enables audiences to travel virtually, to experience the filmed locations at a distance: thus the impulse to visit these locations originates in the imaginary journey on the screen. A third version of the "cinematic tourist" is created when a tourist industry is established in filmed locations, through the products that tourist industries offer when they exploit the film's potential to induce tourism. There is also a fourth type of cinematic tourist that completes the imagined journey of movie watchers. This is the tourist in the flesh, who visits places because they appeared in films, and whose experience of travel may be influenced by film and the attractions that the tourist industry has to offer' (2007: 3).
9. Interestingly, Sordi sings the jazz song that accompanies the scene. In the lyrics, he wishes for the woman who broke his heart to come back to him.
10. I will henceforth refer to this film as *Bello*.
11. On the relationship between *commedia all'italiana* and death, see Lanzoni (2014).
12. We may need to look back at *Passaporto rosso* (Guido Brignone, 1935) and at *Harlem*'s original cut (Carmine Gallone, 1943) in order to find other clubs for Italian emigrants on film.
13. This sequence is based on Sonego's conversations with Italian migrants in Melbourne (see Sonego 2007: 26–30). The writer had a special connection with the continent, as his own father had spent five years in Australia. *Bello* is possibly his most personal picture.
14. The condition of migrant miners was a theme that was always dear to Sonego. As his biographer Tatti Sanguineti recalls, 'His first trip on a production company account was in the second half of the 1950s, when he was surveying the Marcinelle region for a film on the Italian miners killed by the firedamp. A film that was ostracized by our government from the get go and forever. Sonego stayed two weeks in the Ruhr without finding anything that would interest him. On his way back, he stopped in Amsterdam and found, in the red light district, a single miner from Padua who had survived the accident, and who would blow away his salary on a girl, the same one every weekend, enjoying a special rate' (in Sonego 2007: 94). Of course, Sanguineti is referring to the background research for Luciano Emmer's 1961 *La ragazza in vetrina*.

CHAPTER 8

Killing: Criminal Mobilities

At the end of *Anastasia mio fratello ovvero il presunto capo dell'anonima assassini / My Brother Anastasia*[1] (Stefano Vanzina, 1973), a crestfallen Don Salvatore Anastasio (Alberto Sordi) slowly exits the barber shop of the Park Sheraton Hotel in Manhattan, where he has just bade the final farewell to his murdered brother Albert (Richard Conte). The low-angle close-up frames the distraught man's face against imposing New York architecture, the tops of high-rise buildings thrusting themselves into the sky, as if to project his pain up to the heavens. In the next scene, the priest stands on the deck of an ocean liner, heading back to Italy; eyes welling up with tears, he gazes one last time at the Statue of Liberty, an incongruously modern Lower Manhattan's skyline receding in the distance.

Loosely based on Salvatore Anastasio's eponymous memoir (Anastasio and Mosca 1967), the film chronicles the reunion of the infamous Calabrian brothers in New York City, where Albert Anastasia (born Umberto Anastasio) had been rising through the ranks of organized crime since his illegal disembarkation in the United States in 1916. The film begins in December 1949, when Albert sends for his brother, a naive country priest who spends his days playing football with young seminarists in a secluded monastery. By this time, Albert was a dangerous criminal affiliated with gangster Lucky Luciano (1897–1962) and the notorious Murder Inc. – the mafia syndicate's enforcement arm (the 'anonima assassini' in the film's lengthy Italian title). The assassination of real-life gangster Albert Anastasia occurred on 25 October 1957 in the same barber shop, where he was attacked by two gunmen who killed him on the spot. In its closing beats, the film returns to the proverbial scene of the crime, framing Richard Conte in a manner that is consistent with the photographs of the aftermath of Anastasia's murder: fedora-wearing policemen standing over a body lying on the ground, a white sheet covering his face, the leather-trimmed barber chairs splattered with blood.

Coincidentally, one year prior to the release of *Anastasia*, film noir veteran Richard Conte played Mafia boss Emilio Barzini in Francis Ford Coppola's *The Godfather*. In that film's celebrated ending, which crosscuts between a series of assassinations ordered by Michael Corleone (Al Pacino) and the baptism of his godson, Barzini is gunned down on the steps of the Thurgood Marshall United States Courthouse in New York City's Foley Square.[2] The sudden and brutal hit, in other words, is a classic trope of the crime genre since the early silent days, and can be observed in the Prohibition-era masterpieces, in wartime and postwar film noir, in the revisionist pictures of New Hollywood, and beyond.[3]

Anastasia offers a singular treatment of this scene, removing the violent act from view and, conversely, witnessing its effects on a grieving relative. This subdued approach hinges on the intricate and storied relationship between Italian and American cinema, which Mary Ann McDonald Carolan ascribes to 'the Transatlantic Gaze' (2014: 1–14) connecting the two film cultures; according to the scholar, the continuous vibrant exchange between the two countries has produced instances of direct dialogue across a variety of film genres. The transatlantic gaze, in other words, is a way of referencing both cinematic traditions within a singular work that ultimately complicates any notion of Balkanized national industries and aesthetics. While McDonald Carolan does not focus specifically on the crime film, Dana Renga performs precisely such a critical gesture by including essays on both Italian and North American titles in her edited collection *Mafia Movies: A Reader* (2019). As Renga's approach shows, the genre's permeability to questions of ethnicity, culture, race, and gender makes it a particularly valuable site to interrogate cinematic mobilities in relation to national and diasporic identities.

In this chapter, I will investigate a small sample of Italian crime films through the figure of Sordi as an unlikely mobile lawbreaker. In fact, Sordi's turn as weaselly swindler in *I magliari* was not the actor's only foray into criminal mobilities. While his Don Salvatore Anastasio is deeply troubled by his brother's violent fate, and his journey back to Italy is one of grief and melancholy, in Alberto Lattuada's *Mafioso* (1962) it is the Roman actor who pays back his outstanding debts with the Mafia by pulling a gun's trigger in a New York City barber shop, before being returned safely to his family in the peninsula. Moreover, before these Mafia pictures, Sordi had appeared in *Crimen!... And Suddenly It's Murder!* (1960), a comic whodunnit directed by Mario Camerini and shot in Montecarlo in which he played Commendator Alberto Franzetti, an inveterate gambler who is accused of murder alongside two Italian couples. Rodolfo Sonego, who contributed to this film's screenplay, recalls that the team of screenwriters relied on Luciano Vincenzoni's knowledge about gambling, and that they 'began to shoot *Crimen* almost blindly, the actors not having read a script that didn't exist' (qtd in Sanguineti 2015: 194). If this improvisational method would yield miraculous results in *Il diavolo*, the goal-oriented format of the whodunnit, albeit peppered with plenty of comic relief, proved ill-fitted for it, as was the large ensemble cast featured in *Crimen*, which included many (perhaps too many) commanding screen presences like Bernard Blier, Vittorio Gassman, Dorian Gray, Nino Manfredi, Silvana Mangano, and Franca Valeri. Despite these obvious red flags, the film was hugely successful at the box office, to the point of being remade twice, and it exemplifies the kind of genre crossover that characterized much of Italian-style comedy – Mario Monicelli's masterpieces *I soliti ignoti / Big Deal on Madonna Street* (1958) and *La grande guerra* (1959), for instance, successfully combined comedy with the heist picture and the war film respectively.

In the context of cinematic mobilities, *Crimen* must be connected to Sordi's travel comedies, in particular through its use of the railway to reveal information about the characters and their reasons for travel. The opening takes place in the dining car of a train connecting Rome to Montecarlo and Nice, where Remo Capretti (Gassman) is explaining his 'scientific' method to his wife Marina (Mangano) using a portable roulette wheel. Alberto overhears the two and interjects, describing his recovery from his gambling addiction. Sporting pomaded jet-black hair, a moustache, and a pinstripe suit, the suave Franzetti discourages the couple from trying their luck at the green tables. His other interaction on the train is with another Italian couple, Quirino (Manfredi) and Giovanna Filonzi (Valeri); interested in buying their Basset hound, he gives them his contact information on a box of matches, and when Quirino 'forgets' to return his pen to him, the piqued Commendator Alberto chides them: 'Italians? Don't travel, you misers!' Franzetti will direct a variation of this classist (but ultimately self-loathing) comment against Remo after they spend the night gambling together and end up losing everything: 'We are Italians, aren't we? So let's continue, undeterred, to let the foreigners talk about us!' The cruelty of these rebukes stems from Franzetti's distaste for his fellow nationals, a sentiment afforded to him by his wife's distancing wealth. Conversely, in his interactions with the Police Commissioner (Blier), he is overly deferential, losing his sense of self as soon as he learns that the aforementioned box of matches has led the Commissioner to investigate him for the murder around which the film's intricate plot revolves, alongside the two Italian couples, whose reticence to cooperate with the police seems suspicious. Eventually, the bumbling Italians are absolved, and the real culprits are arrested. In the film's closing moments, the characters reunite on the train that originates in Nice and passes through Montecarlo on its way to Rome. When a man is stabbed to death on the train, the Italians reverse their initial attitude towards the authorities: they pull the alarm and congregate around a policeman to give him as much information as they can. Of course, as in the previous case, their stories do not match, and they become suspects themselves.

Unlike the travel comedies, which devote screen time to the locations they visit, *Crimen*'s primary interest is to drive the plot forward via a series of flashbacks – a device pertaining to the narrative discourse of crime fiction. What remains consistent with the films of the 1950s, however, is the attention paid to the mode of transportation and the activities performed therein, such as sleeping, eating, and socializing. Similarly, Sordi's segment in the anthology film *Thrilling* (1965) focused on the recently completed *Autostrada del Sole* (aka A1), a major motorway connecting Milan to Naples via Bologna, Florence, and Rome. A long traffic artery straddling two-thirds of the peninsula, the autostrada was created to boost the Italian economy in the late 1950s by allowing swift transit across its largest metropolitan areas. As often happens in the case of national projects of vast scale, an implicit ranking of communities took place, infrastructure determining who would thrive and who would wither away.

Directed by Carlo Lizzani and written by Rodolfo Sonego (of course), the segment *L'Autostrada del sole* stars Sordi as Fernando Boccetta, an aggressive motorist travelling on the highway's pristine tarmac aboard a 1963 Autobianchi Bianchina Panoramica adorned with stickers of high-performance and motorsport manufacturers such as Ferrari. As Chaim Noy writes regarding bumper stickers (BS),

> the pasting of the sticker unto the car created a new automobile actor: the BS-Car. The new social actor amounts to a gestalt; to a whole that is more meaningful than the sum of its parts. The BS-car is a *discursive, social, and oftentimes also political* vehicle. (Noy 2016: 71; emphasis in the original)

In other words, the aspirational stickers attached to the diminutive Autobianchi forge a vehicle that visually describes Fernando's masculinity and demeanour, spelling out his identity as a motorist and as a citizen. However expertly piloted, the vehicle is no match for the 1965 Fiat 2300 S Coupe driven by a pipe-smoking Milanese who refuses to be overtaken by the overconfident Roman. Eventually, the two collide and Fernando exits his vehicle to confront the other driver, who takes off. The ensuing chase leads them to the snaking ramps of the Orvieto exit, which had been completed in 1964. The clean, smooth, brand-new motorway where Fernando felt so safe (he comments on the experience by stating that 'One is alone on the autostrada, and the radio keeps one in contact with the developed world') is in stark contrast to the dusty and often unpaved country roads where the sideslipping vehicles continue their high-speed journey. Eventually, they arrive at the Albergo della Torre, where the strange ways of the family who run the establishment turn out to be a symptom of murderous behaviour. The events that unfurl at the hotel are largely irrelevant to this analysis, except for a comment made by one of the owners, who confesses to an increasingly suspicious Fernando, 'We used to be rich, but the autostrada ruined us.' The implication for the film's plot, of course, is that now they kill and rob those customers who have the misfortune to happen upon the secluded hotel.

Yet, this statement also encapsulates something profound regarding the nature of vast projects of civic engineering. In fact, mobilities are always relational, intersecting politics, ideology, participation, and power. The motorway is designed to transform large points of interest into an interconnected 'centre', often at the expense of a suddenly marginalized periphery; as Peter Adey writes, quoting J. B. Jackson, the twentieth century's increased 'Mobility failed to emancipate because it instead fostered the unequal positioning of the already marginalized, "the rank and file, particularly those in the countryside, were doomed to immobility and to political inaction"' (Adey 2017: 114). Framed in this way, even pedestrian pictures such as *Crimen* and *L'Autostrada del sole* (pun intended), constitute powerful documents of the growing pains and contradictions of a society that was rapidly evolving with and through auto- and rail mobilities. On one side of the metaphorical coin (or chip, if you will) is the interconnectedness of Italy's capital city with the jet-setting Principality of Monaco, where the wealthy and powerful gamble away fortunes they often conceal in Swiss banks;[4] on the other is a failing family business in the heart of Umbria, cut off from its revenue source (overnighting motorists) by a national project that privileged speed over capillarity. A black comedy about the gambling addiction of Europe's higher echelon is matched by a farce about the meek cannibalizing unsuspecting vacationers.[5]

One of Sordi's most revealing criminal mobilities begins on the factory floor of the Innocenti automobile plant in Lambrate, near Milan, where foreman Antonio Badalamenti (Sordi) is conducting his routine safety rounds. A Sicilian living in Lombardy with his family, Antonio is a serious and dedicated company man who drives one of the marque's products, the popular 1962 Innocenti A40 Mark II, a small hatchback that was almost identical to its Northern European counterpart, the Austin A40 Farina produced by the British Motor Corporation, which licensed the design to

Innocenti. When the Badalamentis leave Milan to vacation in Antonio's fictional hometown of Calamo, his Italian American boss Dr Zanchi gives him a mysterious package to deliver into the hands of the 'family friend' Don Vincenzo (Ugo Attanasio). The family boards the train connecting Milan to Palermo via Messina, reaching the coastal town the following day; on the ferry that shuttles passengers across the strait, Angelo begins to wax lyrical about his native island and the modern infrastructure (including the impressive power lines) that connects it to the continent. The blonde Milanese Marta replies to her excited dark and moustachioed husband, 'I'm watching Italy fade away in the distance. I'm so nostalgic.' Later, when they are about to arrive in the remote Calamo, Marta quips, 'Italy is over.'

In his review of *Mafioso*, the late Yale M. Udoff noted that the film

> is less concerned with the differences between North and South, between Milan and Palermo, than an acute and detailed study of Sicilian customs and manners. [. . .] It is, instead, a study of that strange brotherhood which operates within the Sicilian social system – the Mafia. (Udoff 1965: 48)

Existing in that uncomfortable but productive space between the gangster genre and social satire, *Mafioso* examines organized crime as an institution capable of affecting change on a local (Sicilian), national (Italian), and international scale (USA). In fact, according to Nelson Moe,

> Lattuada's film mimics and deconstructs the stereotype of the Sicilian Mafia in order to offer a dark commentary on the nature of modern capitalism. A key part of this critical and aesthetic project involves both dramatizing and dismantling stereotypes about the north and south of Italy. (Moe 2019: 183)

In Sicily, Don Vincenzo is pleased with the gift Antonio has delivered, which is a coded message from his 'friends' overseas, and calls on him to return the many 'favours' he has bestowed upon him over the years – from the land his father is able to buy at a bargain price, to his own position at Innocenti. Suddenly, Antonio is thrust into an unexpected (mis)adventure that carries him to the other side of the Atlantic, the film's temporarily sunny disposition pivoting quickly into the darker hues of the crime genre. In the extended sequence that documents his journey, Antonio is shuttled through a variety of vehicles: first, he is given the assignment by a menacing Don Vincenzo while they sit in the close quarters of a car; second, the befuddled man is moved to the back of a truck, where he enters a wooden crate; third, he is finally forklifted inside an Alitalia cargo aircraft. The screen goes black, switching to a subjective shot from inside the box. Light filters through the wooden planks, strange loud sounds pierce the ears of a terrified Antonio. Once he arrives at his mysterious destination, the man is uncrated and transferred to the back seat of a 1960 Cadillac Eldorado Biarritz. Framed in a frontal three shot in which he is flanked by two taciturn men, the confounded Antonio appears unable to recognize the landscape he sees through the car's windows. The driver puts the convertible's top down, revealing to the character and to the audience that they have indeed travelled to New York City. Directed by the vertical lines of Manhattan's skyscrapers, Antonio's eyes travel upward, triggering a series of subjective shot-reverse-shots that participate in his marvel at the imposing architecture. A singular parallel with Carmine Gallone's *Harlem* can be traced: in the latter, Massimo Girotti's Tommaso peered through the window of a studio set that stood in for the Commodore Hotel. Given that his visit to Gotham was created on the editing table, splicing together a close-up of his face and stock footage of New York City, the film gave him a high vantage point that spoke of his ability to ultimately prevail over the foreign forces that tried to manipulate him in this strange and hostile land.[6] By 1962, the perspective had radically changed. The Italian man is no longer able to extricate himself from the dehumanizing forces of capital. He is a cog in the (criminal) machine; any resistance is futile, as are pesky principles of legality and truth. Much like in the ending of *Anastasia*, Sordi's long face becomes the emotional counterpoint to an alien cityscape that he observes, defeated and confounded, looking upward, and while *in motion*.[7]

After he is briefed, given a lot to drink, and equipped with a pistol, Antonio is dropped off near the location where he is to assassinate a Mafia rival. Before he can reach his target, an inebriated African American man enters his path by being unceremoniously kicked out of a restaurant where, we learn, he was using the bathroom (Figure 2.7). In English, a language that is clearly unknown to Antonio, the man proceeds to illustrate how this action is fundamentally discriminatory and infringes upon his rights as a citizen. On the one hand, in a strictly narratological sense, this unexpected brush with the language of the civil rights movement serves to increase the scene's suspense by delaying the climactic action that is to follow in the ill-fated Woodcliff Embassy Barber Shop – which stood on 7122 Bergenline Avenue, North Bergen, New Jersey; on the other hand, it is also a clear indication of the film's transatlantic gaze, as it engages with a debate that had become a flashpoint in contemporary American politics (Figure 2.8). Moreover, as Moe notes, 'Ten years before *The Godfather*, Lattuada anticipated (and most likely influenced) Coppola's deconstruction of the time-honoured moral opposition between a "good" (legal, legitimate, official) social and economic order and the "bad" one of the Mafia (criminal, illegitimate, violent)' (2019: 187).

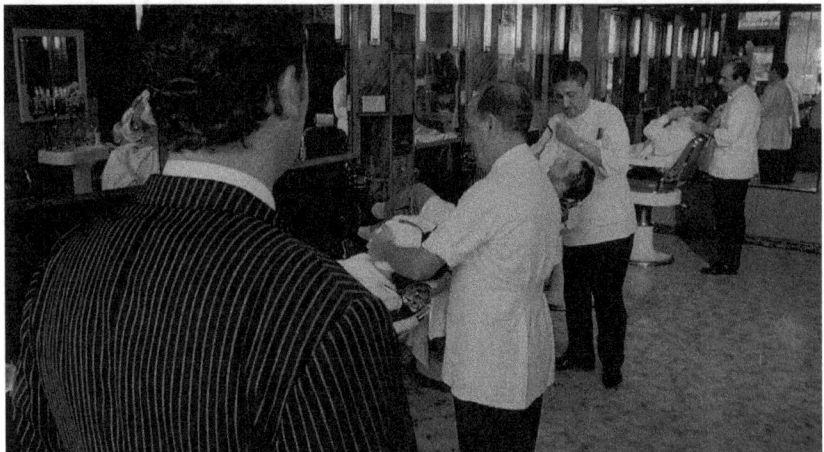

Figures 2.7 and 2.8 Criminal mobilities through the (cinematic) transatlantic gaze.

Connecting identity politics with a barber shop hit, of course, is how *Mafioso* demonstrates itself to be a deeply dialogic text, participating simultaneously in at least two major projects. First, it connects (and therefore implicates) industrial capitalism (Innocenti and the British Motor Corporation) and the migrant labour on which it relies with global (or at least transatlantic) organized crime. Second, in employing a stylized version of the barber shop assassination, it references the Prohibition-era American gangster film, a genre in which (Italian) ethnic stereotypes famously ran rampant. In closing his review, Udoff opines that

> the director's image of American gangsters is derived exclusively, it would seem, from the George Raft and Edward G. Robinson films of the 'thirties and 'forties.

These American Mafia heavies would have better been replaced by some direct observation of their current counterparts. (Udoff 1965: 50)

Yet, this anachronistic depiction of the New York Mafia is necessary to the film's analytical framework, which is based not on realism, but on a systemic deconstruction of the relationships that govern the capitalist machine in which Antonio is a willing participant, and that has profited from institutionalized racism and discrimination, albeit in very different forms, on both sides of the Atlantic. *Mafioso* is a tale of Italian identity, Sicilian masculinity, North–South cultural differences, unevenly developed infrastructure, labour relations, segregation, and diaspora told *through* a porous and hybrid genre that synthesized both the Italian and the American national cinemas.

In his essay on the film's screenplay, Paolo Cherchi Usai recounts that *Mafioso* is based on a true story:

An emissary of the Sicilian Mafia (a 'simple man', according to Lattuada) is smuggled onto a ship and sent to New York on a homicidal mission. A lawyer in Palermo introduces him to noted painter Bruno Caruso, who records the events and paints his portrait, which ends up in Lattuada's house. Producer Antonio Cervi is informed and believes it is good material for a movie. (Cherchi Usai 2009: 219)

In the film, the ship is replaced by an aircraft, but what is retained from the original story is Antonio's cargomobility, a term that, as Adey explains, was coined by Thomas Birtchnell et al. (2015: 1)

to describe what they call an 'orderly disorder' of all sorts of non-human – and sometimes human – traffic that circulates the world as cargo: home appliances, vehicles, electronics, parts, animals, foods, fuel, toys, clothes, building materials, 'waste', weapons, illicit drugs, and illegal migrants – just some of the 'moving materials' that are central to modern social and economic life. (Adey 2017: 242)

Antonio, in other words, is a product of a nascent economy (and a film style) that is simultaneously local (Italian-style comedy) and global (American cinema via the barber shop hit).[8]

If in *Mafioso* the barber shop assassination connects Italian and American cinema, anticipating the hyphenated revisionism of the Italian American cinema of the late 1960s and 1970s, in *Anastasia* the same scene vaults over the divide between historical record and fictionalization. According to Claudio G. Fava, *Anastasia* was a project that originated with Sordi himself, who read Salvatore Anastasio's memoir and lobbied for the film to be made (2003: 241). Tatti Sanguineti adds that Sordi had been working on the film at least since *Fumo di Londra*/*Smoke Over London* (1966), his directorial debut, and that he wished for Sergio Amidei and Rodolfo Sonego to write it, and for Vittorio De Sica to direct it (2015: 410). Only Amidei would join the film's actual production team, and the end result is a far cry from the tonal complexity and stylistic elegance of *Mafioso*.

Yet, the two pictures are connected not only by their central performer and their American setting, but also (and more importantly) by their transatlantic gaze. Unlike Antonio, Don Salvatore Anastasio travels to the United States aboard a luxurious ocean liner, a long sequence that is introduced by documentary footage of real-life Italian migrants leaving the country. His kinship with the powerful Albert Anastasia opens many doors for the oblivious priest, who is moved to a first-class cabin and welcomed to dine at the captain's table. In his personal journal, he attributes the preferential treatment to his brother's reputation, mistaking its root causes for respect and esteem rather than fear. He also anticipates the sight of the New York skyline, a point that returns, once again, to *Harlem*'s observations on the verticalization of American architecture, which the priest reads in altogether different terms: 'Tomorrow we will be in America. I will rise early, because I do not want to miss the grandiose spectacle of the skyscrapers. God has allowed them to be this tall so that people can be nearer to him.' When the ship finally enters New York Harbor, Don Salvatore rushes to the deck, from which he can observe the Statue of Liberty and Lower Manhattan's skyline. As I discussed in this chapter's introductory paragraph, the view is incongruously modern, as it features the Twin Towers of the World Trade Center, which were completed in 1973. Similarly, during the car ride to his brother's mansion in Fort Lee, New Jersey, contemporary infrastructure and modern automobiles are in plain view. In other words, *Anastasia* is a diachronic film whose mise-en-scène is not preoccupied with temporal verisimilitude, but with its position in relation to the history of Italian and American cinema. A small scene reveals the complexity of this historiographic operation: during a montage that depicts the brothers joyfully canvassing the city together, Albert takes Don Salvatore to the barber shop where he will meet his demise; the two get haircuts, and Don Salvatore is embarrassed to admit he has never before had a manicure. When the blonde manicurist bends over in front of him to retrieve her tools, he modestly averts his gaze away from her bottom. Comical in nature, Sordi's gesture recalls Don Pietro Pellegrini's repositioning of an indecorous statuette in Roberto Rossellini's *Roma città aperta / Rome, Open City* (1945). In the Neorealist masterpiece, the priest (Aldo Fabrizi) lends his services and moral fortitude to the partisan resistance, paying the ultimate price in the film's foundational ending. Conversely, in *Anastasia*, Don Salvatore becomes an accessory to his brother's crimes, unwittingly wielding the power of the Anastasio/a surname to accomplish a number of seemingly harmless undertakings, such as the renovation of a local church and the coaching of a youth (American) football team.

While the barber shop assassination is *Anastasia*'s most recognizable nod to its various cinematic sources, the film's crucial sequence is not its grisly ending, but the televized hearings that follow Albert's incarceration, which are modelled on the real-life Kefauver Committee work (1950–1). Nicknamed after its chairman, Senator Carey Estes Kefauver, the United States Senate Special Committee to Investigate Crime in Interstate Commerce was tasked with investigating the activities of organized crime across state borders.[9] In particular, some of the most incendiary replies uttered by mobster Frank Costello (born Francesco Castiglia, 1891–1973) are re-enacted verbatim in the film's extended hearings sequence.[10] Consonantly with its diachronic nature, the film departs from historical record in including a lengthy testimony by a defiant Albert Anastasia in which he proudly discusses his choices and the role he played in organizing the New York dock workers. However, according to Don Salvatore Anastasio's memoir, the mobster behaved differently before the Committee:

> Alberto defended himself calmly, employing all the resources prescribed by the law against accusations. He talked exhaustively about his garment factory in Hazleton, but he refused to speak about his activities between 1919 and 1942. He simply said: 'I don't recall.' (Anastasio and Mosca 1967: 129)[11]

The film's departure from historical record can be understood as another instance of its transatlantic gaze: in fact, when *Anastasia* was released, the Italian American Anti-Defamation League, led by mobster Joseph A. Colombo Sr., was beginning to appropriate the language of the civil rights movement to fight the pejorative stereotyping and the (alleged) discrimination of Italian Americans.[12] Founded in 1970, the League was able to mobilize many Italian Americans who (rightfully) felt demeaned by the entertainment industry because of, ironically, the frequent association of their ethnic background with organized crime. In order to legitimize his fight, Colombo partnered with the Jewish Defense League, which was led by the controversial Rabbi Meir Kahane, who coincidentally was accused of running weapons across state borders (see Kaplan 1971).

Television became the privileged platform for the dissemination of the League's ideas: on 14 April 1971, Colombo appeared on Dick Cavett's popular ABC late-night talk show to argue against the media's problematic depiction of Italian Americans and law enforcement's allegedly unfair targeting of this ethnic group. In *Anastasia*, when questioned by the Kefauver Committee about his activities, Albert launches into a lengthy harangue tinged with nationalism ('I love this country, as I love the one where I was born'), in which he defends his achievements, speaking of the unionization of the New York waterfront workers he spearheaded, and of the dignity his action bestowed upon those who followed him. Albert's rhetoric is heavily reminiscent of Colombo's, although the fictional gangster's tirade is elegantly written and not as self-aware as the real-life mobster's television appearances. Moreover, when he leaves the courthouse flanked by police officers in plainclothes, Richard Conte descends the steps of the Thurgood Marshall United States Courthouse in New York City's Foley Square, the same flight where his *Godfather* character was assassinated by a killer *wearing* a policeman's uniform one year earlier (Figures 2.9 and 2.10). The temporal slippage between *Anastasia*, its source material, and its numerous intertexts is echoed in its various on-screen anachronisms, which include the mid-century costumes worn by the protagonists and the 1970s attire sported by those around them; the period vehicles driven by the characters and the contemporary cars travelling on the same streets; the ocean liner on which Don Salvatore arrives and departs, a relic of days past in the era of commercial aviation; and finally New York's cityscape and skyline, which speak of an entirely different era from the film's mid-century setting.

In conclusion, while much of what happens in *Anastasia* may be seen as a singular revision of and departure from *Harlem*'s plot (whereby it is the immigrant brother who lets organized crime encroach upon his family), the films' endings seem to strangely parallel each other: the older brother perishes, gunned down by a ruthless rival, and the younger brother returns to Italy on an ocean liner, leaving behind that 'America amara' (bitter America)[13] that both lifted and ultimately crushed their kin.[14]

Alberto Sordi would go on to play a variety of shady mobile characters, including the cynical arms dealer in *Finché c'è guerra c'è speranza / While There's War There's Hope* (Alberto Sordi, 1974), but *Anastasia* was his last foray into the sort of criminal mobilities traditionally associated with the gangster genre. After having starred in so many titles with a clear interest in Italian mobilities across the peninsula (and sometimes beyond), from 1966 the popular actor turned his own gaze outward, interrogating national identity and masculinity abroad in a series of films of his own direction. In the next chapter, I will discuss some of these titles in relation to other classic performances by the restless comedian.

Figures 2.9 and 2.10 Acting across cinematic traditions: Richard Conte's transatlantic gaze.

Notes

1. I will refer to this film simply as *Anastasia*.
2. For more on this iconic scene, see Zambenedetti (2019).
3. For more on the treatment of Italian American gangsters in Hollywood, see Bondanella (2006: 172–295).
4. Sordi himself played one such tax-evading capitalist driving his Maserati across the border, from Milan to Lugano, to deposit 100 million lira in a Swiss bank account in *La più bella serata della mia vita* (Ettore Scola, 1972), an adaptation of the 1956 novella *Die Panne* by Friedrich Dürrenmatt.

5. According to Sonego, the episode is inspired by the 'crimes of Alleghe, a series of murders that took place in a small hotel in the area of Belluno', the screenwriter's home town (qtd in Sanguineti 2015: 265).
6. This, of course, is true only of *Harlem*'s postwar cut. In the 1943 version, as I mentioned in Part One, Tommaso loses his brother and returns to Italy a defeated man.
7. The articulation of spatial practices along vertical and horizontal movements is discussed by Henri Lefevbre in *The Production of Space* (1991). The French sociologist notes that 'The arrogant verticality of skyscrapers, and especially of public and state buildings, introduces a phallic or more precisely a phallocratic element into the visual realm; the purpose of this display, of this need to impress, is to convey an impression of authority to each spectator. Verticality and great height have ever been the spatial expression of potentially violent power' (1991: 98).
8. Maurizio De Benedictis comments on the characters Sordi played in the early years of the 1960s, noting the following important changes in his on-screen persona: '1) Sordi is *between* his old character, which risked becoming merely a sketch, and a more marked personage: an Italian in a country that was transforming dramatically (his best role is the one in *Mafioso*, which is both anxious and imperturbable, where the dry, grotesque humour of [screenwriter] Azcona both hardens and gratifies him, like Ferreri does with Tognazzi and Berlanga with Manfredi). 2) The *interaction* with other characters, situations and reality, in such a changing country, who are no longer easily crushed by his emphatic personalism, or "personage-ism", by the narcissist selfishness of both his sketched-out characters and of his scene-stealing ham: the national Albertone. 3) A certain *justification* of the evils and vices of his typical character, which are somehow attributed to chaos in a renewing society or to society *tout court*, to the "modern" world, and so on' (2005: 180–1).
9. For more on the activities of the Kefauver Committee, see Frontani (2016).
10. The passage to which I am referring is the following: Senator Tobey's voice, Question (Q): 'Have you always upheld the Constitution and laws of your state and Nation?' Subjective View (SV). Costello seated at table answers (A): 'I believe I have.' SV. Stenographers. Tobey's voice over. Close Up (CU). Costello. Q: 'Have you ever offered your services to any war effort of this country?' A: 'No.' Q: 'Bearing in mind all that you've gained and received in wealth, what have you ever done for your country as a good citizen?' A: 'Well, I don't know what you mean by that.' Q: 'Well, you're looking back over the years now to that time when you became a citizen and we're now standing 20 odd years after that. You must have in your mind some things you've done that you can speak of as an American citizen, if so, what are they?' A: 'Paid my tax!' See 'US Senate Probe Crime (1951)', British Pathé, available at <https://www.youtube.com/watch?v=WKGganSXFTc> (last accessed 17 August 2020).

11. Refusing to answer the committee's questions actually earned Albert a citation for contempt of Congress. See *New York Herald Tribune* (1951).
12. Renamed the Italian American Civil Rights League (IACRL) in 1974, the organization is currently active in community-based learning. See <https://www.italianamericanleaguenyc.org> (last accessed 17 August 2020).
13. In his book, Don Salvatore echoes the language of Mario Soldati's aforementioned memoir when he declares, 'After I had listened to my brother I would decide whether to remain in New York or to leave, returning to my small town, forgetting this *bitter America* that was already fascinating me so much' (Anastasio and Mosca 1967: 17; my emphasis).
14. I am, of course, referring to *Harlem*'s original ending.

CHAPTER 9

Exploring:
Italian Identity Abroad

As discussed in the previous three chapters, Alberto Sordi starred in a variety of films examining Italian identity in motion, some of which crossed national boundaries to look at the virtues and the vices of a rapidly evolving society from a temporarily external vantage point. The pictures often congealed around specific genres such as travel comedies, social dramas, and crime films – albeit of comedic or satirical intent.[1] In this chapter, I turn my attention to two films that, albeit vastly different in their ambition, can largely be subsumed under the umbrella of the action verb 'exploring' – intended in spatial and geographical terms as well as in existential and human ones. In particular, I will discuss Alberto Sordi's directorial debut *Fumo di Londra/Smoke Over London* (1966) in relation to Ettore Scola's *Riusciranno i nostri eroi a ritrovare l'amico misteriosamente scomparso in Africa/Will Our Heros Be Able to Find Their Friend Who Has Mysteriously Disappeared in Africa?* (1968).

Emboldened by the freeing experience of shooting *Il diavolo* in Sweden *sans* the accoutrements and comforts of big productions, that is, improvising much of the film as he went along, in 1966 Sordi would take the last step towards becoming, as Claudio G. Fava puts it, a film *auteur* in his own right, co-authoring the screenplay for and directing *Fumo di Londra*, which was shot on location in England (2003: 193).[2] While it retains some recognizable qualities of the earlier travel comedies, the film is a considerable step forward for the newly anointed *auteur*, if anything because *gallismo* is not the only force driving the narrative, or at least not its primary one. On the contrary, despite its tongue-in-cheek tone and the numerous gags peppered throughout, *Fumo di Londra* is a clear-eyed and bitter examination of the generational shift that was rapidly changing the face of England and of Europe at large, and of the irrepressible discontent that would soon lead to the wave of protests of May 1968.[3]

The idea for the film was rooted in the persistent xenophilia of the well-to-do Italian bourgeoisie, as Sordi recalls:

When I went to London to shoot *Those Magnificent Men in Their Flying Machines or How I Flew from London to Paris in 25 Hours 11 Minutes*, my friend Peter Sellers told me that the mores were changing, so I thought about writing the story of an antiquarian from Perugia whose dream is to become the perfect gentleman, with umbrella, loafers and the proverbial bowler hat. But when he goes to England, he realises that his model is outdated: the youths grow their hair long, they wear the first miniskirts, and the Beatles are popular . . . (Sordi qtd in Schiavina 1999: 59)

The film reflects this transition in the arc of the main character, Dante Fontana (Alberto Sordi), as he struggles to fit in with the conservative British elites in the film's second act and with the progressive youth in the third, ultimately failing with both. As Dante explains in his voice-over commentary, his reasons for leaving Italy are both personal and professional: an educated, well-mannered, and sophisticated man, he believes that he *deserves* to see London, which he considers, not inaccurately, the world's capital of culture and new trends. In the first act, his desire to assimilate instantly and to look like a perfect English gentleman is accompanied by his rejection of his Italian identity. Two sides of the same coin, these wishes are expressed in progressive stages of ethnic erasure that ultimately backfire: not only does the character try to shed his Italian skin and wear that of an Englishman, by the film's end he also slips into that of an individual half his age, making a mockery of himself. Costumed in a hip velvet suit and a wig of flowing blonde hair, Sordi shows that uncritical xenophilia can lead to a dangerous loss of perspective.[4]

Dante Fontana reaches London on an Alitalia aircraft, as befits the era and his social status. However, he is an inexperienced traveller: as he sits by the window, his voice-over narration explains that he feels somewhat uncomfortable at the thought of flying. Upon his arrival at the London airport, he clashes with the local customs officer, who confiscates his cigarettes and liquor. Similarly, he inadvertently cuts the taxi queue and is quickly reprimanded for it. After he checks into his hotel room, which features a view of Buckingham Palace, Dante hits the stores on St James's Street, purchasing a bowler hat, shoes, an umbrella, a red carnation, and a pipe. Accessorized like a true Englishman, he picks up a copy of *The Times* on a newsstand near Piccadilly Circus and heads over to Buckingham Palace for the changing of the guard. The long montage that accompanies his transformation into a city-dwelling gentleman also signals the beginning of a gradual split between Dante's inner and outer selves that culminates in a sequence reminiscent of a simplified Lacanian mirror stage (Figures 2.11 and 2.12). Still wandering about the city, Dante stops by a store window where he spots a mannequin wearing a tailcoat. Framed from within the window, he closes his eyes and allows himself to

Figures 2.11 and 2.12 Fracturing the (national) self.

slip into daydream. The shot returns to the mannequin, who slowly turns around, revealing that the formal attire is worn by Dante himself, who brings his chic binoculars to his eyes.[5] The cutaway that follows is a subjective view of scenes from an elegant racing track, where the royal family salutes the crowd from a horse-drawn carriage. The sequence ends with Dante wistfully opening his eyes and moving on with his leisurely walk. According to Lacan, the subject's *apperception* (the turning of the self into an object upon viewing one's own image reflected in a mirror) also entails *misrecognition* (seeing a wholesome Ideal-I towards which the subject will perpetually strive). Seen in this way, Dante's store-window 'daydream' is not simply a whimsical fantasy expressing the desire for English bespoke clothing, but something much more meaningful and somewhat alarming: it is the expression of a fractured self, the projection of an unattainable rewriting of one's own biography, the fashioning of a new identity dislodged from one's own culture and background. Adrift across national boundaries, Dante's ego becomes dependent on external signifiers (such as morning dress) for its own self-definition.

Dante continues to roam around the city, visiting its most prominent sights, yet his appearance is that of a local. The disguise is so accurate that a group of Southern Italian tourists mistake him for a conservatively dressed Englishman, and they ask to have their picture taken with him, with London Bridge in the background. Dante is flattered by this honest mistake and plays along, gladly posing for the photograph; but when one of the children hits the strange man on the head, the illusion is shattered. Dante breaks character and scolds the kid: 'Nice, boy! Be nice! People, don't give yourself away for what we are!' This line, of course, is almost identical to the one the actor uses in *Crimen* to rebuke his fellow Italian gamblers in Montecarlo for their unruly behaviour, as discussed in Chapter 8. Clearly, Dante's attempt at cloaking himself with Britishness and to conceal his real identity betrays his insecurity with regards to his Italian origins. He wishes for his compatriots to behave appropriately and, in his (fractured) mind, tries to set an example. The joke, however, is on him, because his (national) shame is not shared by all Italians abroad. The befuddled tourists reply to his comment with a dry 'Who's this guy?', which draws attention to the silliness of Dante's enterprise. By rejecting his Italianness and by failing at being truly English (which, of course, is an impossible proposition), he is left without a clear sense of self.

While signalling a new direction in Sordi's career, *Fumo di Londra* is also a film that capitalizes on the actor's enormous popularity by nodding to his signature roles and gags. For instance, when choosing a restaurant for dinner, Dante scoffs at the many neon signs promising Italian delicacies (Trattoria La Dolce Vita, Ristorante La Colombina d'Oro, Hostaria Capri, and so on) and asks a policeman to recommend a 'typical English restaurant'. However, when the food he is served turns out to be an unappetizing jellied concoction with beady eye-like decorations, the film cuts to a close-up of a saddened Sordi, only to zoom back and reveal that the man is indeed resignedly eating a large bowl of spaghetti in an Italian restaurant. Just as the wannabe Yankee Nando Moriconi had rejected 'American' food in the career-making *Un americano a Roma* (Steno, 1954), twelve years later Dante Fontana begrudgingly returns to his culinary roots in *Fumo di Londra*.[6]

Albeit imperfect, his English gentleman disguise manages to fool people, with the only result being that it makes things more difficult for him. At the prestigious auction house Christie's, the antiquary meets the Duchess of Bradford (Amy Dalby), who asks him to extend his stay and visit her castle, in the hope of showing him an Etruscan sculpture – which will turn out to be a forgery. Dante, excited at the prospect of mingling with the British aristocracy, travels to the English countryside wearing an elegant three-piece attire complete with pocket square, leather gloves, and a fashionable six-panel plaid deerstalker hat. He is supposed to meet the Duchess's driver at the station, but the driver is told to look for an Italian man, while Dante is again dressed like an upper-class Englishman. When Dante asks the station master for help, he comments, 'Oh my God, you are Italian? You look like a real Englishman!', to which the flattered Dante replies, 'Thank you very much, what a wonderful compliment.' Naturally, the joke is on the Italian, because the station master retorts, 'Not really, your car has left!' Once more, Dante's attempt at (outward) assimilation is successful, but does not bear good fruit. He has to walk all the way to the castle, where he is mistaken by one of the Duchess's butlers for a local tourist visiting the extravagant estate and is made to pay for entry. His incredible ability to camouflage himself works against him; forced to make his presence known to his hostess, he calls to her from a balcony as she is preparing to leave for a hunt. The act is deemed reprehensible by the butler, who indignantly points out to him that 'this is not Rome, you know!' When the misunderstanding is finally cleared up, Dante is properly welcomed among the distinguished guests, and invited to join the hunt, for which he is furnished with a red equestrian outfit and a horse that he is incapable of riding. Once again, Dante attempts to erase his ethnicity, and he gets his comeuppance by causing a riding accident. While this plot device of action and retribution frustrates the character's project and provides many of the film's comic moments, it also alerts the audience to its absurdity. Dante's aspirations are inherently flawed, as is his interest in Lady Elizabeth (Fiona Lewis), the Duchess's niece – a potential love interest who is less than half the protagonist's age.

After he inadvertently destroys the forged sculpture and is chased from the castle by a barrage of gun and cannon fire, Dante boards the train back to London, where he runs into the young woman, who is heading back to her boarding school. Here, the films employs the travel comedy narrative device of having characters reveal something fundamental about themselves while in motion: Elizabeth hints to Dante that she has an active sex life, and Dante (in voice-over) confesses that, despite the woman's young age, he wishes to pursue her. If in *Fumo di Londra*'s first two acts Sordi's critique was equally directed at Italian xenophilia *and* at British superciliousness, the film's third act turns to the Bakhtinian carnivalesque for its skewering of England's youth culture, which at the time was beginning to percolate into the peninsula. In the hope of reconnecting with Elizabeth, Dante postpones his departure and visits her college, only to find out that she has left it and moved to Richmond, where England's mods are converging.[7] When he visits the town's 'Youth Club' to find Elizabeth, Dante is hopelessly out of place in his dark suit and bowler hat. The teenage girl takes him to a hip party where the host derides his clothes for being too conventional and offers to dress him appropriately, remarking that England's youth has embraced gender fluidity, and that 'Women's fashion and men's fashion don't exist any more as such. Fortunately, the difference between the sexes is disappearing' – and so are the traditional sexual mores with which Dante is concerned, Elizabeth instructs him, as she invites the Italian to kiss Angel (Elizabeth Rutter), another girl at the party.[8]

It is important to underscore that, while on the surface Elizabeth seems to behave like a sexually liberated 'unruly woman', as theorized by Kathleen Rowe, Sordi himself was by no means a feminist, and no such connotation should be attributed to his films. Elizabeth's character has the specific function of luring the old satyr into the bacchanal where his (sexual) inadequacy finally catches up with him. It is after this sobering realization that the carnival is brought (forcefully) to an abrupt end by the intervention of law enforcement. As Rowe writes, 'gender inversion can also set into motion a destabilization of the binary categories of gender, opening the way to more fluid forms of sexuality before the hero and heroine are reinscribed into the norms of a more conventionally figured heterosexuality' (1995: 118). In fact, unlike anarchy, which can be permanent, the social inversions enacted by the carnival must be temporary by definition; 'as a kind of dress rehearsal for revolution, carnival suspends hierarchical distinctions, barriers, and prohibitions. It installs a qualitatively different kind of communication based on "free and familiar contact"' that includes 'banquet imagery of feasts and symposia', transvestitism, drag, and gender-bending. 'By focusing on the shared physiological processes of bodily life – copulation, birth, eating, drinking, and defecation – the carnivalesque offers a *temporary* suspension of hierarchy and prohibition' (Stam et al. 2015: 70–1; my emphasis).

Donning a blond wig, a double-breasted blue velvet jacket, a shirt with a prominent jabot, and a multicoloured cravat, Dante asks for Elizabeth's opinion:

Dante: Do you like me?
Elizabeth: Yes!
Dante: Am I like one of you?
Elizabeth: Yes!
Dante: Elizabeth, what will they think about me?
Elizabeth: They don't think. To them, it's as if you didn't exist.

Elizabeth exposes the absurdity of Dante's obsession by pointing out that nobody at the party is truly concerned with his presence, let alone with his appearance. She does, however, recognize that the disguise, albeit absurd, is successful, and her opinion is reinforced in a gag that replicates the earlier one: at daybreak, Dante leaves the party with a group of youngsters and heads to Carnaby Street, where they leisurely browse antique stores. Two Italian men with thick Roman accents mock the assembly of English youths for their bizarre clothes and long hair. Dante breaks character again and, in passing, finishes the man's sentence, echoing his *romanesco* language, thereby turning him into the object of his own joke.[9]

When the rowdy mod crowd comes to blows with a group of rockers, Dante implores a leather-clad, motorcycle-riding brute who has targeted him for a beating to spare him because, he confesses, 'I am not one of you, my name is Dante Fontana, from Perugia. I am not young like you, I am old. I have a wife and children', to which the aggressor replies, 'yellow-livered clown!'[10] By outing himself, Dante finally comes to terms with the impossibility of his endeavour: he is (literally) forced to reconcile himself with his true (national) identity, surrendering the ability to camouflage himself that the fracturing of his self had temporarily afforded him. Eventually the police break up the fight, Dante is arrested, and, in the following sequence, he wears his usual clothes while being escorted to an Alitalia aircraft headed to Italy.

While *Fumo di Londra* is by no means a great film, it does signal a shift in the way travel comedies understood and portrayed Italians in relation to other cultures. To recapitulate, *Parigi è sempre Parigi* postulated difference as antinomies: Italy versus France, provincial versus cosmopolitan, simple versus sophisticated, unrefined versus genteel, with the story of Franco and Christine elegantly bridging the two cultures. *Brevi amori a Palma di Maiorca* played up its male characters' *gallismo* and emphasized conquest as an essential component of tourism. *Il diavolo* established a new way of shooting films abroad and elaborated on the issue of Italian peripatetic *gallismo* by contrasting it with Northern European gender relations. *Fumo di Londra* complicates this picture even further by introducing the notion of shame at one's nationality which, as Jaqueline Reich (2004) noted, is the flip side of *gallismo*. In *Il diavolo*, Amedeo cannot find a partner because he is unequipped to understand the culture that surrounds him; likewise, when Lady Elizabeth propositions *Fumo di Londra*'s Dante with a suggestive note, he ends up wandering around the Duchess's castle at night-time, unable to find her room. Having squandered the opportunity of a romantic adventure, Dante turns his efforts entirely to divesting himself of the remnants of his Italian identity, which betrays his inability to accept, or to interpret correctly, his position in the world. This sentiment, which *Fumo di Londra* investigates extensively, informs Sordi's subsequent mobile pictures, which also progressively abandon lowbrow humour in favour of sophisticated social critique, while also revealing their deep entanglement with issues of migration and diaspora. In fact, as Steve Della Casa writes, the film expresses the director's 'narrative desire for close examination that critics always failed to acknowledge, and that has a fundamental role in Sordi's transition from iconoclastic genius (in the first part of his career) to pensive moralist (in his last films)' (2018: 99).

In the late 1960s, Sordi's cinematic explorations became ever more ambitious and far reaching, both in his own directorial projects and in the films in which he acted. Such is the case of Ettore Scola's *Riusciranno i nostri eroi a ritrovare l'amico misteriosamente scomparso in Africa*[11] (Ettore Scola, 1968), a scorching indictment of European colonialism that blends the story of a (singular) Italian migration with the stylistic elements of the travel comedy – as I discussed in Chapter 6. One the one hand, this multilayered, Janus-like text reflects on the complex legacy of colonialism at a time when decolonization was under way, examining how Italian culture was still imbued with Eurocentric notions. On the other hand, it introduces a new figure in the landscape of Italian mobility, that of the *existential migrant*, which would become a recurring character in the cinema of the late 1980s and 1990s.[12]

The great actor had worked on films either shot or simply set in the African continent numerous times before: he was an uncredited extra in Carmine Gallone's notorious *Scipione l'Africano* (1937); he had a small part in *Giarabub* (Goffredo Alessandrini, 1942); he starred in Ferruccio Cerio's *I quattro bersaglieri* (aka *Tripoli, bel suol d'amore*, 1954), which was set against the backdrop of the Italo-Turkish war of 1911–12; and he acted opposite David Niven (and Amedeo Nazzari) in Guy Hamilton's *The Best of Enemies* (1961), a film about the demise of Italy's (Fascist) empire. In other words, Sordi participated in films that championed the colonial enterprise, as well as in the postwar critique of the same experience. While *Riusciranno* does not discuss directly Italy's colonial history, it uses Sordi's well-oiled *italiano all'estero* character to illustrate the difficult position of a European subject in a land that had suffered so many years under colonial rule, which certainly was a preoccupation Italy shared with the countries that had participated in the 'scramble for Africa'.[13]

By the time they collaborated on *Riusciranno*, Sordi and Scola had been friends many years; as a matter of fact, Sordi credited Scola's transition from the radio to the film industry to his intercession: 'I introduced Ettore to Ruggero Maccari, the screenwriter, and he began working on several screenplays with him' (Sordi qtd in Schiavina 1999: 83). Scola had a long apprenticeship as a screenwriter before he debuted behind the camera in

Se permettete parliamo di donne/Let's Talk About Women (1964), which was penned by Maccari, and he subsequently co-wrote the screenplay of every film he directed. *Riusciranno* was authored with veteran screenwriting duo Agenore Incrocci and Furio Scarpelli (better known as Age-Scarpelli), who were also responsible for *La grande guerra*, *The Best of Enemies*, *Mafioso*, and many more films in which Sordi appeared.

Loosely based on Joseph Conrad's *Heart of Darkness* (1899), *Riusciranno* tells the story of Fausto di Salvio (Alberto Sordi), a wealthy publisher who feels oppressed by his family and their profligate bourgeois lifestyle, and decides to fly to Angola to locate his brother-in-law, Oreste 'Titino' Sabatini (Nino Manfredi), who has been missing for a year. But the journey is only partially motivated by this search and rescue operation; bored with Rome and its urban comforts, Fausto is admittedly in need of an adventure. He drags along his reluctant accountant Ubaldo Palmarini (Bernard Blier) – who plays Sordi's straight man and provides most of the comic relief. Their mission goes quickly awry: their 1958 Land Rover 109 series II is stolen, they actively oppose episodes of racism and exploitation, and they almost get themselves killed by a gang of mercenaries and poachers. Eventually Fausto and Ubaldo find Titino, who has become the head of an indigenous tribe. Initially reticent, Titino agrees to return to Italy with them, but soon after the ship sets sail he jumps off to swim back to his adoptive tribe.

Riusciranno was shot almost entirely on location in Angola, which in 1968 was still a Portuguese colony and would remain such until 11 November 1975. Scola chose this particular location precisely because 'in this Portuguese colony colonialism still included episodes of racism and abuse', which punctured Fausto's idealized (and inherently colonial) notions of the African continent (Scola and Bertini 1996: 84). In the film, Scola uses racism as a way to evoke and critique Italy's complex relationship with its own history as a colonial power; for instance, after they lose their car, Fausto and Ubaldo get a ride from a Portuguese couple, Fernando (Edgar Montiero) and Florinda (Claude De Solms). The four get to a river crossing, but the bridge has collapsed. The Portuguese man assembles a team of black Angolans to hold up the structure. They descend into the water and form a human chain, while the portly Fernando cracks a whip to keep them in position under the weight of the bridge, eventually driving his jeep over them. At the edge of the frame, Fausto and Ubaldo witness the scene in silence, but a close-up of their faces reveals their disapproval.

Scola translates into images what Aimé Césaire postulated in his famous 1950 essay *Discourse on Colonialism*: the Martiniquan professor argued that 'colonization works to *decivilize* the colonizer, to *brutalize* him in the true sense of the word, to degrade him, to awaken him to buried instincts, to covetousness, violence, race hatred, and moral relativism' ([1950] 2000: 35; emphasis in the original). In other words, Césaire reverses the scheme upon which European colonialism was predicated: the 'savages' are not the colonized subjects, to whom Europeans are supposedly bestowing the gift of civilization, but the colonizers themselves, who must unleash their inner monster in order to create and justify the artificial hierarchization of races and nations that is inherent to colonial thought. And, Césaire continues, with the horrors of colonialism 'a poison has been distilled into the veins of Europe and, slowly but surely, the continent proceeds toward savagery' ([1950] 2000: 35–6).

In this scene, the Portuguese man of course is the savage, and the colonized people are made to literally carry the weight of his monstrosity. After the 1965 Austin Mini Moke crosses over to the other shore, the Italians politely excuse themselves and refuse to continue travelling with the couple. Florinda understands the real nature of their change of heart, and tells her husband, 'It's because of the way we treat the blacks.'[14] The Portuguese man is outraged at the Italians' judgement of him, and the argument escalates to blows. After the scuffle, which the Italians win, the couple drives off, and Fausto and Ubaldo continue their journey on foot. Three men leave the circle formed by the crowd of Angolans who had silently watched the brawl, and jokingly mimic the Europeans' behaviour, rolling around in the dirt to entertain the bystanders. Initially, the scene seems to displace the Italians' guilt for their own history as brutal colonizers onto the Portuguese, absolving them of their crimes because they have the courage to stand up to the couple and side with the Angolans. But as the last shot reveals, the Angolans do not differentiate between the white men in safari outfits. Fausto and Ubaldo's heroic gesture, which visually translates into a clumsy tussle between three overweight middle-aged men, is only a moment of comic relief in a long history of oppression, and the Italians' assertion of the higher moral ground can only be regarded as hypocritical and historically myopic.

When Arjun Appadurai writes about ethnically motivated violence, he outlines two concepts that can be productive in understanding the relationship between the European characters and their surroundings: he employs the notions of focalization and transvaluation as defined by the social anthropologist Stanley Jeyaraja Tambiah. Focalization is the 'denudation of local incidents and disputes of their particulars of context and aggregating them' (Tambiah qtd in Appadurai 1996: 151); this process is akin to the reification of colonial subjects and the lack of historical specificity regarding the atrocities inflicted upon them. Transvaluation is the 'parallel process of assimilating particulars to a larger, collective, more enduring, and therefore less context-bound, cause of interest' (Tambiah qtd in Appadurai 1996: 151); the colonizer's poor understanding of the colonized's culture, history, and circumstances is therefore functional to the interests of the colonial enterprise. Appadurai writes that

> both focalization and transvaluation take their energy from macroevents and processes (cascades) that link global politics to the micropolitics of streets and neighborhoods. Synchronically, these cascades provide the material for linking processes of focalization and transvaluation. That is, they provide material for the imaginations of actors at various levels for reading meanings into local and contingent events, just as they provide the alibi for inscribing long-standing scripts about ethnic manipulations and conspiracies onto apparently trivial street events. (Appadurai 1996: 152–3)

In other words, the street tussle is only another 'cascade' that underscores how the perverse logics of colonialism, manifested by focalization and transvaluation, have been interiorized by all 'actors' (the Portuguese, the Angolans, and the Italians, even though the latter temporarily side with the colonized).

The fact that *Riusciranno* was shot in an African country that was still under the influence of European imperialism does resonate in several instances in its narrative. Both its central characters, Fausto and Titino, are susceptible to the continent's seductions, but Fausto understands this through the epistemological formulations of a Global North still largely imbued with colonial thinking. In the first moments of the film's second act, before the loss of transport technology forces him to reckon with the problematic nature of his own received ideas, Fausto fashions himself into a *seeing-man* who, according to Mary Louise Pratt, is 'the white male subject of European landscape discourse – he whose imperial eyes passively look out and possess' (2008: 9). Scola emphasizes opticality in his film, not simply by focalizing the narrative through Fausto's subjectivity, but by employing a variety of strategies of distortion and manipulation of his gaze. For instance, when he stands before the majestic Kalandula Falls, Fausto sheds a single tear from behind his mirrored sunglasses. The shot begins with an extreme close-up of Sordi's face, and slowly pulls out as the tear rolls down his cheek, the waterfall reflected in his 'seeing' equipment (Figure 2.13). Scola's reflexive approach is even more apparent when Fausto first arrives in Luanda, donning a full safari outfit, complete with cameras and firearms. He begins to enthusiastically shoot the locals with his small film camera, capturing their image for his own consumption (and that of his family and friends back home); but one of his 'subjects', a man who sports a Western, blue, two-piece suit, is also equipped with a larger,

Figures 2.13 and 2.14 The imperial seeing-man in the cinematic mirror.

more modern camera, which he turns on the tourist (Figure 2.14). In the era of decolonization, Fausto's ethnographic mannerisms, let alone his entire attitude towards the African continent and its peoples, are outdated and inherently problematic. The local man's reappropriation of the colonial commodifying gaze goes beyond autoethnography;[15] by reclaiming his ability to originate such a gaze, and not simply to suffer it, he reverses the power relations between the characters.

Fausto's inability to truly understand the continent he sets out to explore is exposed from the get-go, and the journey will slowly chip away at all his assumptions; his initial identification with the seeing-man of colonial discourse is questioned as the narrative unfolds and his certainties are eroded by first-hand experience. As the director puts it, 'by the end of his journey he is pervaded by an almost Conrad-like disquietude full of doubts and dissatisfactions' (Scola 1996: 85). At the outset, Fausto is infused with Western consumerism and arrogance, values that are slowly but progressively abandoned throughout the film, as he gradually divests himself (not of his own volition, of course) of his possessions and comforts.[16]

Titino, conversely, 'goes native' by embracing the mores of the host culture wholeheartedly and, as the film's concluding scene suggests, even romancing a local woman, who tears up at the sight of his (temporary) departure. When Fausto finally finds his long-lost brother-in-law, the latter sports long, braided hair, his skin is tanned, he wears many necklaces and bracelets, and he asks Fausto and Ubaldo how 'white people' express a certain concept or say a word – as if whiteness were not an attribute of his own identity as well.[17] According to a term suggested by Michael Hardt and Antonio Negri, Titino's apparently superficial 'conversion' to the tribe's lifestyle could be understood as an *anthropological exodus*, which to Hardt and Negri is

> important primarily because here is where the positive, constructive face of the mutation begins to appear: an ontological mutation in action, the concrete invention of a first *new place in the non-place*. This creative evolution does not merely occupy any existing place, but rather invents a new place; it is a desire that creates a new body; a metamorphosis that breaks all the naturalistic homologies of modernity. (Hardt and Negri 2000: 215–16; emphasis in the original)

Of course, positing a remote location in the Angolan countryside as a non-place for the reinvention ('mutation') of a European man's identity is an inherently colonial gesture. In forging a 'new body' for his exodus from the strictures of modernity, Titino has appropriated the signifiers of a culture that does not belong to him. Unfortunately, the film remains oblivious to this issue; as film critic Maria Coletti writes, 'Titino is, after all, a typical antihero of Italian-style comedy, who represents the art of getting by to the nth degree – so much so that if he is in Africa, he is even able to make the rain fall' (2002: 187).

But Titino is also a transitional figure that is at the dawn of a new kind of Italian mobility propelled more by existential angst than by economic necessity. In the films of the 1980s and 1990s, the next generation of characters leaving the peninsula will do so for destinations that are (in the majority of the cases) not inscribed in the historical narrative of the diaspora. Neither full emigrants nor simply tourists, they reject the well-explored paths established by the great migrations and position themselves at the margins of the 'diasporic public spheres' (Appadurai 1996: 147). As their motivation is very rarely of a financial nature, they seek alternatives that befit their existential restlessness, their thirst for diversity and less homogenized cultures, and their disillusionment with post-industrial, metropolitan Italy.[18]

The foremost representative of this new kind of mobile cinema is director Gabriele Salvatores, whose collaborations with actor Diego Abatantuono have often retrodden the trails blazed by Sordi. Of particular significance to this chapter is *Marrakech Express* (1989), which is also based on *Heart of Darkness* and borrows heavily from *Riusciranno*. In this film, four friends in their late thirties are summoned by Teresa (Cristina Marsillach), a woman who claims to be the girlfriend of their long-lost friend Rudy (Massimo Venturiello). They are to collect 30 million lira and travel to Marrakech, Morocco, in order to bail their friend out of jail, where he is being detained on drug-smuggling charges. The four embark on a road trip across Italy, France, Spain, and Morocco, gradually rekindling their long-forgotten friendship in the course of the journey. But they are being scammed: when the occasion present itself, Teresa vanishes with the money and the jeep in which they are travelling. The four decide to venture south of Marrakech, across the desert, where they hope to find Rudy and Teresa. After a long and perilous journey via bus, on bicycles, and on foot, they find the mischievous friend and learn that he had been living in the inhospitable land for years, working at his life's dream: farming the desert. He had conceived the scam at their expense because he needed the money in order to purchase a drill and extract water – a technologically superior solution to Titino's rainmaking prayer. Eventually, they forgive Rudy and help him accomplish the impossible task of finding water underneath the dunes. Two of them will return home, while two will continue, indefinitely, their existential roaming. The issue undermining *Marrakech Express*'s superficially third-worldist project, however, is that,

> while the film gently derides the behaviour of materialistic, bourgeois Italians abroad and highlights the unease of individuals from the post-1968 generation who have become embedded within the capitalist system, its own visual objectification and commodification of Moroccan culture suggests that, as an art form, the film has absorbed exactly the same value system that it purports to satirize. (Hope 2009: 11)

Plainly put, the criticism William Hope levels against Salvatores's film applies to Scola's picture as well.

If, on the one hand, *Riusciranno* introduced this new type of existentially restless post-capitalist character, on the other hand, the film fits into the cinematic tradition that, by continuing to focus on the plethora of Italian mobilities, and in particular on those involving border crossings, interrogates the position occupied by Italy (and Italians) on a global scale – in social and political terms. An example of this continuing reflection is provided by a scene in which Fausto and Ubaldo are captured by Belgian mercenaries, whose leader (José María Mendoça) explains his ambiguity towards Italy in a strange spiel: 'We are always close to loving Italy, but Italy always does little thing [sic] to make us hate her. I think the opposite: we are always close to hating Italy, but Italy always does little thing to make us love her.'[19]

In fact, Titino's vanishing aside, Fausto's real reason for his journey to Africa is not too dissimilar to that of Dante Fontana – Sordi's character in *Fumo di Londra*. Disenchanted with their domestic humdrum, these affluent men long for experience, knowledge, and excitement, and they embark on adventures in which they allow themselves to question their identities and their certainties, and in the process they harshly criticize their own nationality; for instance, when Fausto is frustrated with Oreste's pettiness, he yells at him, 'What is this! Let's always give ourselves away with everyone!'[20] The line repeats, almost verbatim, Dante's scolding comment towards the Italian family he meets in London, as well as the words spoken by Sordi against Remo, Vittorio Gassman's character in *Crimen*. Ultimately, *Riusciranno*'s wide-ranging condemnation of European colonialism rings a bit hollow, especially if compared with contemporaneous films that tackled it with aplomb, such as Gillo Pontecorvo's anticolonial masterpiece *La battaglia di Algeri / The Battle of Algiers* (1966) and Pier Paolo Pasolini's *Appunti per un'Orestiade africana / Notes Towards an African Orestes* (1970). Nonetheless, it is *a* condemnation at a time when Italian cinema was struggling to reckon with the legacy of the country's involvement in the colonial enterprise. Unfortunately, much of this work was undermined, or at least delayed, by the popularity of Luigi Scattini's exotic/erotic trilogy: *La ragazza dalla pelle di luna / Moon Skin* (1972), *La ragazza fuoristrada* (1972), and *Il corpo / The Body* (1974). This new series of objectifying orientalist fantasies focused on the male conquest of black bodies and exotic landscapes, launching a *filone* (sub-genre) whose racist and misogynistic effects continue to ripple through Italian culture to this day.

Notes

1. I would contend that Sordi's travel comedies plant the seed for the future *cinepanettoni* and *cinecocomeri*, the annual Christmas and summer romps that depict the adventures of Italians abroad, and that for over fifty years have

dominated the Italian box office charts. At the time of writing, the critical vacuum on this quintessentially Italian film genre is astonishing. The most comprehensive research on the topic today can be found in O'Leary (2013). While the putative patient zero of this tradition is considered Carlo Vanzina's 1983 *Vacanze di Natale*, I would argue that the travel comedies of the 1950s are where the interest for Italian mobile cinematic masculinities began.

2. As is well known, in the mid-1950s a new understanding of film art came to the fore, famously spearheaded by a group of intellectuals gravitating around the French magazine *Cahiers du Cinéma*. They called it *la politique des auteurs*, or *auteur* theory, as Andrew Sarris dubbed it for the English-speaking world in his canonical article 'Notes on the *Auteur* Theory in 1962' (1962/3). The main tenet of *auteur* theory is the re-evaluation of the figure of the director, who, these critics argue, can be elevated from craftsman to author status; as a consequence, the films of a certain *auteur* can be studied not only individually, in relation to their genre or the canon, but also as part of an artist's oeuvre, as one piece in the larger canvas of their career. This overarching approach allows for a better understanding of the *auteur*'s poetics and their position in film history. When the theory was in the process of being devised, many Italian directors, such as Rossellini, Visconti, and De Sica, already understood themselves as *auteurs*; before the *Cahiers* critics engaged with their work, they enjoyed the status of founding fathers of Neorealism, and that of film artists all round. The next generation of filmmakers, including those whose films are analysed in this book, achieved such status after *auteur* theory became a consolidated approach in film scholarship in the early 1960s. My approach, which seeks to understand how screen mobilities reflect or complicate notions of national identity, is not an auteurist approach, but a longitudinal, historical, and sociological investigation that traces the stylistic and thematic commonalities and discrepancies across a wide-ranging body of work. Approaches of this nature tend to downplay the importance of a single individual as the creative force behind the finished product, while privileging larger structures – studios, genre, political climate – as responsible for a film's distinguishing features. However, when reflecting on the body of work of a prolific film presence (before and behind the camera) such as Alberto Sordi, it is fundamental to take into account the individual choices made by the performer/screenwriter/director within and without the confines of narrative and generic conventions. Moreover, in order to fully appreciate the creator's artistic intervention, it is also crucial to understand the political and socio-economic climate in the nation's history at a specific juncture in time – in this case, the relatively abrupt transition from the postwar to reconstruction and the economic boom.

3. On *Fumo di Londra* as a template for Sordi's subsequent directorial efforts, see Della Casa (2018).

4. This act of concealing identity and modifying one's appearance to an extreme degree is a trope that reappears in several films, most notably in

Pane e Cioccolata / Bread and Chocolate (Franco Brusati, 1974), in which Nino Manfredi dyes his hair blond in order to look Germanic and to assimilate into an ostensibly segregated Swiss society. Interestingly, Goffredo Fofi reports that Franco Brusati first offered the lead role to Alberto Sordi, who asked to direct the film in his stead. Brusati declined, and the part went to Nino Manfredi, who co-authored the screenplay (2004: 147). In this film, an Italian waiter in Switzerland has his visa rescinded after he is caught urinating on a tree. This event precipitates him into the nightmare of clandestine work, shaking his sense of self and pushing him into increasingly humiliating scenarios. As film critic Masolino d'Amico summarizes, '*Pane e cioccolata* is certainly not a typical Italian-style comedy. Brusati was not a comedy man either. But the grotesque, crooked, expressionistic tone of the result is in tune with the era' (2008: 232).

5. Of course, this scene also brings to mind Vittorio De Sica's mannequin in *I grandi magazzini* (Mario Camerini, 1939), another film in which role-playing and national identity are intertwined.
6. The opening sequence of *I magliari*, which takes place at an Italian restaurant as well, is also certainly part of *Fumo di Londra*'s intricate intertext, which in its turn informs a similar gag in *Un tassinaro a New York* (Alberto Sordi, 1987).
7. Interestingly, Michelangelo Antonioni's *Blow-Up*, which similarly explored the culture of Swinging London, was also released in 1966.
8. According to Della Casa (2018: 95), the relationship between Dante and Angel was supposed to evolve in a number of scenes that were cut from the film's theatrical version.
9. By speaking Roman argot, Sordi temporarily steps out not only of his mod disguise, but of Dante Fontana entirely, reclaiming his own native regional language. In other words, rather than working within the diegesis, the gag articulates the intricate relationship between the actor's off-screen persona and his performance in the film.
10. Clearly, this is another example of Sordi's self-referentiality. In the final moments of Mario Monicelli's 1959 *La Grande Guerra*, Oreste Jacovacci (Sordi) and Giovanni Busacca (Vittorio Gassman) are executed by an Austrian platoon. While Busacca dies heroically, refusing to give any information to the arrogant commanding office, Jacovacci's last words are, 'I don't know anything! I am a coward! Everyone knows that.'
11. For reasons of legibility, I will refer to this film simply as *Riusciranno*.
12. See the introduction to Hall and Williams (2002). The permutations of mobility portrayed here blur the boundaries between migration, travel, and tourism in and around the era of transnational and global fluxes, thanks also to progress in transportation and communication technology, which transformed the Italian emigrant from the meek rural worker of recent memory into a flexible (world) citizen. Filmic representations of this new figure, whom I define as an *existential migrant*, depict him as prone more to cultural

nomadism than to emigration. Some directors, such as Gabriele Salvatores, will make this character a permanent feature of their cinema.
13. According to Claudio G. Fava, 'Scola's film attempted to cast the Sordi character against a different background: an Africa that was suspended between the fantastical and the political, balanced between old colonialism and a new air of independence' (2003: 212).
14. Fernando, Florinda, and all the other characters Fausto and Ubaldo meet in Angola speak a language that I would describe as a simplified, Italian-friendly Portuguese. In this scene, the woman says 'è per a nossa maneiras de tratar as pretos'.
15. I am borrowing Mary Louise Pratt's terminology. She defines autoethnography or autoethnographic expression as 'instances in which colonized subjects undertake to represent themselves in ways that *engage with* the colonizer's terms' (2008: 9).
16. For a brilliant psychoanalytic reading of Fausto's personality, see the chapter on *Riusciranno* in Piotti and Senaldi (2002).
17. Of course, Titino's trajectory, his agenda, and his representation are incredibly problematic for very apparent reasons. Ultimately, the film is unaware of its own inherent racism. For a detailed unpacking of *Riusciranno*'s own colonial unconscious, see Luijnenburg (2014).
18. For more on this, see Malavasi (2005).
19. Il Leopardo, as this character is nicknamed, speaks a mixture of French, Italian, and Portuguese. The actual words are: 'Noi siamo sempre vicini a amare Italia, ma Italia fare sempre piccola cosa che si fa odiare. Io penso il *contraire*: noi siamo sempre vicini a odiare Italia, ma Italia fare sempre piccola cosa per farsi amare.'
20. 'E che è? E facciamoci sempre riconoscere da tutti!'

CHAPTER 10

Drilling: (Auto)Mobile Satires of Global Petroculture

With the exception of the opening scene, Alberto Sordi's third directorial project *Un Italiano in America* (1967) was shot entirely on location in the United States, and it was based on the real-life experience of Sicilian-American painter and automobile racer Salvatore Scarpitta (1919–2007). Rodolfo Sonego, the veteran writer of travel comedies who co-authored *Brevi amori a Palma di Maiorca*, *La ragazza in vetrina*, and *Il diavolo*, among many others, had originally penned the screenplay for producer Dino De Laurentiis, who in the late 1950s had hoped to have it made by Paramount Pictures and directed by Mario Monicelli. According to Sonego, Paramount took control of the pre-production and determined he should be flanked by legendary novelists John Fante and William Saroyan to produce an English-language script that could be shot casting American actors (qtd in Sanguineti 2015: 268–78). The project was eventually acquired by Columbia Pictures, which shelved it for almost a decade. Sordi resurrected it and teamed up again with screen legend Vittorio De Sica, who agreed to play the role of Sordi's father, which established Sordi as the natural heir to De Sica's throne as the biggest comedy star in the Italian film industry.[1]

Sordi plays Giuseppe Marozzi, a down-to-earth pump attendant working at a Gulf-owned petrol station in Rome who is approached by an American embassy attaché on behalf of his long-lost father. The latter is alive and awaiting his adult son in the United States. Giuseppe flies to New York and meets the suave Lando Marozzi on live television – the Italians being the object of ridicule on the part of the American audience. The man promises to take his son on a cross-country journey to Memphis, where he allegedly owns a villa and many oil rigs. But Lando is not the man Giuseppe was hoping to meet; he turns out to be a gambler who squanders every penny they have, and then leaves his son stranded in the middle of rural America. Giuseppe eventually makes it to Memphis on his own, where he learns that Lando's property amounts to a small house and a Gulf petrol station. Since his father is in jail for his outstanding gambling debts, the lot is entirely in the hands of Evelyn, a kind divorcee with two children to feed. Come full circle, Giuseppe gladly returns to his old profession in Memphis, helping the woman run the establishment and raise her children.

In his 1967 review of the film, legendary critic Tullio Kezich wrote:

> Sordi still talks about the America that swallowed our migrant fathers and often never returned them, or that sometimes let them reappear as rich men. A sociological reality that was transformed, in the folklore of poor countries, into a veritable cult. (Kezich qtd in Fava 2003: 206)

While Kezich's contemporaneous appraisal focuses primarily on the relationship between the Italian diaspora and the flow of global capital, a modern re-evaluation of *Un italiano in America* cannot fail to notice that Sonego and Sordi, once again, anticipate some of the concerns to which many twenty-first-century debates are devoted, including extraction culture, oil mobilities, and energy (un)sustainability in the Anthropocene. In particular, the filmmakers probe a fundamental question about oil's undeniable impact on the twentieth century, as formulated by Sheena Wilson, Adam Carlson, and Imre Szeman in their volume *Petrocultures*:

> Given the geopolitics of the twentieth century, which has been shaped to an inordinate degree around struggles over oil and gas, why have fossil fuels been thematised in so few of the fictions of the petro-hegemon of the century, the United States? (Wilson et al. 2017: 6)

According to *Un Italiano in America*, the answer is as multifaceted as it is intrinsic to cinematic mobilities: first, at a textual level, Giuseppe's inter- and transcontinental journey is powered by oil, from his initial im/mobility at the Rome petrol station all the way to its Memphis equivalent, via the large helicopter that delivers him to the rooftop helipad of the New York broadcasting skyscraper, to the 1967 Lincoln Continental the TV show gifts them, all the way to the modest Greyhound bus. Second, at the intertextual level, the film's roots plunge deep into the history of Italian cinema and its myth of American wealth through extraction – as depicted, for instance, in George Stevens's *Giant* (1956). Third, at the level of genre, *Un Italiano in America* is a road movie of the European variety, which film scholar David Laderman defines as follows:

> While obviously sharing some traits with the American existentialist 1970s road movie, the European journey on film distinguishes itself with important features: characters on the road out of necessity rather than choice, seeking work, family, or

a home; less valorization of the individual Road Man or the outlaw couple, more emphasis on the traveling group; less fetishism of the automobile; less emphasis on driving as high-speed action-spectacle. The European road movie foregrounds the meaning of the quest journey more than the mode of transport; revelation and realization receive more focus than the act of driving. (Laderman 2002: 248)[2]

In fact, Sordi's film is undeniably rooted in the travel comedies of the 1950s, where 'revelation and realization' were symbiotic with all kinds of mobility, including social and sexual. The American road and its chimeras charm the fickle Lando, but not the earthbound Giuseppe, whose journey of discovery quickly mutates into one of sustenance. However, *Un Italiano in America* does fetishize its petrol-powered vehicles, but only to eventually dismantle their appeal as symbols of wealth or individual freedom.

Similarly to what happened with Amedeo Nazzari's character in *Il gaucho*, which was based on his past 'im/mobile' roles, the casting of De Sica in the part of the inveterate gambler and womanizer Lando Marozzi establishes an intertextual relationship with Mr Brown, a second-generation Italian American *automobile* magnate who returns to Italy and falls for an Italian girl in Baldassarre Negroni's *Due cuori felici* – a character the young De Sica played back in 1932.[3] Yet the intertextual connections are even deeper and more intricate, since they expand to De Sica's off-screen persona; in fact, to the attentive viewer, Lando's personality can recall that of the legendary singer, actor, and director. Indeed, Vittorio De Sica was himself a heavy gambler, and he did have children with two women, but the most notable similarity is evident when Lando also maintains he has a past in the American film world:

Giuseppe: You worked as an actor?
Lando: Uh, five years in Hollywood, romantic genre. Poor Jean Harlow died in my arms. What, you didn't know?
Giuseppe: I know nothing about you, Dad . . .
Lando: I went into the movies as a joke, and I became Hollywood's best-paid actor. I always wore a tailcoat, Latin lover, you know . . .

Lando's alleged career in Hollywood recalls De Sica's early days in the Italian film industry; but this parallel is more than just a wink at the audience. Indeed, while it is true that in the 1930s the legendary actor was a dapper matinée heartthrob, it is also undeniable that in American cinema, 'if there is any stereotypical image of Italians that has a longer history than the gangster, it is the "Latin Lover"', as Peter Bondanella observes (2006: 133). Lando's 'Romeoization' on foreign soil is to be understood as a cheap and exploitative gimmick the conman embraced, a travesty of De Sica's true greatness at home and abroad. By giving 'American' audiences just what they would expect out of him, he plays right into the stereotype they (not-so-secretly) want him to be; it is a 'subversive deployment of the stereotype' (Stam et al. 2015: 99).

However, Lando's self-stereotyping strategies are purely performative, and are aimed at exploiting whoever is fooled by them; in that, they recall Sordi's performances-within-the-performance as Totonno in Rosi's *I magliari*. The director highlights the manipulative nature of Lando's behaviour in one of the film's most notable sequences: Giuseppe and Lando's televized reunion. After he accepts the deal the embassy attaché offers him, the modest Giuseppe is helicoptered to the Manhattan studios that broadcast the show and sent immediately to make-up. In the dressing room, Giuseppe is not prepared for the momentary emotional shock he will suffer at seeing his father for the first time in thirty years. Instead, he undergoes a stereotyping process orchestrated by the show's producer and executed by the hair and make-up stylists. From a loudspeaker, the producer's disembodied voice controls the operation: 'What is Giuseppe dressed as?', he asks, making sure that Giuseppe's image will conform to the Italian archetypes he has in mind. On a swivel chair, facing the camera, Giuseppe is spun several times and transformed into various characters: Harlequin, a *carabiniere*, a *bersagliere*, and finally a gondolier (Figure 2.15).[4]

Even if the discombobulated man is from Viterbo, near Rome, the idea of sending Giuseppe onstage dressed up like a Venetian boatman agrees with the producer, who turns the duo into caricatures. The befuddled Giuseppe plays along, repeating 'Thank you, America' at every turn, and so does his father, whose double-breasted pinstripe suit, thin black moustache, two-tone shoes, driving gloves, pocket square, and red carnation lapel make him into the stereotypical Latin lover he supposedly played on-screen for so many years. At the sight of his long-lost son, Lando even

Figure 2.15 Strategies of (mediated) self-stereotyping.

pretends to be overwhelmed with emotion and faints, only to spring back to his feet thanks to his formidable pills as soon as the commercial break ends.

If we employ the terminology developed by historian Daniel J. Boorstin in the 1960s, this staged reunion could be understood as a 'pseudo-event', in that it serves little to no purpose for its subjects, other than to be performed for an audience and to be at the service of advertisements (see Boorstin 1964). While Lando is in control of his image and of the stereotyping process (he fully embraces his nickname of 'Mandolino'), and can play according to the rules of television, Giuseppe is too naive and ill-equipped to understand that he is being consumed as a novelty, just like the Italian food popularized in the commercial breaks that punctuate the reunion. 'Let's go to Italy! Let's eat spaghetti!' is the slogan that accompanies the image of an American family struggling to get the wormy noodles on the tines of their forks. Just like spaghetti, Lando and Giuseppe must be commodified in order to be of any value in American society; but as the commercial shows, the exotic food proves elusive to the American actors, who smile their way through their pasta fiasco, and so are the two Italians, costumed as they may be. In fact, when Sordi cuts to the studio audience, they are shown laughing cruelly at Giuseppe's uneasiness in front of the camera and at his ridiculous attire, coming across as shallow and simple-minded. Ultimately, Sordi's true audience is Italian moviegoers, which is why the scene is not constructed as a simple one-way mirror but as a chain of looks: it works along an 'us watching them watching us' pattern, in which the notion of 'them' (Americans) is one partly created by 'us' (Italians) in response to Cocacolonization, the pervasive and capillary globalization of American culture of which oil, as well as consumer goods and other cultural symbols, has been one of the primary lubricants, vehicles, and engines.

After a night in the gargantuan penthouse of the New York Hilton, the duo embarks on an ill-fated road trip across the United States motivated by Lando's business dealings, which consist of acquiring land for oil extraction with the money given to them by the TV show. Images of offshore oil platforms, derricks, and pipelines punctuate the landscape traversed by the Italians aboard their telephone-equipped four-door sedan – a luxury that amazes Giuseppe, and that recalls *Harlem*'s Tommaso Rossi's first impressions of 'American' technology. They reach Los Angeles, and then proceed back east through Las Vegas, where they are forced to separate by Lando's creditors. Giuseppe is beaten and robbed, ends up on a Greyhound bus that crosses New Mexico, and reaches San Antonio, where he meets his half-sister Pamela, an exotic dancer with dreams of one day

Figure 2.16 Satirizing (American) petroculture: pushing the Model T.

achieving extravagant affluence. Forced to hitchhike his way to Memphis, he is picked up by a cowboy driving a 1926 Ford Model T, arguably the first mass-produced petrol-powered automobile, and one of the most recognizable icons of American modernization. In a gesture that punctures the myth of Fordism and other efficiency-based management and production theories, of which the Model T is the physical four-wheel manifestation, Sordi shows that Giuseppe reaches his destination not by travelling inside the symbolic vehicle, but by pushing it (Figure 2.16).

During their journey, Giuseppe and his father stop by a derrick that, according to Lando, is the oldest in the field, having been active for fifty years. As they solemnly salute the piece of equipment, Lando becomes emotional and proclaims his love for it, swearing that one day Giuseppe will love it too, because with every oscillation of the drill its owner gets richer. Lando exhibits an unwavering faith in what Mark Simpson terms *lubricity*,

> the texture and mood requisite to the operations of neoliberal petroculture. Lubricity offers smoothness as cultural common sense, promoting the fantasy of a frictionless world contingent on the continued, intensifying use of petro-carbons from underexploited reserves in North America. It thereby contributes to the contemporary *mobility* regime that, idealizing smooth flow, mystifies so as to maximize the violent asymmetries of movement and circulation globally. (Simpson 2017: 289; my emphasis)

Lando's 'lesson' to his pragmatic son is predicated on an unworried and unending exploitation of natural resources, one of the fundamental tenets of neoliberalism; his emotions are tangled up in the derrick's continuous oscillations, which mirror his endless quest for social and economic climbing. However, as Giuseppe's trajectory will make salient, neoliberal petroculture is far from frictionless, but in fact brings into sharp relief the systemic blockages (racial and sexual discrimination, corporatocracy, economic inequality, market fundamentalism, mass incarceration, financialization, and so on) its functioning produces – or even necessitates.

Un Italiano in America is a trenchant critique not only of America as the supposed land of opportunity, but of a global economic system, anticipating much of the commentary set forth by Michelangelo Antonioni in his celebrated *Zabriskie Point* (1970); but while the latter focuses on the rise of counterculture (the future), the former stops at eulogizing the diaspora and its disappointments (the past). In fact, Lando's (probably apocryphal) quick rise to the top in Hollywood is mirrored by an even faster descent not only into anonymity but into captivity, since at the end of the film he appears, handcuffed, in the back of a police vehicle. Giuseppe himself is only marginally more successful than his delusional father, but he is realistically anchored to the minutiae of petrol (oil as mobility), instead of dreaming of extraction (oil as capital).

Giuseppe's encounter with his half-sister Pamela in a strip club in San Antonio, Texas, is another notable scene in which Sordi delivers an acerbic critique of the kind of unfettered capitalism in which the United States and its allies are imbricated. From behind the counter, a topless Pamela recites Lando's trite, clichéd speech about easy riches and fast social climbing, to which a pragmatic Giuseppe replies ('but you are naked'). Pamela dismisses the man's level-headedness as lack of imaginative power, which she attributes to his nationality: 'but you are an Italian, you can't understand', she says, ending the conversation. Both the interlocutors fail to relate to each other's arguments and prefer to stick to what is familiar to them, even if neither of them has been unable to make much of themselves. Sordi levels the field between the petrol pump attendant and the topless barmaid, making them examples of how Italian and American society alike can fail their people, the former for not encouraging them to dream big, the latter for allowing them to dream too big.

Ultimately, Sordi privileges Giuseppe's meek pragmatism over Lando's vain ambition. But is through this character that the director deconstructs and satirizes the repercussions of petroculture on the migrant narrative; as Domenico Campana puts it, Lando is

> consumed by the complex love-hate relationship with the adoptive country; he is forced to live on his wits yet he still clings onto an idea of America as a lottery in which, with cunning and luck, the paper boy can become a Mr. Ford. (Campana qtd in Fava 2003: 206–7)

Conversely, Giuseppe is ultimately able to adjust to the host society because his pragmatism is not too dissimilar from that of Evelyn, who shows him 'the real face of industrious, bourgeois America', as Campana concludes (qtd in Fava 2003: 207).

Notes

1. Sordi himself will figuratively pass the baton to Carlo Verdone in *In viaggio con papà* (1982), his 'spiritual' follow-up to *Un Italiano in America*. Directed by Sordi and co-written by Sonego, Sordi, and Verdone, this pot-boiler pits an ageing Lothario (Sordi) against a young moralist (Verdone) over an accidental road trip from Rome to Liguria. Aboard his father's luxurious 1982 Mercedes Benz 240 D, the naive commune-dwelling, animal rights and environmental activist will encounter a vision of life fraught with cynicism and vice, and ultimately driven by *gallismo*. Through a series of misadventures, the estranged relatives gradually become reacquainted, learning from one another. Their rough edges smoothed out, in the end they embrace each other's flaws and embark, this time willingly, on another road trip together.
2. In order to discuss how the national cinemas of the Old World shaped the road movie genre, Laderman (2002) analyses six films, among which are some timeless classics: *La strada* (Federico Fellini, 1954), *Wild Strawberries* (Ingmar Bergman, 1957), *Weekend* (Jean-Luc Godard, 1967), *Kings of the Road* (Wim Wenders, 1976), *Vagabond* (Agnès Varda, 1985), and *Bandits* (Katja von Garnier, 1997). Laderman chose a representative sample of films from the main film industries of the continent – Italy, France, Sweden, and Germany – embracing a time span of almost forty years.
3. As discussed in Part One of this book, the successful Italian or Italo-American who returned to Italy was a common trope in Fascist-era cinema; similar characters appear in *Terra di nessuno* (Mario Baffico, 1939), *Due milioni per un sorriso* (Mario Soldati, 1939), and *La bisbetica domata* (Ferdinando Maria Poggioli, 1942).
4. Sordi did play a skirt-chasing gondolier in Dino Risi's 1958 comedy *Venezia, la luna e tu*. His choice of the same costume for *Un Italiano in America* could be understood as a cheeky return to his iconic role, but also as the specific type of transtextuality called allusion, which 'can take the form of a verbal or visual evocation of another film, hopefully as an expressive means of commenting on the fictional world of the alluding film' (Stam et al. 1992: 206).

Conclusion to Part Two: Driving Across (Screen) Borders

In 1983, Alberto Sordi took his seat behind the wheel of a yellow Fiat Ritmo, a small, five-door hatchback manufactured by the Italian automaker between 1978 and 1988, to play the role of Pietro Marchetti, an ageing Roman taxicab driver with a penchant for idle chatter. When he picks up a call from Via Margutta, the driver is amazed to discover that his client is none other than famed director Federico Fellini (playing himself), who elects to sit next to the star-struck driver. As they drive to Cinecittà, Pietro showers the embarrassed Fellini with praise, voting him 'the greatest scientist of the cinemas of the entire world', reciting his biography with an astounding degree of precision, playing him a tape with Nino Rota's *La passerella di 'Otto e mezzo'* (the soundtrack from Fellini's own 1963 masterpiece *8½*), and launching into a round-up of his films' most memorable characters. For the first five minutes Fellini is dumbfounded by the barrage of words unleashed at him by the personable driver. Barely keeping himself from laughing, the director eventually tells Piero that he is headed to Cinecittà to do a bit part in a movie directed by Alberto Sordi, confessing that he is always uneasy when he is asked to step in front of the camera. The driver enquires about the part, and Fellini tells him that they will play themselves as they are now, older *vitelloni* that have not changed much with age. Pietro then notes that Fellini and Sordi made the eponymous movie together, and quotes the famous gesture made by the Roman actor (himself) in the 1954 picture.[1] When they finally reach Cinecittà, an impatient Alberto Sordi welcomes Fellini at the door of the soundstage, wearing the same blue jacket as Pietro.[2]

This largely improvised metacinematic vignette exemplifies how, through the character of Pietro Marchetti, Sordi circles back to examine his own career, achievements, gags, motifs, and ideas across two films: *Il tassinaro* (1983), and the sequel *Un tassinaro a New York* (1987), which he directed and co-wrote – the first with Age-Scarpelli, the second with Sonego. As Sarah Sharma writes, the taxi links local space to global space as it transports between airports, hotels, shopping centers, and business districts. It services the elderly and the infirmed, the too drunk to drive, and those not wanting to walk alone. It is a public space of transit; moving capital, serving safety, giving tours, and providing local knowledge. (Sharma 2010: 185)

If the automobile is the object that defined the twentieth century, engendering deep changes at all levels of industry, urban planning, land development, environmental protection (or lack thereof), and culture (both local and global), then taxicab drivers, in their symbiotic relationship with this world-shaping machine, emerge as the most representative figures of our time.³

Sordi, of course, is not the first filmmaker to intuit that by probing into the life of this inherently mobile character, one can reveal deep societal struggles – the list of such films is too long to cite here, but Martin Scorsese's *Taxi Driver* (1976) is the most obvious reference. However, in the context of Italian cinematic mobilities, Sordi's late career choice, which was made at a moment when the industry was beginning to move away from the comforts of genre filmmaking and reviving the figure of the film *auteur*, proved prescient. This is not to say, of course, that either of the *tassinaro* films is in any way remarkable, quite the contrary; rather shoddily shot and edited, they are expressions of a social and political conservatism that was gradually transforming Sordi's characters into stiff moralists, caricatures prone to a vulgarity that anticipated the imminent rise of *cinepanettoni*, Italy's populist genre par excellence. Nevertheless, it is impossible not to note the similarities between *nouveau auteur* Nanni Moretti's happenstance encounter with Hollywood star Jennifer Beals during his peregrinations on a white Vespa in *Caro Diario/Dear Diary* (1993) and Piero Marchetti's awkward flirting with Italy's once popular actress Silvana Pampanini, whom he mistakes for Sylva Koscina. In the vignettes that punctuate *Il tassinaro*'s very loose narrative, Sordi offers the back seat of his Ritmo to stars, curious characters, and even politicians. Of note is the cameo by the honourable Giulio Andreotti, leader of the Christian Democratic Party and the most prominent politician of the First Republic, at the time Italy's vice prime minister. Andreotti was the historic enemy of Italian Neorealist cinema: the 1949 Andreotti Law, promulgated when he was the state undersecretary in charge of entertainment, mandated that screenplays be vetted before they could obtain state funds, which translated into a form of pre-emptive censorship aimed at curtailing the resources of filmmakers wishing to expose Italy's problems. In Sordi's taxicab, Andreotti proposes a problematic reform of higher education: restricting access to universities to a limited number of select students. At the time, Italy's post-secondary institutions were open to all, independently of wealth, background, or preparation – a democratic principle that had governed the Italian education system at least since the postwar period. Early in the film, Piero appears to be a vocal labour organizer who participates in a successful strike against unlicensed cabs, yet he acts obsequiously with figures such as Andreotti, from whom he tries to extract a 'recommendation' for his soon-to-graduate engineer son.

In *Un tassinaro a New York*, which hinges on a crudely sketched-out international mafia affair, the practice of seeking the benevolence of the powerful to find steady employment for his son is what sets the plot into motion. In his review of the 'transatlantic' sequel, Tullio Kezich notes that the director

> has become lenient with his character; Sordi makes him into a naive backslapper, he envelops him in a simulation of agreeableness. One wonders how thirty years ago he would have demolished this obsequious taxicab driver who bows before his double-breasted-suit-wearing clients, calling them 'your excellency,' extracting recommendations for his son, and always siding with the establishment. (Kezich qtd in Fava 2003: 287)

In *Il tassinaro*, Sordi's attempts to capture lower-middle-class Italian life in the rituals of Piero's multigenerational family translate into expressions of cultural staleness and political disengagement; for instance, when they gather in front of the household's sole TV set to watch the weekly episodes of *Dallas* (an American series about the vicissitudes of a Texas oil baron that aired from 1978 to 1991), the exhausted *pater familias* expresses his disdain for the foreign import by slipping into sonorous snoring. The next day he collects some loud tourists from the eponymous American city at the airport; incapable of appreciating the beauty and history of Rome, the couple ends up irritating Pietro, who buries them under a thick coat of insults. Barely outlined stereotypes, these characters shoulder the weight of Sordi's coarse cultural critique, which pits Italy against the United States (or any other country) in a nationalistic contest unfavourably rigged in favour of the former.

In the same film, Sordi takes another stab at a critique of global petroculture in a scene shot at the Cavalieri Hilton, Rome's most luxurious hotel, where a group of offensively stereotypical 'Saudi Arabians' is partying with a platoon of escorts driven to the campus by a fleet of taxicabs. Pietro and his colleague Fernanda (Marilù Tolo) are invited to stay for dinner, and they oblige but take a seat at a secluded table. Eventually they get up and slow dance, and the Sheik 'Alj Ciucci' (Julian Jenkins) flings food at Pietro to amuse himself and his company.[4] The driver reacts to the offence, a fact that freezes the wealthy 'Arabs' and their guests into a stupor; the Sheik then threatens Pietro by reminding him that 'In this country, one in two cars burns petrol from my nation',[5] pointing to the extraordinary geopolitical power of his (and any) oil-rich state. The toothless critique of OPEC's world power expressed in this gag pales in comparison with the caustic clarity of *Un Italiano in America*, in which Sordi managed to anatomize American (petro)cultural imperialism by exposing its inequalities, underscoring its environmental harm, and connecting it to the intergenerational trauma experienced by those touched by the Italian diaspora.

Similarly, *Un tassinaro a New York* returns to the American continent (the film was shot almost entirely on location in New York and Miami), but fails to gain a deep understanding of the society it wishes to critique, relying instead on bi-dimensional stereotypes and tiresome vignettes. Tatti Sanguineti writes that

> As in all the films Sordi shot abroad, besides the spaghetti, every ten minutes of film there are 45 seconds of b-roll: jingles, atmospheric shots, landscapes, and the usual things one knows will be there, such as policemen on horseback in Central Park. *That's America*. (2015: 269; the sentence in italics appears in English in the original)

While Sordi's ability to 'act across borders' might have waned in the 1980s, it is undeniable that, both as an actor and a director, he remained engaged in an exploration of Italian mobilities via cinematic journeys until the end. As the public figure that was most equated with *italianità* in the second half of the twentieth century, he was uniquely positioned to comment on the country's many structural and cultural transformations. Elena M. Past writes that 'Fellinian films document the beginning of Italy's dependence on the automobile, simultaneously charting the seductive appeal of car culture and its tendency to isolate and exclude' (2020: 349). It is only fitting, then, that Sordi would turn to Federico Fellini to reflect on the thirty years that had elapsed between their last project together, *I vitelloni* (1953), and the making of *Il tassinaro*.

But the jovial meta-conversation that closes Sordi's film is not the director's sole homage to his friend's towering genius: a much deeper affection for Fellini shines through an earlier scene when Pietro takes a call from Quartiere don Bosco. Named after the Italian pedagogue and patron of schoolchildren, it is Cinecittà's neighbourhood, and its streets appear briefly in Fellini's *La dolce vita*. Pietro's passenger is a quiet older man, Mr Donato (Orazio Stracuzzi), who carries a large duffle bag, a character that recalls the mysterious *l'uomo del sacco* (the man with the sack, played by Leo Catozzo), the charitable wanderer encountered by the sex worker protagonist in *Le notti di Cabiria*. The passenger is directed to Caracalla, where he needs to meet Esther (Maria Scagnetti), a prostitute and the mother of the baby he is carrying in the bag. When they find her, the woman gently takes the child and proceeds to nurse him in the street. The concluding notes of the Triumphal March from Verdi's *Aida* can be heard in the distance, coming from the outdoor Auditorium Caracalla, where a performance of the opera is taking place. After the child has finished nursing, he falls asleep, and the mother returns him to Mr Donato, who is revealed to be the caretaker of the building where Esther and her baby live. Donato and the child climb into the back seat of Pietro's taxicab and drive off, but the car soon comes to a stop, giving way to a religious procession that crosses its path. Intoning a chant devoted to the Madonna del Divino Amore, the believers' voices temporarily drown out Verdi's music, the flames of their torches mirroring the fires lit by the prostitutes in the background. A similar night-time procession also appears before Cabiria and her colleagues, and it is at the Sanctuary of the Madonna del Divino Amore that the woman drops to her knees and prays for her life to change. The scene's concluding long shot frames the procession in the foreground, the yellow Ritmo in the middle ground, and the Baths of Caracalla in the background, its historic arches lit with the colours of the Italian flag. As the two songs compete for the audience's attention, the taxicab drives off into the night (Figure 2.17).

If Fellini had underscored the symbiotic relationship between N/Lazzari's mid-century stardom and (auto)mobility in his fortuitous nighttime encounter with Cabiria, the *flâneuse* prostitute of the Passeggiata

Figure 2.17 Stacking the iconic deck: Catholicism, Romanitas, Verdi, Fellini, and Sordi.

Archeologica (where the Baths of Caracalla are located), in this scene Sordi connects his own on-screen peregrinations to a broader narrative of quintessentially Italian cinema and culture at large, epitomized simultaneously by the figures of the legendary director and the composer most strongly associated with the Risorgimento. Through the character of the world-weary, populist taxicab driver, Sordi seems to (rightfully) place himself in this pantheon of illustrious Italians, himself a stratum in the bedrock of *Romanitas* and Catholicism that, to him, were the cultural roots of a nation that he decided to explore from within and, as this book's second part has attempted to demonstrate, from without.

Notes

1. In the English edition of Tullio Kezich's biography of Federico Fellini, the gesture is described as flipping the bird (2007: 133). To be more precise, Sordi gives them the 'umbrella gesture' ('il gesto dell'ombrello'), by slapping the crook of his right arm with his left hand. It is an offensive gesture that roughly translates into 'up yours'.
2. Film critic Valerio Caprara notes that this is the film's only redeeming sequence: 'The unfailing Fellini offers a hand to the tired showman, allowing him to close the film with a bravura sequence all improvised, a sort of testament to the greatness that was. I suggest we clip out the sequence, which is truly breathtaking, for Sordi's future pantheon' (qtd in Fava 2003: 277).
3. The advent of ride-sharing companies such as Uber and Lyft has both complicated and solidified this symbiosis. On this, see Sharma (2017).
4. The Sheik's improbable name phonetically could be understood as 'here are the donkeys' ('ciucci') in Roman dialect; Giuseppe Gioacchino Belli compares cardinals ('Minenze') and 'ciucci' in his sonnet *Er pittore de Sant'Agustino* (1886: vol. 2, 171). In Mario Monicelli's 1981 *Il Marchese del Grillo*, Sordi's character cites a line from Belli's 1832 sonnet *Li soprani Der Monno vecchio*: 'Iö sò io, e vvoi nun zete un cazzo' (I am who I am, and you are nothing) (1886: vol. 2, 49). I am grateful to Damiano Acciarino for bringing these connections between Sordi's lines and Belli's vernacular poems to my attention.
5. Again, the man's Italian is imperfect, so as to signify his foreignness: 'in questo paese, un'automobile sì e una no viaggia con benzina di mia nazione'.

Filmography

4 passi fra le nuvole (1942; *Four Steps in the Clouds*). Director: Alessandro Blasetti.
L'albero di Adamo (1936; *Adam's Tree*). Director: Mario Bonnard.
Amarcord (1973). Director: Federico Fellini.
Un americano a Roma (1954; *An American in Rome*). Director: Steno.
Anastasia mio fratello ovvero il presunto capo dell'anonima assassini (1973; *My Brother Anastasia*). Director: Stefano Vanzina.
L'angelo bianco (1955; *The White Angel*). Director: Raffaello Matarazzo.
Anni difficili (1948). Director: Luigi Zampa.
L'anonima Roylott (1936). Director: Raffaello Matarazzo.
Apparizione (1943; *Apparition*). Director: Jean de Limur.
Appunti per un'Orestiade africana (1970; *Notes Towards an African Orestes*). Director: Pier Paolo Pasolini.
L'argine (1938). Director: Corrado D'Errico.
L'assedio dell'Alcazar (1940; *The Siege of the Alcazar*). Director: Augusto Genina.
Assenza ingiustificata (1939; *Unjustified Absence*). Director: Max Neufeld.
Avanti c'è posto . . . (1942; *Before the Postman*). Director: Mario Bonnard.
Il bandito (1946; *The Bandit*). Director: Alberto Lattuada.
Bandits (1997). Director: Katja von Garnier.
La battaglia di Algeri (1966; *The Battle of Algiers*). Director: Gillo Pontecorvo.
Bellissima (1950). Director: Luchino Visconti.
Bello, onesto, emigrato Australia sposerebbe compaesana illibata (1971; *A Girl in Australia*). Director: Luigi Zampa.
Ben-Hur: A Tale of the Christ (1925). Director: Fred Niblo.
Berlin: Die Sinfonie der Großstadt (1927; *Berlin: Symphony of a Great City*). Director: Walter Ruttman.
The Best of Enemies (1961). Director: Guy Hamilton.
La bisbetica domata (1942; *The Taming of the Shrew*). Director: Ferdinando Maria Poggioli.
Blow-Up (1966). Director: Michelangelo Antonioni.
Brevi amori a Palma di Maiorca (1959). Director: Giorgio Bianchi.
Il brigante Musolino (1950; *Cowboy Girl*). Director: Mario Camerini.
Camicia nera (1933; *Black Shirt*). Director: Giovacchino Forzano.
Il cammino della speranza (1950; *The Path of Hope*). Director: Pietro Germi.

Campo de' fiori (1943; *The Peddler and the Lady*). Director: Mario Bonnard.
La cantante dell'opera (1933). Director: Nunzio Malasomma.
Caro Diario (1993; *Dear Diary*). Director: Nanni Moretti.
La casa del peccato (1938). Director: Max Neufeld.
Catene (1949; *Chains*). Director: Raffaello Matarazzo.
Il cavaliere senza nome (1941). Director: Ferruccio Cerio.
Cavalleria (1936; *Cavalry*). Director: Goffredo Alessandrini.
La cena delle beffe (1942; *The Jester's Supper*). Director: Alessandro Blasetti.
Cenere (1917). Director: Febo Mari.
Centomila dollari (1940; *A Hundred Thousand Dollars*). Director: Mario Camerini.
Chi è senza peccato . . . (1952). Director: Raffaello Matarazzo.
Chi sei tu? (1939; *Who Are You?*). Director: Gino Valori.
Il cielo brucia (1958; *The Sky Burns*). Director: Giuseppe Masini.
Come scopersi l'America (1949; *How I Discovered America*). Director: Carlo Borghesio.
Conflicto inesperado (1948). Director: Ricardo Gascón.
La congiuntura (1965; *Hard Times for Princes*). Director: Ettore Scola.
La contessa di Parma (1936; *The Duchess of Parma*). Director: Alessandro Blasetti.
Il corpo (1974; *The Body*). Director: Luigi Scattini.
Cose dell'altro mondo (1939). Director: Nunzio Malasomma.
Costa Azzurra (1959). Director: Vittorio Sala.
Crimen (1960; *. . . And Suddenly It's Murder!*). Director: Mario Camerini.
Il critico (1913; *The Critic*). Director: Febo Mari.
Cronaca di un amore (1950; *Story of a Love Affair*). Director: Michelangelo Antonioni.
Cuandos los ángeles duermen (1947). Director: Ricardo Gascón.
Dagli Appennini alle Ande (1916; *From the Apennines to the Andes*). Director: Umberto Paradisi.
Delitto d'amore (1974; *Crime of Love*). Director: Luigi Comencini.
Il delitto di Giovanni Episcopo (1947; *Flesh Will Surrender*). Director: Alberto Lattuada.
Il diavolo (1963; *To Bed or Not to Bed*). Director: Gianni Polidori.
Disonorata senza colpa (1954). Director: Giorgio Walter Chili.
Divorzio all'italiana (1961). Director: Pietro Germi.
The Docks of New York (1928). Director: Joseph von Sternberg.
La dolce vita (1960). Director: Federico Fellini.
Don Juan de Serralonga (1949). Director: Ricardo Gascón.
La donna della montagna (1944; *The Mountain Woman*). Director: Renato Castellani.
Dopo divorzieremo (1940; *Then We'll Get a Divorce*). Director: Nunzio Malasomma.
Dora Nelson (1939). Director: Mario Soldati.

Due cuori felici (1932; *Two Happy Hearts*). Director: Baldassarre Negroni.
Due milioni per un sorriso (1939). Director: Mario Soldati.
È sbarcato un marinaio (1940). Director: Piero Ballerini.
Ein bißchen Liebe für Dich (Zwei Glückliche Herzen) (1932; *A Bit of Love*). Director: Max Neufeld.
L'emigrante (1915; *The Emigrant*). Director: Febo Mari.
Emigrantes (1948). Director: Aldo Fabrizi.
A Farewell to Arms (1957). Director: Charles Vidor.
Fari nella nebbia (1942; *Headlights in the Fog*). Director: Gianni Franciolini.
I figli di nessuno (1951; *Nobody's Children*). Director: Raffaello Matarazzo.
Finché c'è guerra c'è speranza (1974; *While There's War There's Hope*) Director: Alberto Sordi.
Fontamara (1980). Director: Carlo Lizzani.
Frente de Madrid aka *Carmen fra i rossi* (1939). Director: Edgar Neville.
Fumo di Londra (1966; *Smoke Over London*). Director: Alberto Sordi.
Fuochi d'artificio (1938). Director: Gennaro Righelli.
Gangs of New York (2002). Director: Martin Scorsese.
Il gaucho (1964). Director: Dino Risi.
Germania anno zero (1948; *Germany Year Zero*). Director: Roberto Rossellini.
Germanin – Die Geschichte einer kolonialen Tat (1943). Director: Max V. Kimmich.
Giant (1956). Director: George Stevens.
Giarabub (1942). Director: Goffredo Alessandrini.
Giorni felici (1942). Director: Gianni Franciolini.
Un giorno in pretura (1954; *A Day in Court*). Director: Steno.
Un giorno nella vita (1946; *A Day in the Life*). Director: Alessandro Blasetti.
Gli uomini, che mascalzoni! (1932; *Men, What Rascals!*). Director: Mario Camerini.
The Godfather (1972). Director: Francis Ford Coppola.
Good Morning Babilonia (1987; *Good Morning Babylon*). Directors: Paolo and Vittorio Taviani.
Grand Hotel (1932). Director: Edmund Goulding.
Il grande appello (1936; *The Great Appeal*). Director: Mario Camerini.
La grande guerra (1959; *The Great War*). Director: Mario Monicelli.
I grandi magazzini (1939; *Department Store*). Director: Mario Camerini.
Grattacieli (1943). Director: Guglielmo Giannini.
Harlem aka *Knockout!* (1943/1946). Director: Carmine Gallone.
Intolerance (1916). Director: D. W. Griffith.
L'invasore (1943/1949; *The Invader*). Director: Nino Giannini.
In viaggio con papà (1982). Director: Alberto Sordi.
Un Italiano in America (1967). Director: Alberto Sordi.
Joe il rosso (1936). Director: Raffaello Matarazzo.
Kean: genio e sregolatezza (1956). Director: Francesco Rosi.
Kings of the Road (1976). Director: Wim Wenders.

Ladri di biciclette (1948; *Bicycle Thieves*). Director: Vittorio De Sica.
Luciano Serra pilota (1938; *Luciano Serra, Pilot*). Director: Goffredo Alessandrini.
Mafioso (1962). Director: Alberto Lattuada.
I magliari (1959; *The Swindlers*). Director: Francesco Rosi.
Malinconico autunno (1958; *Melancholic Autumn*). Director: Raffaello Matarazzo.
Mamma mia, che impressione! (1951). Director: Roberto Savarese.
Il Marchese del Grillo (1981). Director: Mario Monicelli.
Marrakech Express (1989). Director: Gabriele Salvatores.
Mille lire al mese (1939). Director: Max Neufeld.
Mimì metallurgico ferito nell'onore (1972; *The Seduction of Mimi*). Director: Lina Wertmüller.
Una moglie americana (1965; *Run for Your Wife*). Director: Gian Luigi Polidoro.
Montevergine (La grande luce) (1939). Director: Carlo Campogalliani.
Napoletani a Milano (1953; *Neapolitans in Milan*). Director: Eduardo de Filippo.
Ninotchka (1939). Director: Ernst Lubitsch.
Non c'è bisogno di denaro (1933). Director: Amleto Palermi.
La notte delle beffe (1939). Director: Carlo Campogalliani.
Le notti di Cabiria (1957; *Nights of Cabiria*). Director: Federico Fellini.
Oh! Qué mambo aka *Il giovane Leone* (1959). Director: John Berry.
L'onorevole Angelina (1947). Director: Luigi Zampa.
Ossessione (1943; *Obsession*). Director: Luchino Visconti.
Pane e Cioccolata (1974; *Bread and Chocolate*). Director: Franco Brusati.
Paper Moon (1973). Director: Peter Bogdanovich.
Parigi è sempre Parigi (1951; *Paris is Always Paris*). Director: Luciano Emmer.
Partire (1938; *Departure*). Director: Amleto Palermi.
Passaporto rosso (1935; *Red Passport*). Director: Guido Brignone.
Il peccato di Rogelia Sanchez (1939; *The Sin of Rogelia Sanchez*). Director: Carlo Borghesio.
Pépé le Moko (1937). Director: Julien Duvivier.
La più bella serata della mia vita (1972). Director: Ettore Scola.
La puerta abierta (1957; *The Open Door*). Director: César Fernández Ardavín.
Le Quai des brumes (1938; *Port of Shadows*). Director: Marcel Carné.
I quattro bersaglieri aka *Tripoli, bel suol d'amore* (1954). Director: Ferruccio Cerio.
Racconti d'estate (1958; *Love on the Riviera*). Director: Gianni Franciolini.
La ragazza dalla pelle di luna (1972; *Moon Skin*). Director: Luigi Scattini.
La ragazza fuoristrada (1972). Director: Luigi Scattini.
La ragazza in vetrina (1961; *Woman in the Window*). Director: Luciano Emmer.
Rebel Without a Cause (1955). Director: Nicholas Ray.
Riusciranno i nostri eroi a ritrovare l'amico misteriosamente scomparso in Africa (1968; *Will Our Heros Be Able to Find Their Friend Who Has Mysteriously Disappeared in Africa?*). Director: Ettore Scola.
Roma città aperta (1945; *Rome, Open City*). Director: Roberto Rossellini.

Rubacuori (1931). Director: Guido Brignone.
Sancta Maria aka *La muchacha de Moscú* (1941; *Saint Maria*). Directors: Pier Luigi Faraldo and Edgar Neville.
Sanguepazzo (2008; *Wild Blood*). Director: Marco Tullio Giordana.
Santa Rogelia aka *Il peccato di Rogelia Sanchez* (1940; *Saint Rogelia*). Director: Federico Moreno Torroba.
Satyricon (1969). Director: Federico Fellini.
Scampolo (1941). Director: Nunzio Malasomma.
Scarpe grosse (1940). Director: Dino Falconi.
Lo sceicco bianco (1952; *The White Sheik*). Director: Federico Fellini.
Scipione l'Africano (1937; *Scipio Africanus: The Defeat of Hannibal*). Director: Carmine Gallone.
Il seduttore (1954). Director: Franco Rossi.
Se permettete parliamo di donne (1964; *Let's Talk About Women*). Director: Ettore Scola.
Senso (1954). Director: Luchino Visconti.
La sfida (1958). Director: Francesco Rosi.
Signori, in carrozza! (1951; *Rome-Paris-Rome*). Director: Luigi Zampa.
I soliti ignoti (1958; *Big Deal on Madonna Street*). Director: Mario Monicelli.
Il sorpasso (1962; *The Easy Life*). Director: Dino Risi.
Sotto la croce del Sud (1938; *Under the Southern Cross*). Director: Guido Brignone.
Sottozero (1987; *Below Zero*). Director: Gian Luigi Polidoro.
La strada (1954). Director: Federico Fellini.
Stramilano (1930). Director: Corrado D'Errico.
Sunrise: A Song of Two Humans (1927). Director: F. W. Murnau.
Le svedesi (1960). Director: Gian Luigi Polidoro.
Il tassinaro (1983). Director: Alberto Sordi.
Un tassinaro a New York (1987). Director: Alberto Sordi.
Taxi Driver (1976). Director: Martin Scorsese.
Terra madre (1931; *Mother Earth*). Director: Alessandro Blasetti.
Terra di nessuno (1939; *No Man's Land*). Director: Mario Baffico.
La terra trema (1948). Director: Luchino Visconti.
Il testimone (1946; *The Witness*). Director: Pietro Germi.
Those Magnificent Men in Their Flying Machines; Or, How I Flew from London to Paris in 25 Hours 11 Minutes (1965). Director: Ken Annakin.
Thrilling (1965). Directors: Ettore Scola, Carlo Lizzani, and Gian Luigi Polidoro.
Tormento (1950; *Torment*). Director: Raffaello Matarazzo.
Torna! (1953). Director: Raffaello Matarazzo.
Tragica notte (1942; *Tragic Night*). Director: Mario Soldati.
I tre aquilotti (1942). Director: Mario Mattoli.
Tutti a casa (1960). Director: Luigi Comencini.
L'ultima carrozzella (1943; *The Last Wagon*). Director: Mario Mattoli.

Umberto D. (1952). Director: Vittorio De Sica.
Vacanze d'inverno (1959). Directors: Camillo Mastrocinque and Giuliano Carnimeo.
Vacanze di Natale (1983). Director: Carlo Vanzina.
Vagabond (1985). Director: Agnès Varda.
Venezia, la luna e tu (1958). Director: Dino Risi.
Vertigo (1958). Director: Alfred Hitchcock.
Viaggio in Italia (1950; *Journey to Italy*). Director: Roberto Rossellini.
Il vigile (1960). Director: Luigi Zampa.
I vitelloni (1953). Director: Federico Fellini.
Volver a la vida (1951; *Return to Life*). Director: Carlos F. Borcosque.
Weekend (1967). Director: Jean-Luc Godard.
Wild Strawberries (1957). Director: Ingmar Bergman.
The Young Lions (1958). Director: Edward Dmytryk
Zabriskie Point (1970). Director: Michelangelo Antonioni.

Bibliography

Adamson, Walter L. (2001), 'Avant-Garde Modernism and Italian Fascism: Cultural Politics in the Era of Mussolini', *Journal of Modern Italian Studies*, 6, 2, 230–48.
Adey, Peter (2017), *Mobility*, 2nd edn, New York: Routledge.
Adey, Peter, David Bissell, Kevin Hannam, Peter Merriman, and Mimi Sheller (eds) (2014), *The Routledge Handbook of Mobilities*, New York: Routledge.
Aguilar, Santiago (2002), *Edgar Neville: Tres sainetes criminales*, Madrid: Filmoteca Española.
Akhtar, Salman (1999), 'The Immigrant, the Exile, and the Experience of Nostalgia', *Journal of Applied Psychoanalytic Studies*, 1, 2, 123–30.
Allum, Felia (2014), 'Understanding Criminal Mobility: The Case of the Neapolitan Camorra', *Journal of Modern Italian Studies*, 19, 5, 583–602.
Anastasio, Salvatore and Benedetto Mosca (1967), *Anastasia mio fratello*, Rome: Edizioni di Novissima.
Angelucci, Gianfranco (2007), 'Il guardaroba di Nazzari', in Arnaldo Colasanti and Ernesto Nicosia (eds), *Amedeo Nazzari. Rigore e pathos*, Rome: Archivi del Novecento, 109–14.
Anile, Alberto (2018), 'Sputare sul pubblico. Sordi contro lo spettatore, fuori e dentro il film', *Bianco e Nero: Rivista Quadrimestrale del Centro Sperimentale di Cinematografia*, LXXIX, 592, September–December, Rome: Edizioni del CSC, 50–6.
— (2020), *Alberto Sordi*, Rome: Edizioni Sabinæ.
Appadurai, Arjun (1996), *Modernity at Large: Cultural Dimensions of Globalization*, Minneapolis: University of Minnesota Press.
Aprà, Adriano (ed.) (2009), *Alberto Lattuada. Il cinema e i film*, Venice: Marsilio.
Argentieri, Mino (2003), *L'occhio del regime*, Rome: Bulzoni Editore.
Aristarco, Guido (1996), *Il cinema fascista: Il prima e il dopo*, Bari: Edizioni Dedalo.
Arvidsson, Adam (2003), *Marketing Modernity: Italian Advertising from Fascism to Postmodernity*, New York: Routledge.
Baratieri, Daniela (2005), '*Bengasi – Bengasi anno '41*: The Evidence of Silences in the Transmission of Memory', in Jaqueline Andall and Derek Duncan (eds), *Italian Colonialism: Legacy and Memory*, New York: Peter Lang, 75–98.
Barattoni, Luca (2014), *Italian Post-Neorealist Cinema*, Edinburgh: Edinburgh University Press.

Barbaro, Umberto (1939), 'La VII Esposizione di Venezia', *Bianco e Nero: Rassegna di arte critica e tecnica del film*, III, 9, 30 September, Rome: Edizioni Italiane, 3–13.
Baron, Cynthia and Sharon Marie Carnicke (2006), *Reframing Screen Performance*, Ann Arbor: University of Michigan Press.
Bayman, Louis (2015), *The Operatic and the Everyday in Postwar Italian Film Melodrama*, Edinburgh: Edinburgh University Press.
Bazin, André (2011), *André Bazin and Italian Neorealism*, ed. Bert Cardullo, New York: Continuum.
Bazzoffia, Alessandro, Massimo Bottini, and Antonio Mencarelli (2003), *I giovani e I luoghi dell'istruzione dello svago e dello sport nella cultura degli anni trenta in Italia*, Città di Castello: Monte Meru Editrice.
Belli, Giuseppe Gioachino (1886), *Sonetti romaneschi*, ed. Luigi Morandi, Città di Castello: S. Lapi Tipografo-Editore.
Ben-Ghiat, Ruth (1996), 'Envisioning Modernity: Desire and Discipline in the Italian Fascist Film', *Critical Inquiry*, 23, 1, 109–44.
— (2001), *Fascist Modernities: Italy, 1922–1945*, Berkeley: University of California Press.
— (2015), *Italian Fascism's Empire Cinema*, Bloomington: Indiana University Press.
Ben-Ghiat, Ruth and Mia Fuller (eds) (2005), *Italian Colonialism*, New York: Palgrave Macmillan.
Ben-Ghiat, Ruth and Stephanie Malia Hom (eds) (2016), *Italian Mobilities*, New York: Routledge.
Bernardini, Paola, Teresa Lobalsamo, Joanne Granata, and Alberto Zambenedetti (eds) (2016), *Federico Fellini: Riprese, riletture, (re)visioni*, Florence: Franco Cesati Editore.
Bertellini, Giorgio (2003), 'Colonial Autism: Whitened Heroes, Auditory Rhetoric, and National Identity in Interwar Italian Cinema', in Patrizia Palumbo (ed.) (2003), *A Place in the Sun: Africa in Italian Colonial Culture from Post-Unification to the Present*, Berkeley: University of California Press, 255–78.
— (2010), *Italy in Early American Cinema*, Bloomington, IN: Indiana University Press.
Bertonelli, Elena and Luigi M. Lombardi Satriani (eds) (1991), *Emigrazione e immigrazione: Catalogo*, Milan: Editoriale Jaca Book.
Bertozzi, Marco (2000), 'Visualizing the Past: The Italian City in Early Cinema', *Film History*, 12, 322–9.
Betti, Carmen (1984), *L'Opera Nazionale Balilla e l'educazione fascista*, Florence: La Nuova Italia.
Bianco e Nero: Rassegna di arte critica e tecnica del film (1938), II, 9, 30 September, Rome: Edizioni Italiane.
Bianco e Nero: Rassegna di arte critica e tecnica del film (1939), III, 9, 30 September, Rome: Edizioni Italiane.

Bianco e Nero: Rassegna di arte critica e tecnica del film (1943), VII, 6, June, Rome: Edizioni Italiane.
Bianco e Nero: Rivista Quadrimestrale del Centro Sperimentale di Cinematografia (2018), LXXIX, 592, September–December, Rome: Edizioni del CSC.
Bini, Andrea (2011), 'The Birth of Comedy Italian Style', in Flavia Brizio-Skov (ed.), *Popular Italian Cinema Culture and Politics in a Postwar Society*, London: I.B Tauris, 107–52.
Birtchnell, Thomas, Satya Savitsky, and John Urry (eds) (2015), *Cargomobilities: Moving Material in a Global Age*, New York: Routledge.
Boggio, Cecilia (2003), 'Black Shirts/Black Skins: Fascist Italy's Colonial Anxieties and *Lo Squadrone Bianco*', in Patrizia Palumbo (ed.) (2003), *A Place in the Sun: Africa in Italian Colonial Culture from Post-Unification to the Present*, Berkeley: University of California Press, 279–98.
Bolton, Lucy and Christina Siggers Mason (eds) (2010), *Italy on Screen: National Identity and Italian Imaginary*, New York: Peter Lang.
Bolzoni, Francesco (1986), *I film di Francesco Rosi*, Rome: Gremese Editore.
Bonaguidi, Alberto (1990), 'Italy', in Charles B. Nam, William J. Serow, and David F. Sly (eds), *International Handbook on Internal Migration*, New York: Greenwood Press, 239–55.
Bondanella, Peter (2006), *Hollywood Italians: Dagos, Palookas, Romeos, Wise Guys, and Sopranos*, New York: Continuum.
Boorstin, Daniel J. (1964), *The Image: A Guide to Pseudo-events in America*, New York: Harper & Row.
Brancati, Vitaliano (1973), *Il borghese e l'immensità. Scritti 1930–1954*, Milan: Bompiani.
Brizio-Skov, Flavia (ed.) (2011), *Popular Italian Cinema Culture and Politics in a Postwar Society*, London: I.B. Tauris.
Brunetta, Gian Piero (1979), *Storia del cinema Italiano: 1895–1945*, Rome: Editori Riuniti.
Bruni, David (2013), *Commedia degli anni Trenta*, Milan: Il Castoro.
Buffa, Maria Evelina (2008), *Amedeo Buffa in arte Nazzari*, Cantalupo in Sabina: Edizioni Sabinæ.
Burke, Frank (1996), *Fellini's Films*, New York: Twayne Publishers.
Camaiti Hostert, Anna and Anthony Julian Tamburri (eds) (2002), *Screening Ethnicity: Cinematographic Representations of Italian Americans in the United States*, Boca Raton, FL: Bordighera Press.
Canella, Maria and Sergio Giuntini (eds) (2009), *Sport e fascismo*, Milan: FrancoAngeli.
Capomolla, Rinaldo, Marco Mulazzani, and Rosalia Vittorini (2008), *Case del Balilla: Architettura e fascismo*, Milan: Electa.
Carratalá, Juan Antonio Ríos (2007), *Una arrolladora simpatía: Edgar Neville: de Hollywood al Madrid de la posguerra*, Barcelona: Editorial Ariel.
Casadio, Gianfranco (1989), *Il grigio e il nero: Spettacolo e propaganda nel cinema italiano degli anni Trenta (1931–1943)*, Ravenna: Longo Editore.

Casadio, Gianfranco, Ernesto G. Laura, and Filippo Cristiano (1991), *Telefoni bianchi: Realtà e finzione nella società e nel cinema italiano degli anni Quaranta*, Ravenna: Longo Editore.
Cascone, Claudia (2006), *Il Sud di Lina Wertmüller*, Naples: Lettere Italiane.
Casella, Paola (1998), *Hollywood Italian: Gli italiani nell'America di celluloide*, Milan: Baldini & Castoldi.
Cattini, Alberto (2001), 'Tra un'immigrazione e l'altra. Tentazioni, in Suso Cecchi d'Amico, Giuseppe Patroni Griffi, and Francesco Rosi, *I magliari: Sceneggiatura originale dell'omonimo film di Francesco Rosi*, Mantua: Publi Paolini, 7–48.
Cavallo, Pietro (2010), *Viva l'Italia: Storia, cinema e identità nazionale (1932–1962)*, Naples: Liguori Editore.
Cecchi, Emilio (1997), *Saggi e Viaggi*, ed. Margherita Ghilardi, Milan: Arnoldo Mondadori Editore.
Cecchi d'Amico, Suso, Giuseppe Patroni Griffi, and Francesco Rosi (2001), *I magliari: Sceneggiatura originale dell'omonimo film di Francesco Rosi*, Mantua: Publi Paolini.
Cederna, Antonio (2006), *Mussolini urbanista: Lo sventramento di Roma negli anni del consenso*, Venice: Corte del fontego.
Certeau, Michel de (1988), *The Practice of Everyday Life*, trans. Steven Rendall, Berkeley: University of California Press.
Césaire, Aimé [1950] (2000), *Discourse on Colonialism*, trans. Joan Pinkham, New York: Monthly Review Press.
Cherchi Usai, Paolo (2009), 'Mafioso', in Adriano Aprà (ed.) (2009), *Alberto Lattuada. Il cinema e i film*, Venice: Marsilio, 219–22.
Choate, Mark (2008), *Emigrant Nation: The Making of Italy Abroad*, Cambridge, MA: Harvard University Press.
Cicognetti, Laura and Luisa Servetti (2003), *Migranti in celluloide: Storici, cinema ed emigrazione*, Foligno: Editoriale Umbra.
Cipolloni, Marco and Gian Luigi De Rosa (2001), *'La materia di cui sono fatti i sogni': Le Americhe di celluloide dell'emigrazione italiana*, Salerno: Edizioni del Paguro.
Coladonato, Valerio and Paolo Noto (2017), 'In the Eyes of the Beholder: The Tourist Gaze and Gender in 1950s Italian Comedies', *La Valle dell'Eden*, 31, 111–19.
Colasanti, Arnaldo and Ernesto Nicosia (eds) (2007), *Amedeo Nazzari: Rigore e pathos*, Rome: Archivi del Novecento.
Coletti, Maria (2002), 'Alla ricerca dell'innocenza perduta. "Riusciranno i nostri eroi . . .?"', in Vito Zagarrio (ed.), *Trevico – Cinecittà. L'avventuroso viaggio di Ettore Scola*, Venice: Marsilio, 184–90.
Conley, Tom (2007), *Cartographic Cinema*, Minneapolis: University of Minnesota Press.
Corrado, Andrea and Igor Mariottini (2013), *Cinema e autori sulle tracce delle migrazioni*, Rome: Ediesse.

Cowie, Elizabeth (1993), '*Film Noir* and Women', in Joan Copjec (ed.), *Shades of Noir*, New York: Verso, 121–65.
Cresswell, Tim and Tanu Priya Uteng (2008), 'Gendered Mobilities: Towards an Holistic Understanding', in Tanu Priya Uteng and Tim Cresswell (eds), *Gendered Mobilities*, Burlington, VT: Ashgate, 1–12.
Cwerner, Saulo (2009), 'Introducing Aeromobilities', in Saulo Cwerner, Sven Kesselring, and John Urry (eds) (2009), *Aeromobilties*, New York: Routledge, 1–21.
Cwerner, Saulo, Sven Kesselring, and John Urry (eds) (2009), *Aeromobilties*, New York: Routledge.
D'Acierno, Pellegrino (1999), 'Cinema Paradiso: The Italian American Presence in American Cinema', in Pellegrino D'Acierno (ed.), *The Italian American Heritage*, New York: Garland Publishing, 563–690.
D'Amelio, Maria Elena (2018), 'The Ideal Man: Amedeo Nazzari, Fatherhood, and Italy's Melodramatic Masculinity', *gender/sexuality/italy*, 5, <http://www.gendersexualityitaly.com/2-the-ideal-man-amedeo-nazzari-fatherhood-and-italys-melodramatic-masculinity/> (last accessed 17 August 2020).
d'Amico, Masolino (2007), 'Ritratto dell'attore', in Arnaldo Colasanti and Ernesto Nicosia (eds), *Amedeo Nazzari. Rigore e pathos*, Rome: Archivi del Novecento, 11–14.
— (2008), *La commedia all'italiana: La commedia all'italiana. Il cinema comico dal 1945 al 1957*, Milan: Saggiatore.
De Benedictis, Maurizio (2005), *Acting: Il cinema dalla parte degli attori*, Rome: Avagliano Editore.
De Bernardinis, Flavio (2007), 'Le contraddizioni della nostalgia: *Il gaucho*', in Arnaldo Colasanti and Ernesto Nicosia (eds), *Amedeo Nazzari: Rigore e pathos*, Rome: Archivi del Novecento 101–4.
De Grazia, Victoria (1981), *The Culture of Consent: Mass Organization of Leisure in Fascist Italy*, Cambridge: Cambridge University Press.
Della Casa, Steve (2018), 'Al passo con i mods. Ambizioni e tagli da *Fumo di Londra*, la sua prima regia', *Bianco e Nero: Rivista Quadrimestrale del Centro Sperimentale di Cinematografia*, LXXIX, 592, September–December, Rome: Edizioni del CSC, 93–9.
De Santi, Pier Marco (1988), *I film di Paolo e Vittorio Taviani*, Rome: Gremese editore.
De Santis, Giuseppe (1943), 'Harlem', *Cinema*, VIII, 1, 10 May, no. 165, 280.
Duggan, Christopher (2007), *The Force of Destiny: A History of Italy Since 1796*, New York: Houghton Mifflin.
Einaudi, Luigi (1900), *Un principe mercante*, Turin: Fratelli Bocca Editori.
Ember, Carol R., Melvin Ember, and Ian A. Skoggard (eds) (2004), *Encyclopedia of Diasporas: Immigrant and Refugee Cultures Around the World*, New York: Kluwer Academic/Plenum.
Falasca-Zamponi, Simonetta (1997), *Fascist Spectacle: The Aesthetics of Power in Mussolini's Italy*, Berkeley: University of California Press.

Fava, Claudio G. (2003), *Alberto Sordi*, Rome: Gremese Editore.
Featherstone, Mike, Scott Lash, and Roland Robertson (eds) (1997), *Global Modernities*, London: Sage Publications.
Film Lexicon (1959), vol. 2, Rome: Bianco e Nero.
Fofi, Goffredo (2004), *Alberto Sordi: L'Italia in bianco e nero*, Milan: Mondadori.
Forgacs, David (1990), *Italian Culture in the Industrial Era, 1880–1980: Cultural Industries, Politics and the Public*, Manchester: Manchester University Press.
Franco, Mario (2007), 'Un incontro ai limiti del paradosso', in Arnaldo Colasanti and Ernesto Nicosia (eds), *Amedeo Nazzari: Rigore e pathos*, Rome: Archivi del Novecento, 91–6.
Francia di Celle, Stefano and Enrico Ghezzi (eds) (2004), *Mister(o) Emmer: l'Attenta distrazione*, Turin: Torino Film Festival.
Franklin, Adrian (2014), 'Tourist Studies', in Peter Adey, David Bissell, Kevin Hannam, Peter Merriman, and Mimi Sheller (eds), *The Routledge Handbook of Mobilities*, New York: Routledge, 74–84.
Freund, Peter and George Martin (eds) (1993), *The Ecology of the Automobile*, New York: Black Rose Books.
Frontani, Michael R. (2016), ' "Narcotic": Constructing the Mafia – The Nationally Televised New York Hearings of the Kefauver Committee, March 1951', *Italian American Review*, 6, 2, 173–202.
Fullwood, Natalie (2015), *Cinema, Gender, and Everyday Space: Comedy, Italian Style*, New York: Palgrave Macmillan.
Gabaccia, Donna (2000), *Italy's Many Diasporas*, Seattle: University of Washington Press.
Gentile, Emilo (2009), *La Grande Italia: The Myth of the Nation in the 20th Century*, Madison: University of Wisconsin Press.
Giacobini, Silvana (2018), *Albertone: Alberto Sordi, una leggenda italiana*, Milan: Cairo Editore.
Giacovelli, Enrico (2002), *Breve storia del cinema comico in Italia*, Turin: Lindau.
— (2003), *Un italiano a Roma: La vita, i successi, le passioni di Alberto Sordi*, Turin: Lindau.
Gianferrara, Lidia (1988), *Cinema ed emigrazione*, Bologna: Barghigiani.
Ginsborg, Paul (1990), *A History of Contemporary Italy: Society and Politics 1942–1988*, London: Penguin Books.
Glick Schiller, Nina (2004), 'Long-Distance Nationalism', in Carol R. Ember, Melvin Ember, and Ian A. Skoggard (eds), *Encyclopedia of Diasporas: Immigrant and Refugee Cultures Around the World*, New York: Kluwer Academic/Plenum, 570–80.
Governi, Giancarlo (2010), *Alberto Sordi, l'italiano*, Rome: A Curcio.
Grande, Maurizio and Orio Caldinon (2003), *La commedia all'italiana*, Rome: Bulzoni.
Grandi, Dino (1941), *Bonifica umana: decennale delle leggi penali e della riforma penitenziaria, Volume 1*, Ministero di Grazia e Giustizia.

Gubitosi, Giuseppe (1998), *Amedeo Nazzari*, Bologna: Il Mulino.
Guha, Ranajit (2011), 'The Migrant's Time', in Saloni Mathur (ed.), *The Migrant's Time: Rethinking Art History and Diaspora*, Williamstown, MA: Sterling and Francine Clark Art Institute, 3–9.
Gundle, Stephen (2013), *Mussolini's Dream Factory: Film Stardom in Fascist Italy*, New York: Berghahn.
— (2017), 'The Question of Italian National Character and the Limits of Commedia all'italiana: Alberto Sordi, Federico Fellini, and Carlo Lizzani', in Frank Burke (ed.), *A Companion to Italian Cinema*, Chichester: John Wiley & Sons, 198–214.
Günsberg, Maggie (2005), *Italian Cinema: Gender and Genre*, New York: Palgrave Macmillan.
Hall, Colin Michael and Allan M. Williams (2002), *Tourism and Migration: New Relationships between Production and Consumption*, Dordrecht: Kluwer Academic.
Hardt, Michael and Antonio Negri (2000), *Empire*, Cambridge, MA: Harvard University Press.
Harlem (1943), *Cinedoc n. 9 dal film omonimo, produzione Cines*, Rome: Anonima Documento Editrice.
Hay, James (1987), *Popular Film Culture in Fascist Italy: The Passing of the Rex*, Bloomington: Indiana University Press.
Higate, Paul (ed.) (2003), *Military Masculinities: Identity and the State*, Westport, CT: Praeger.
Hipkins, Danielle E. (2016), *Italy's Other Women: Gender and Prostitution in Italian Cinema, 1940–1965*, Oxford: Peter Lang.
Hope, William (2009), 'Gabriele Salvatores' *Marrakech Express* and *Mediterraneo*: Capitalist Dystopias, the Marxist Sublime, Nascent Radicalism', *The Italianist*, 29, 115–31.
Iaccio, Pasquale (ed.) (2003), *Non solo Scipione: Il cinema di Carmine Gallone*, Naples: Liguori Editore.
Innocenti, Marco (1999), *Telefoni bianchi amori neri*, Milan: Mursia.
Ipsen, Carl (2007), 'La Più Grande Italia: The Italianization of Argentina', in Marc S. Rodriguez and Anthony Grafton (eds), *Migration in History: Human Migration in Comparative Perspective*, Rochester, NY: University of Rochester Press, 35–52.
Jarratt, Vernon (1951), *The Italian Cinema*, New York: Macmillan.
Kaplan, Morris (1971), 'Kahane and Colombo Join Forces to Fight Reported U.S. Harassment', *New York Times*, 14 May, 1.
Kezich, Tullio (2006), *Federico Fellini: His Life and Work*, New York: Farrar, Straus and Giroux.
Klevan, Andrew (2004), *Film Performance: From Achievement to Appreciation*, London: Wallflower.
Laderman, David (2002), *Driving Visions: Exploring the Road Movie*, Austin: University of Texas Press.

Landy, Marcia (1988), *Fascism in Film: the Italian Commercial Cinema, 1931–1943*, Princeton, NJ: Princeton University Press.
— (1998), *The Folklore of Consensus: Theatricality in the Italian Cinema 1930–1943*, Albany: State University of New York Press.
— (2008), *Stardom, Italian Style: Screen Performance and Personality in Italian Cinema*, Bloomington: Indiana University Press.
Lanzoni, Rémi Fournier (2014), 'Chronicles of a Hastened Modernisation', in Peter Bondanella (ed.), *The Italian Cinema Book*, London: BFI, 188–94.
La Prensa (1951), Review of *Volver a la vida*, *La Prensa*, 12 January.
Lefevbre, Henri (1991), *The Production of Space*, trans. Donald Nicholson-Smith, Cambridge, MA: Blackwell.
Lenzi, Umberto (2009), *Terrore ad Harlem*, Introduction by Gianfranco De Cataldo, Rome: Coniglio.
Leonardi, Andrea, Alberto Cova, and Pasquale Galea (1997), *Il Novecento economico italiano: Dalla grande guerra al 'miracolo economico'*, Bologna: Monduzzi.
Levi, Carlo (2006), *Christ Stopped at Eboli*, trans. Mark Rotella, New York: Farrar, Straus and Giroux.
Luijnenburg, Linde (2014), 'The Grotesque as a Tool/Deconstructing the Imperial Narrative in Two *commedie all'italiana* by Ettore Scola', *Incontri: Rivista Europea di Studi Italiani*, 29, 2, 43–54.
Maccari, Mino (1928), *Il trastullo di Strapaese*, Florence: Vallecchi Editore.
McDonald Carolan, Mary Ann (2014), *The Transatlantic Gaze: Italian Cinema, American Film*, Albany: State University of New York Press.
Mainardi, Michele (2004), *A mare col Duce: Le colonie estive nel Salento Fascista*, Novoli: Bibliotheca Minima.
Malavasi, Luca (2005), *Gabriele Salvatores*, Milan: Il Castoro.
Mancini, Elaine Carol (1985), *Struggles of the Italian Film Industry During Fascism, 1930–1935*, Ann Arbor, MI: UMI Research Press.
Maurri, Enzo (1981), *Rose scarlatte e telefoni bianchi: appunti sulla commedia italiana dall'Impero al 25 luglio 1943*, Rome: Edizioni Abete.
Mekdjian, Sarah (2014), 'Cinematic Maps of Mobile Borders and Cross-Border Migrations', *Annales de Géographie*, 695–6, 1, 784–804.
Merriman, Peter (2014), 'Roads', in Peter Adey, David Bissell, Kevin Hannam, Peter Merriman, and Mimi Sheller (eds), *The Routledge Handbook of Mobilities*, New York: Routledge, 196–204.
Mezzadra, Sandro (2012), 'The New European Migratory Regime and the Shifting Patterns of Contemporary Racism', in Christina Lombardi-Diop and Catarina Romeo (eds), *Postcolonial Italy: Challenging National Homogeneity*, New York: Palgrave Macmillan, 37–50.
Mida, Massimo and Lorenzo Quaglietti (1980), *Dai telefoni bianchi al neorealismo*, Bari: Laterza.
Moe, Nelson (2019), 'Modernity, Mafia Style: Alberto Lattuada's *Mafioso*', in Dana Renga (ed.), *Mafia Movies: A Reader*, 2nd edn, Toronto: University of Toronto Press, 183–7.

Mollica, Vincenzo and Alessandro Nicosia (2004), *Sordi segreto: Un italiano a Roma*, Rome: Gangemi Editore.
Morgan, Philip (2004), *Italian Fascism, 1915–1945*, New York: Palgrave Macmillan.
— (2007), *The Fall of Mussolini: Italy, the Italians, and the Second World War*, Oxford: Oxford University Press.
Mussolini, Benito (1951–63), *Opera omnia di Benito Mussolini*, 36 vols, ed. Edoardo Susmel and Duilio Susmel, Florence: La Fenice.
Nacci, Michela (1989), *L'antiamericanismo in Italia negli anni trenta*, Turin: Bollati Boringhieri.
Nadal, María Luisa Burguesa (1999), *Edgar Neville: Entre el humor y la nostalgia*, Valencia: Institució Alfons el Magnànim.
Nam, Charles B., William J. Serow, and David F. Sly (eds) (1990), *International Handbook on Internal Migration*, New York: Greenwood Press.
Naremore, James (1988), *Acting in the Cinema*, Berkeley: University of California Press.
Negri, Adelchi (1909), *Sul valore della bonifica umana come mezzo di lotta contro la malaria*, Pavia: Tipografi Cooperativa.
New York Herald Tribune (1951), 'Crime Committee Votes to Cite Albert Anastasia', 2 April, 5.
Nicoloso, Paolo (2008), *Mussolini architetto: Propaganda e paesaggio urbano nell'Italia Fascista*, Turin: Einaudi.
Nicosia, Ernesto (2007), 'Amedeo Nazzari sulla scena internazionale', in Arnaldo Colasanti and Ernesto Nicosia (eds), *Amedeo Nazzari. Rigore e pathos*, Rome: Archivi del Novecento, 5–9.
Noy, Chaim (2016), 'The Semiotics of (Im)mobilities: Two Discursive Case Studies of the System of Automobility', in Giuseppina Pellegrino (ed.), *The Politics of Proximity: Mobility and Immobility in Practice*, Abingdon: Routledge, 61–81.
O'Leary, Alan (2013), *Fenomenologia del cinepanettone*, Rome: Rubbettino.
O'Rawe, Catherine (2014), *Stars and Masculinities in Contemporary Italian Cinema*, New York: Palgrave Macmillan.
— (2017), 'Back for Good: Melodrama and the Returning Soldier in Post-War Italian Cinema', *Modern Italy*, 22, 123.
Past, Elena (2020), 'Environmental Fellini: Petroculture, the Anthropocene, and the Cinematic Road', in Frank Burke, Marguerite Waller, and Marita Gubareva (eds), *A Companion to Federico Fellini*, Hoboken, NJ: Wiley-Blackwell, 347–60.
Pende, Nicola (1933), *Bonifica umana razionale e biologia politica*, Florence: Cappelli.
Pennacchi, Antonio (2008), *Fascio e martello: Viaggi per le città del Duce*, Rome: Editori Laterza.
Peters, Kimberley (2015), 'Drifting: Towards Mobilities at Sea', *Transactions of the Institute of British Geographers*, 40, 2, 262–72.

Pieterse, Jan Nederveen (1997), 'Globalization as Hybridization', in Mike Featherstone, Scott Lash, and Roland Robertson (eds), *Global Modernities*, London: Sage Publications, 45–68.
Pietrangeli, Antonio (1943), 'Harlem', *Bianco e Nero: Rassegna di arte critica e tecnica del film*, VII, 6, June, Rome: Edizioni Italiane, 32–5.
Piotti, Antonio and Marco Senaldi (2002), *Maccarone, m'hai provocato! La commedia italiana del Piccolo Sé*, Rome: Bulzoni Editore.
Pomerance, Murray and Kyle Stevens (eds) (2018), *Close-Up: Great Cinematic Performances*, Edinburgh: Edinburgh University Press.
Pratt, Mary Louise (2008), *Imperial Eyes: Travel Writing and Transculturation*, 2nd edn, New York: Routledge.
Primer Plano (1951), Review of *Volver a la vida*, *Primer Plano*, March.
Pruzzo, Piero and Enrico Lancia (1983), *Amedeo Nazzari*, Rome: Gremese Editore.
Pucci, Laura (2012), 'Remapping the Rural: The Ideological Geographies of Strapaese', in Angela Dalle Vacche (ed.), *Film, Art, New Media: Museum Without Walls?*, New York: Palgrave Macmillan, 178–95.
Raffaelli, Sergio (1992), *La lingua filmata: Didascalie e dialoghi nel cinema italiano*, Florence: Le Lettere.
Ranieri, Tino (1955), *Alberto Sordi*, Milan: Sedit.
Reich, Jacqueline (2004), *Beyond the Latin Lover: Marcello Mastroianni, Masculinity, and Italian Cinema*, Bloomington: Indiana University Press.
Renga, Dana (ed.) (2019), *Mafia Movies: A Reader*, 2nd edn, Toronto: University of Toronto Press.
Restivo, Angelo (2002), *The Cinema of Economic Miracles: Visuality and Modernization in the Italian Art Film*, Durham, NC: Duke University Press.
Ricci, Steven (2008), *Cinema and Fascism: Italian Film and Society, 1922–1943*, Berkeley: University of California Press.
Rigoletto, Sergio (2010), 'The Italian Comedy of the the Economic Miracle: *L'italiano medio* and Strategies of Gender Exclusion', in Lucy Bolton and Christina Siggers Mason (eds), *Italy on Screen: National Identity and Italian Imaginary*, New York: Peter Lang, 33–47.
Rodriguez, Marc S. and Anthony T. Grafton (eds) (2007), *Migration in History: Human Migration in Comparative Perspective*, Rochester, NY: University of Rochester Press.
Rosselli, Alberto and Bruno Pampaloni (2005), *Il Ventennio in celluloide*, Rome: Edizioni Settimo Sigillo.
Rossi, Fabio (2006), *Il linguaggio cinematografico*, Rome: Aracne.
— (2007), *Lingua italiana e cinema*, Rome: Carocci.
Rowe, Kathleen (1995), *The Unruly Woman: Gender and the Genres of Laughter*, Austin: University of Texas Press.
Ruffin, Valentina and Patrizia D'Agostino (1997), *Dialoghi di regime*, Rome: Bulzoni.

Sanfilippo, Matteo (ed.) (2009), *L'emigrazione italiana sugli schermi*, Viterbo: Sette città.
Sanguineti, Tatti (2015), *Il cervello di Alberto Sordi: Rodolfo Sonego e il suo cinema*, Milan: Adelphi.
— (2018), 'Un Italiano in Brasile. Un progetto cinematografico lungo vent'anni', *Bianco e Nero: Rivista Quadrimestrale del Centro Sperimentale di Cinematografia*, LXXIX, 592, September–December, Rome: Edizioni del CSC, 77–92.
Sarris, Andrew (1962/3), 'Notes on the *Auteur* Theory in 1962', *Film Culture*, Winter, 1–8.
Savio, Francesco (1975), *Ma l'amore no: Realismo, formalismo, e propaganda nel cinema italiano di regime (1930–1943)*, Milan: Sonzogno.
Sawchuk, Kim (2014), 'Impaired', in Peter Adey, David Bissell, Kevin Hannam, Peter Merriman, and Mimi Sheller (eds), *The Routledge Handbook of Mobilities*, New York: Routledge, 409–20.
Schiavina, Maria Antonietta (ed.) (1999), *Alberto Sordi: Storia di un commediante*, Milan: Baldini & Castoldi.
Scola, Ettore (2010), 'Ettore Scola', in Giancarlo Governi, *Alberto Sordi, l'italiano*, Rome: A Curcio, 93–100.
Scola, Ettore and Antonio Bertini (1996), *Il cinema e io*, Rome: Officina edizioni.
Shakespeare, William (1997), 'The Taming of the Shrew' (1590–2), *The Riverside Shakespeare*, 2nd edn, vol. 1, ed. G. Blakemore Evans, New York: Houghton Mifflin.
Sharma, Sarah (2010), 'Taxi Cab Publics and the Production of Brown Space After 9/11', *Cultural Studies*, 24, 2, 183–99.
— (2017), 'Speed Traps and the Temporal: Of Taxis, Truck Stops, and TaskRabbits', in Judy Wajcman and Nigel Dodd (eds), *Societies of Speed*, Oxford: Oxford University Press, 131–51.
Sheller, Mimi and John Urry (2000), 'The City and the Car', *International Journal of Urban and Regional Research*, 24, 737–57.
— (2006), 'The New Mobilities Paradigm', *Environment and Planning A*, 38, 207–26.
Silone, Ignazio (1960), *Fontamara*, trans. Harvey Fergusson II, New York: Atheneum Publishers.
Simpson, Mark (2017), 'Lubricity: Smooth Oil's Political Frictions', in Sheena Wilson, Adam Carlson, and Imre Szeman (eds) (2017), *Petrocultures: Oil, Politics, Culture*, Montreal: McGill-Queen's University Press, 287–318.
Sonego, Rodolfo (2007), *Diario australiano*, Rome: Adelphi.
Stam, Robert, Robert Burgoyne, and Sandy Flitterman-Lewis (1992), *New Vocabularies in Film Semiotics: Structuralism, Post-Structuralism and Beyond*, New York: Routledge.
Stam, Robert with Richard Porton and Leo Goldsmith (2015), *Keywords in Subversive Film/Media Aesthetics*, Malden, MA: John Wiley & Sons.
Steimatsky, Noa (2008), *Italian Locations: Reinhabiting the Past in Postwar Cinema*, Minneapolis: University of Minnesota Press.

— (2020), 'Backlots of the World War: Cinecittà 1942–1950', in Brian R. Jacobson (ed.), *In the Studio: Visual Creation and Its Material Environments*, Los Angeles: University of California Press, 122–42.
Stewart, Susan (1984), *On Longing: Narratives of the Miniature, the Gigantic, the Souvenir, the Collection*, Baltimore: Johns Hopkins University Press.
Talese, Gay (1992), *Unto the Sons*, New York: Alfred A. Knopf.
Tamburri, Anthony Julian (1991), *To Hyphenate or Not to Hyphenate: The Italian/American Writer: An Other American*, Montreal: Guernica.
Taviani, Paolo and Vittorio Taviani (1987), *Good Morning Babylon*, London: Faber & Faber.
Thomas, Peter (2014), 'Railways', in Peter Adey, David Bissell, Kevin Hannam, Peter Merriman, and Mimi Sheller (eds), *The Routledge Handbook of Mobilities*, New York: Routledge, 214–24.
Thompson, Doug (1991), *State Control in Fascist Italy: Culture and Conformity, 1925–1943*, Manchester: Manchester University Press.
Torre, Christian Franco (2015), *Edgar Neville: Duende y misterio de un cineasta español*, Santander: Shangrila Textos Aparte.
Torriglia, Anna Maria (2002), *Broken Time, Fragmented Space: A Cultural Map for Postwar Italy*, Toronto: University of Toronto Press.
Troisio, Luciano (ed.) (1975), *Le riviste di Strapaese e Stracittà: Il Selvaggio – L'Italiano '900'*, Treviso: Canova.
Tzanelli, Rodanthi (2007), *The Cinematic Tourist: Explorations in Globalization, Culture and Resistance*, London: Routledge.
Udoff, Yale M. (1965), 'Mafioso by Alberto Lattuada and Dino De Laurentiis', *Film Quarterly*, 18, 3, 48–50.
Urry, John (2000), *Sociology Beyond Societies: Mobilities for the Twenty-First Century*, Florence, KY: Routledge.
— (2007), *Mobilities*, Cambridge: Polity Press.
Vargau, Marina (2016), 'La figura della flâneuse nel film *Le notti di Cabiria* di Federico Fellini', in Paola Bernardini, Joanne Granata, Teresa Lobalsamo, and Alberto Zambenedetti (eds), *Federico Fellini: Riprese, riletture, (re)visioni*, Florence: Franco Cesati Editore, 81–94.
La Vita Cinematografica (1915), VI, special issue, December, Turin: Galleria Nazionale.
Walks, Alan (ed.) (2015), *The Urban Political Economy and Ecology of Automobility: Driving Cities, Driving Inequality, Driving Politics*, New York: Routledge.
Wall, Alex and Stefano De Martino (eds) (1988), *Cities of Childhood: Italian Colonies of the 1930s*, London: Architectural Association Publications.
Walters, William (2015), 'Migration, Vehicles, and Politics: Three Theses on Viapolitics', *European Journal of Social Theory*, 18, 4, 469–88.
Wilson, Sheena, Adam Carlson, and Imre Szeman (eds) (2017), *Petrocultures: Oil, Politics, Culture*, Montreal: McGill-Queen's University Press.
Woodward, Rachel and K. Neil Jenkings (2014), 'Soldier', in Peter Adey, David Bissell, Kevin Hannam, Peter Merriman, and Mimi Sheller

(eds), *The Routledge Handbook of Mobilities*, New York: Routledge, 358–66.

Zagarrio, Vito (ed.) (2002), *Trevico – Cinecittà. L'avventuroso viaggio di Ettore Scola*, Venice: Marsilio.

— (2004), *Cinema e fascismo: Film, modelli, immaginari*, Venice: Marsilio.

Zambenedetti, Alberto (2010), 'New Coinages for Old Phenomena: From *Terrone* to *Extracomunitario* and Beyond', in Grace Russo Bullaro (ed.), *From Terrone to Extracomunitario: New Manifestations of Racism in Contemporary Italian Cinema*, Leicester: Troubador Publishing, 1–24.

— (2012), *Italians on the Move: Towards a History of Migration Cinema*, PhD thesis, New York University.

— (2017), 'Keeping the Faith: Fallen Soldiers and Catholic Iconography in Late Fascist War Cinema', *The Italianist*, 37, 2, 176–91.

— (2019), 'The Godfather: Scene Analysis – The Baptism/Murder', in Dana Renga (ed.), *Mafia Movies: A Reader*, 2nd edn, Toronto: University of Toronto Press, 371–2.

Zambetti, Sandro (1976), *Francesco Rosi*, Florence: La nuova Italia.

Index

A reference in *italics* indicates a figure.

Adamson, Walter L., 41
Adey, Peter, 30, 53, 90, 165, 169
aeromobilities
   the aviator as romantic hero, 28–30
   the honourable pilot figure, 26–7
   I tre aquilotti, 119
   Il cielo brucia / The Sky Burns, 31–3
   see also *Luciano Serra pilota / Luciano Serra, Pilot*
Akhtar, Salman, 89, 99
Alessandrini, Goffredo
   Giarabub, 24–5, 119, 183
   see also *Luciano Serra pilota / Luciano Serra, Pilot*
Alfa Romeo, 113, 116
Allum, Felia, 142
americani
   Catene / Chains, 86–7
   Centomila dollari / A Hundred Thousand Dollars, 28–30, 37, 52–3
   corrupt *americani*, 86–7
   Due cuori felici / Two Happy Hearts, 39–40, 50, 53, 55 n.8, 196
   in Fascist-era cinema, 41–3, 50
   Joe il rosso, 58 n.29
   La bisbetica domata / The Taming of the Shrew, 37–8, 50–2
   label of, 37
   Montevergine (La grande luce), 42–3, 50
   Nazzari's portrayals of, 37
   return migrant figure, 42, 50–1, 86–7
   Terra di nessuno / No Man's Land, 50
Amidei, Sergio, 69
Anastasio, Salvatore, 161, 171
Andreotti, Giulio, 203–4
Angelucci, Gianfranco, 108
Antonioni, Michelangelo
   Cronaca di un amore / Story of a Love Affair, 123
Appadurai, Arjun, 75, 124, 185–6

Argentina
   Amedeo Nazzari in, 102
   Il gaucho, 19 n.5, 37, 77, 99–103
   Italian migration to, 2, 49–50
auteur theory, 191 n.2, 203
automobilities
   Alfa Romeo Giulietta model, 113, 116
   Amedeo Nazzari's pre- and post-war vehicular mobility, *106*
   Amedeo Nazzari's love of cars, 109 n.2
   Bello, onesto, emigrato Australia sposerebbe compaesana illibata / A Girl in Australia, 157–8
   bumper stickers, 164
   cars as status symbols, 92, 103 n.2
   gendering of, 103 n.1, 113, 114
   I magliari, 144, 146, 149–50
   Il vigile, 154
   Italian car culture, 113
   L'Autostrada del sole, 164–5
   Le notti di Cabiria / Nights of Cabiria, 107–8
   Mafioso, 165–7
   mobility of taxi drivers, 202–4
   Racconti d'estate / Love on the Riviera, 124, 132–3
   Rallye del Cinema, 113–16, *114*, *115*
   term, 19 n.7
   tourism mobilities, 124
   in travel comedies, *131*
   Vacanze d'inverno, 130–2

Baffico, Mario
   Terra di nessuno / No Man's Land, 40, 41, 42, 43, 48–9, 50
Ballerini, Piero, 38
Bayman, Louis, 86, 92
Ben-Ghiat, Ruth, 17, 20 n.12, 24, 50
Berry, John
   Oh! Qué mambo, 124, 125–7, 133

Bertellini, Giorgio, 3
Bertozzi, Marco, 6
Bianchi, Giorgio
   Brevi amori a Palma di Maiorca, 124, 128, 133–6, 182
Bini, Andrea, 117, 154
Blasetti, Alessandro
   Terra madre/Mother Earth, 57 n.15
Bolzoni, Francesco, 139–40
bonifica umana (human reclamation), 20 n.12
Boorstin, Daniel J., 198
Borcosque, Carlos F.
   Volver a la vida/Return to Life, 102
Barattoni, Luca, 101
Brignone, Guido
   Passaporto rosso, 48, 140, 142
   Sotto la croce del Sud/Under the Southern Cross, 24
Brunetta, Gian Piero, 42–3, 48
Burke, Frank, 108–9

Calzolari, Giuseppe, 116
Camerini, Mario
   Centomila dollari/A Hundred Thousand Dollars, 28–30, 37, 52–3
   Crimen!/. . . And Suddenly It's Murder! 162–4, 165
   Il grande appello/The Great Appeal, 25
Campana, Domenico
   In viaggio con papà, 200
Campogalliani, Carlo
   La notte delle beffe, 41
   see also *Montevergine (La grande luce)* (Campogalliani)
Caprara, Valerio, 207 n.2
cartography
   bilocation devices, 44–5
   maps in *Luciano Serra pilota/Luciano Serra, Pilot*, 28, 34 n.9
   Montevergine (La grande luce), 44, 45–6, 45
   print-reel montage *Centomila dollari*, 30
Catene/Chains (Matarazzo)
   corrupt *americani*, 86–7
   matres dolorosae, 86, 87, 88
   migrant nostalgia, 87–8
   return migration, 88–9
   Roberto Murolo's songs, 88, 89
   social mobility in, 87–8
Cattini, Alberto, 142–3
Cecchi, Emilio, 69, 71

Cerio, Ferruccio
   I quattro bersaglieri, 119–20
Certeau, Michel de, 4–5
Césaire, Aimé, 184–5
Cherchi Usai, Paolo, 169
Choate, Mark, 54 n.2
cinema impegnato (engaged cinema), 139
Coladonato, Valerio, 125
Colombo Sr, Joseph A., 171–2
colonialism
   The Best of Enemies, 117–18, 120, 183
   cinematic legacy of, 123–4
   decivilisation of the coloniser, 184–5
   Empire Cinema, 17
   focalisation and transvaluation in, 185–6
   I quattro bersaglieri, 119–20
   inter-African mobility, 25
   Luciano Serra pilota/Luciano Serra, Pilot, 25
   orientalist fantasies, 190
   redemptive colonial spaces in empire cinema, 17, 24–5
   see also Ethiopia; *Riusciranno i nostri eroi a ritrovare l'amico*
Comencini, Luigi
   Delitto d'amore/Crime of Love, 10 n.13
commedia all'italiana (Italian-style comedy) canon, 133
Coppola, Francis Ford
   The Godfather, 162, 167, 172
Cresswell, Tim, 9 n.10, 86
crime genre
   flashbacks, 164
   sudden assassinations in, 162
criminal mobilities
   American organized crime, 37, 171
   Anastasia mio fratello/My Brother Anastasia, 82 n.27, 161–2, 169–71, 172
   Camorra/magliari networks, 142
   Crimen!/. . . And Suddenly It's Murder! 162–4, 165
   Harlem, 61, 66
   Mimì metallurgico ferito nell'onore/The Seduction of Mimi, 10 n.13, 159 n.4
   modes of transportation, 163–4
   see also *I magliari* (Rosi); *Mafioso* (Lattuada)
Cwerner, Saulo, 31, 32

De Benedictis, Maurizio, 174 n.8
De Bernardinis, Flavio, 101, 103 n.3
De Santis, Giuseppe, 69–70

De Sica, Vittorio
  Due cuori felici / Two Happy Hearts,
    39–40, 50, 53, 55 n.8, 196
  as a leading man, 16, 55 n.8, 196–7
  Partire / Departure, 55 n.8
  Un Italiano in America, 194, 196
  Vacanze d'inverno, 131
Della Casa, Steve, 183
Duse, Eleonora, 1–2

Emmer, Luciano
  Il cammino della speranza / The Path of Hope, 128
  La ragazza in vetrina / Woman in the Window, 126, 130, 150
  Parigi è sempre Parigi / Paris is Always Paris, 127, 129, 134, 136 n.4
Empire Cinema
  of the Fascist era, 17, 24
  human mobility in, 23, 24, 25
  term, 17
  see also colonialism; *Luciano Serra pilota / Luciano Serra, Pilot*
Ethiopia
  The Best of Enemies, 117–19, 120, 183
  Italian colonialism, 25
  Second Italo-Abyssinian War, 63
  Second Italo-Ethiopian War, 24, 25

Fabrizi, Aldo
  Emigrantes, 140, 142, 144
Fascist regime
  anti-American sentiments of the Fascist era, 53, 61, 64, 66–9, 77
  aviation ethos, 26
  figure of the returned migrant, 39–41
  human mobility policies, 15–16, 17, 18, 23, 53
  internal migration during, 15, 17, 140, 141
  xenophobia of, 41–2, 53
Fellini, Federico
  I vitelloni, 116
  in *Il tassinaro*, 202, 205–7
  La Dolce Vita, 70, 107, 108, 126, 135, 136, 205
  Le notti di Cabiria / Nights of Cabiria, 16–17, 107–9
Forgacs, David, 10 n.13
Franciolini, Gianni
  Racconti d'estate / Love on the Riviera, 124, 132–3
Franco, Mario, 90

Franklin, Adrian S., 124
Fullwood, Natalie, 103 n.1, 113–14
Fumo di Londra / Smoke Over London (Sordi)
  Italian identity in, 177–80, *178*, 182, 190
  narrative trajectory, 176–8
  sexuality and sexual liberation, 180–1
  youth culture, 181–2

Gabaccia, Donna, 3
Gallone, Carmine
  career, 61
  Scipione l'Africano / Scipio Africanus: The Defeat of Hannibal, 61, 183
  see also *Harlem* (Gallone)
gender
  of automobiles, 103 n.1, 113, 114
  Brevi amori a Palma di Maiorca, 135–6
  gendered practices of mobility, 9 n.10
  gendered terrain of Italian cinema, 5
  homme and *femme fatale* figures, 87
  mediated mobilities, 92, *93*
  in melodramas, 85, 86, 87
  narratives of mobility and, 86
  postmenopausal woman figures, 88, 91
  sexual tourism, 125–6, 127
Giacovelli, Enrico, 124
Ginsborg, Paul, 140, 154
Glick Schiller, Nina, 30
Governi, Giancarlo, 121 n.1
Grande, Maurizio, 10 n.12
Gubitosi, Giuseppe, 44, 52, 104 n.6
Guha, Ranajit, 96
Gundle, Stephen, 38, 52, 116
Günsberg, Maggie, 86, 87, 88, 91

Hamilton, Guy
  The Best of Enemies, 117–19, 120, 183
Hardt, Michael, 188
Harlem (Gallone)
  anti-Americanism in, 61, 64, 66–70, 73–4, 77
  the Cinecittà's set, 70, 73, 74
  ethnic and racial depictions in, 65–6, 73–5
  ideological milieu of, 61–2
  Italian migration to America, 61, 64, 71–2, 73
  narrative trajectory, 63, 75–6
  nationalist rhetoric in, 77–9
  opening sequence, 71–3
  original 1943 cut, 62–3, 71, 72–3, 75, 78
  parallels with *Il gaucho*, 77

Harlem (Gallone) (*cont.*)
  parallels with *Mafioso*, 167
  positive models of diasporic citizenship, 75, 77–8
  postwar cut of, 62, *63*, 64, 65, 66, 69, 71, 73, 75
  print-reel montage, 76
  Second Italo-Abyssinian War in, 63, 65
  social mobility in, 75–7, 78
  stock footage, 70, 73, 74
Hay, James, 31, 65–6
Hipkins, Danielle, 94
Hope, William, 189

I magliari/*The Swindlers* (Rosi)
  automobility, 144, 146, 149–50
  Belinda Lee in, 134, 141
  commercial sex, 145–7
  critical reception of, 148–9
  labour mobilities to Northern Europe, 134, 139, 140–1
  marginality in, 141–2
  narrative trajectory, 141–2
  opening sequence, 143
  organized crime and chain migration themes, 142–5, 147–8
identity
  Alberto Sordi's Italian cinematic identity, 6, 116, 117–18
  Amedeo Nazzari's Italian cinematic identity, 6, 117
  emigrant songs, 88, 89, 90, 91
  Fumo di Londra/*Smoke Over London*, 177–80, 182, 190
  Il gaucho, 100–1
  Italian Americans, 171–2
  Italian *gallismo* (machismo), 151–2, 153, 155
  leisure travel and, 125, 129
  on-screen constructions of national identity, 4–5, 6
im/mobilities
  È sbarcato un marinaio, 38–9, 43, 52, 89
  Malinconico autunno/*Melancholic Autumn*, 38
  masculinity and family responsibilities, 38–9
  of Nazzari's characters, 6–7, 37, 48, 49, 52–3, 98 n.3
  in postwar melodramas, 86
  Sancta Maria/*La muchacha de Moscú*, 39
imprisonment
  alongside migration, 88
  Catene/*Chains*, 88
  Harlem, 64, 65, *69*
  L'angelo bianco/*The White Angel*, 94–5
  Montevergine (La grande luce), 42, 44, 46–7, *47*, 88
internal migration
  during the Fascist era, 15, 17, 140, 141
  Mimì metallurgico ferito nell'onore/*The Seduction of Mimì*, 10 n.13, 159 n.4
  see also labour mobilities
Italian cinema
  Alfieri Law, 53
  bonifica umana (human reclamation) in, 20 n.12
  car culture in, 113
  cinema impegnato (engaged cinema), 139
  cinematic expression, 1–2
  commedia all'italiana (Italian-style comedy) canon, 133
  conversion narratives, 31
  coverage of World War II, 62
  during the Fascist regime, 16
  as a gendered terrain, 5
  as high art, 1
  links with the diaspora, 123
  national identity building, 5, 6, 125
  relationship with American cinema, 68, 162, 167, 168–9, *168*, 170, 171
  representations of the migrant experience, 2–3, 5
  star system, 101
Italy
  consumer culture, 117, 119, 122 n.8, 125
  economic boom, 3, 101, 124

Jewish Defense League, 171
journeys
  Centomila dollari/*A Hundred Thousand Dollars*, 29–30
  harbours in *Catene*/*Chains*, 52
  harbours in *Harlem*, 71
  harbours of *È sbarcato un marinaio*, 38–9, 89
  maps in *Luciano Serra pilota*/*Luciano Serra, Pilot*, 28, 34 n.9
  montage of *Montevergine*, 44–5, *45*
  visual devices for, 44–5
  see also cartography

Kezich, Tullio, 107, 108, 116, 195, 204

La bisbetica domata/*The Taming of the Shrew* (Poggioli)
  americano figure in, 51
  narrative trajectory, 51–2
  Nazzari's partnership with Lilia Silvi, 37–8
  return migration in, 50–1
labour mobilities
  Bello, onesto, emigrato Australia sposerebbe compaesana illibata/*A Girl in Australia*, 139, 154–8
  Delitto d'amore/*Crime of Love*, 10 n.13
  Emigrantes, 140, 142, 144
  during the Fascist era, 15, 17, 140, 141
  I magliari/*The Swindlers*, 134, 139, 140–6
  Il diavolo/*To Bed or Not to Bed* (Polidori), 124, 139, 151–4, 163, 182
  migrants as disenfranchised working class, 17, 18
  Passaporto rosso/*Red Passport*, 48, 140, 142
  social mobility and, 76–7
  South to North during the economic boom, 3, 10 n.13
Laderman, David, 195–6
Lancia, Enrico, 33 n.4, 57 n.17, 102
Landy, Marcia, 30, 31, 122 n.7
Lattuada, Alberto *see* Mafioso (Lattuada)
Lefevbre, Henri, 174 n.7
leisure travel *see* tourism mobilities
Levi, Carlo, 49
Limur, Jean de
  Apparizione/*Apparition*, 105–7, 109
Lizzani, Carlo
  L'Autostrada del sole, 164–5
Luciano Serra pilota/*Luciano Serra, Pilot* (Alessandrini)
  aviation ethos, 26–7, 119
  colonialism and the diaspora, 25
  homecoming of migrants, 23–4, 40
  narrative trajectory, 26
  parallels with *Il grande appello*/*The Great Appeal*, 25
  patriotism of return migration, 25, 30–1
  pointlessness of migration, 27
  stills, *29*

Maccari, Mino, 41–2
Mafioso (Lattuada)
  automobilities, 165–6
  barber shop assassination, 162, 168, 169
  cargomobilities, 166–7, 169
  film's transatlantic gaze, 167, 168–9
  local/national/international spheres of the Mafia, 166, 169
  narrative trajectory, 165–7
  parallel with *Harlem* (Gallone), 167
Malasomma, Nunzio, 37
Mari, Febo
  Cenere, 1–2
  cinema as high art, 1
  L'emigrante/*The Emigrant*, 2–3, 6, 8 n.3, 8 n.4
Marotta, Giuseppe, 154
Martera, Luca, 81 n.14
Masini, Giuseppe
  Il cielo brucia/*The Sky Burns*, 31–3
Mastrocinque, Camillo
  Vacanze d'inverno, 123–4, 130–2, 133
Mastroianni, Marcello, 120, 135–6
Matarazzo, Raffaello
  Catene/*Chains*, 86–90
  im/mobilities, 37
  Joe il rosso, 58 n.29
  L'anonima Roylott, 81 n.16
  Malinconico autunno/*Melancholic Autumn*, 38–9, 95, 96–7
  melodramas, 85
  Torna! 87, 88
Mattoli, Mario
  I tre aquilotti, 119
McDonald Carolan, Mary Ann, 162
McLuhan, Marshall, 30
Mekdjian, Sarah, 47
melodramas
  Chi è senza peccato..., 95–6
  the family unit, 85, 86
  female characters, 88
  gender, 85, 86, 87
  I figli di nessuno/*Nobody's Children*, 91–2
  L'angelo bianco/*The White Angel*, 91, 92–5
  Malinconico autunno/*Melancholic Autumn*, 38–9, 95, 96–7
  in post-war Italian cinema, 85–6
  Roberto Murolo's participation in, 88–9, 90–1
  social mobility in, 87–8
  Tormento, 90
  Torna! 87, 88
  see also *Catene*/*Chains*
Merriman, Peter, 158
Mezzadra, Sandro, 4, 10 n.13

migrants
  as disenfranchised working class, 17, 18
  existential migrants, 183
  temporal asynchronicity of, 99
migration
  alongside imprisonment, 88
  assimilation of migrants, 78–9
  early cinematic representations of the migrant experience, 2–3
  La Grande Italia concept, 78–9
  numbers of Italian migrants, 3
  positive models of diasporic citizenship, 75, 77–8
  social mobility and, 27, 40–1
  to South America, 2, 24
  threat of emigration, 17, 18
  see also internal migration; return migration
military mobilities
  The Best of Enemies, 117–19, 120, 183
  cinematic legacy of, 123–4
  Cronaca di un amore / Story of a Love Affair, 123
  I quattro bersaglieri, 119–20
mobilities
  differential mobilities, 134–5
  in Empire Cinema, 23, 24
  during the Fascist era, 15–16, 17, 18, 23, 53
  gendered practices and, 9 n.10
  inter-African mobility, 25
  in the Italian film industry, 3–4
  La Grande Italia concept, 78–9
  large infrastructure projects and, 164–5
  in marginal colonies and the diaspora, 23
  mediated mobility, 30
  of the mid-century, 123
  national identities and, 4–5
  physical displacement through montage sequences, 44–6
  in post-war Italian cinema, 140
  scholarship on, 4
  see also aeromobilities; criminal mobilities; labour mobilities; migration; sexual mobilities; social mobility; tourism mobilities
Moe, Nelson, 166, 167
Monaco, Eitel, 68
Montevergine (La grande luce) (Campogalliani)
  americano figure in, 43
  cartographic devices, 44–5, *45*

  immigrant nostalgia and return migration, 42, 43, 48–9, 50
  imprisonment, 42, 44, 46–7, *47*, 88
  narrative trajectory, 46–7
  parallels with *Passaporto rosso / Red Passport*, 48
  Peruvian subplot, 48
  reconciliation through the power of religion, 43–4
  Strapaese in, 37, 41
Morgan, Philip, 34 n.12
Murolo, Roberto, 88–9, 90
Mussolini, Benito
  on Ethiopia, 25
  involvement with *Luciano Serra pilota / Luciano Serra, Pilot*, 33 n.6
  on Italian migration, 17, 18
  see also Fascist regime
Mussolini, Vittorio, 26

Nacci, Michela, 68
Nazzari, Amedeo
  americani characters, 37, 50
  Apparizione / Apparition, 105–7, 109
  in Argentina, 102
  The Best of Enemies, 117–19, 120, 183
  career, 5, 16–17
  Centomila dollari / A Hundred Thousand Dollars, 28–30, 37, 52–3
  È sbarcato un marinaio, 38–9, 43, 52, 89
  emotional expressiveness of, 28
  I quattro bersaglieri, 119–20
  Il cielo brucia / The Sky Burns, 31–3
  Il gaucho, 19 n.5, 37, 77, 99–103
  im/mobile characters, 6–7, 37, 48, 49, 52–3, 98 n.3
  La bisbetica domata / The Taming of the Shrew, 37–8, 50–2
  La notte delle beffe, 41
  Le notti di Cabiria / Nights of Cabiria, 16–17, 107–9
  in Matarazzo's melodramas, 85
  pater familias persona, 19 n.6, 32, 44, 58 n.22, 85, 96–7, 107
  pre-and post-war vehicular stardom, *106*
  on-screen personas, 6, 28, 105–7, 116, 117
  Terra di nessuno / No Man's Land, 40, 41, 42, 43, 48–9, 50
  Volver a la vida / Return to Life (Borcosque), 102

work with Lilia Silvi, 38
  see also *Catene/Chains* (Matarazzo); *Harlem* (Gallone); *Il gaucho* (Risi); *Luciano Serra pilota/Luciano Serra, Pilot*; melodramas; *Montevergine (La grande luce)*
Negri, Antonio, 188
Negroni, Baldassarre
  Due cuori felici/Two Happy Hearts, 39–40, 50, 53, 55 n.8, 196
Neorealism
  aesthetic renewal of, 61
  Amedeo Nazzari's work, 16
  Andreotti Law, 203
  depictions of urban mobility, 109
  memorialization of the resistance, 32
  Roma città aperta/Rome, Open City (Rossellini), 170
  stock characters of, 107, 109
Neville, Edgar
  Sancta Maria/La muchacha de Moscú, 39
Nicosia, Ernesto, 5
Noël, Magali, 126
Noto, Paolo, 125
Noy, Chaim, 164

O'Rawe, Catherine, 5, 9 n.10

Pampaloni, Bruno, 66
Paradisi, Umberto
  Dagli Appennini alle Ande/From the Apennines to the Andes, 8 n.4
Pasinetti, Francesco, 70, 71
Past, Elena M., 205
Perón, Eva, 102
Pesce, Alberto, 152
Peters, Kimberley, 97
petroculture
  in American film, 195
  cultural critiques of in *Il tassinaro*, 204–5
  lubricity of, 199
  see also *Un Italiano in America* (Sordi)
Pieterse, Jan Nederveen, 17
Pietrangeli, Antonio, 66–7, 68
Poggioli, Ferdinando Maria, 37
  see also *La bisbetica domata/The Taming of the Shrew* (Poggioli)
Polidori, Gianni
  Il diavolo/To Bed or Not to Bed, 124, 139, 151–4, 163, 182
Pruzzo, Piero, 33 n.4, 57 n.17, 102

railways
  cinematic symbolism of, 151, 163
  Crimen/. . . And Suddenly It's Murder! 162–4, 165
  during the Fascist regime, 15–16, 151
  gendered mobilities, *93*, 94
  Il diavolo/To Bed or Not to Bed, 124, 139, 151–4, 163, 182
  Parigi è sempre Parigi/Paris is Always Paris, 127, 129, 134, 136 n.4
  Signori, in carrozza!/Rome-Paris-Rome, 154
  tourism mobilities and, 124
  Vacanze d'inverno, 130, *131*, 132, 151
Ranieri, Tino, 116
Reich, Jacqueline, 135–6
religion
  I figli di nessuno/Nobody's Children, 91
  Il tassinaro, 206
  in the melodramas of Matarazzo, 91
  reconciliation through the power of religion, 43–4
  Sancta Maria/La muchacha de Moscú, 39
Renga, Dana, 162
return migration
  of *americani*, 42, 50–1, 86–7
  Catene/Chains, 88–9
  the figure of in Fascist-era cinema, 39–41
  Harlem, 68–9
  immigrant nostalgia and, 42, 43, 48–50, 75, 88–9, 99–100, 129
  long-distance nationalism of the returnee, 30–1, 77–8
  patriotism of return migration, 25, 30–1, 77–8
  redemptive return of the migrant, 24–5
Ricci, Steven, 54 n.1
Risi, Dino
  Il gaucho, 19 n.5, 37, 77, 99–103
  Riusciranno i nostri eroi a ritrovare l'amico misteriosamente scomparso in Africa (Scola)
    Angolan location of, 184, 186
    changing European identities, 187–9, 190
    critiques of, 189–90
    Heart of Darkness (Conrad) and, 184, 189
    as an indictment of European colonialism, 183, 184–5, 186–8, *187*, 189–90
    narrative trajectory, 184

Rosi, Francesco
  La sfida, 139
  sociopolitical themes in the work of, 139
  see also *I magliari* (Rosi)
Rosselli, Alberto, 66
Rossellini, Roberto
  Roma città aperta/Rome, Open City, 170

Sala, Vittorio
  Costa Azzurra, 124, 128–30, 133
Salvatores, Gabriele
  Marrakech Express, 189
Sanguineti, Tatti, 150, 160 n.14, 205
Sanson, Yvonne, 85, 87
Sawchuk, Kim, 134–5
Scarpitta, Salvatore, 194
Scattini, Luigi, 190
Scola, Ettore
  career, 183–4
  Se permettete parliamo di donne/Let's Talk About Women, 184
  see also *Riusciranno i nostri eroi a ritrovare l'amico*
sexual mobilities
  Bello, onesto, emigrato Australia sposerebbe compaesana illibata/A Girl in Australia, 155–7
  Brevi amori a Palma di Maiorca, 135–6
  commercial sex in *I magliari/The Swindlers*, 145–7
  Costa Azzurra, 124, 128–30
  depictions of homosexuality, 127, 128, 129–30
  in *Fumo di Londra/Smoke Over London*, 180–1
  gallismo (machismo), 151–2, 153, 155
  Il diavolo/To Bed or Not to Bed, 151–3
  in labour mobility films, 139
  Oh! Qué mambo, 125–6
  orientalist fantasies, 190
Sharma, Sarah, 202–3
Silone, Ignazio
  Fontamara, 15
Silvi, Lilia, 38
Simpson, Mark, 199
skyscrapers
  Anastasia mio fratello/My Brother Anastasia, 170
  Harlem, 70, 71, 167, 170
  Luciano Serra pilota/Luciano Serra, Pilot, 29
  Mafioso, 167
  spatial expressions of, 70–1, 174 n.7

social mobility
  within Fascist-era cinema, 40–1
  Harlem, 75–7, 78
  in melodramas, 87–8
  and migration, 27, 40–1
  physical mobilities and, 27
  in travel comedies, 125, 127, 131–2, 133
Soldati, Mario, 25, 61, 82 n.24
Sonego, Rodolfo
  Anastasia mio fratello/My Brother Anastasia, 170
  collaborations with Alberto Sordi, 132, 150, 154
  Costa Azzurra, 128, 130
  Crimen/. . . And Suddenly It's Murder! 162
  I magliari/The Swindlers, 134
  Il vigile, 154
  L'Autostrada del sole, 164
  theme of migrant miners, 160 n.14
  Un Italiano in America, 194
Sordi, Alberto
  Anastasia mio fratello/My Brother Anastasia, 82 n.27, 161–2, 169–71, 172
  Bello, onesto, emigrato Australia sposerebbe compaesana illibata/A Girl in Australia, 139, 154–8
  The Best of Enemies, 117–19, 120, 183
  Brevi amori a Palma di Maiorca, 124, 128, 133–6, 182
  career, 116–17, 120, 126, 174 n.8, 176, 202
  character of Pietro Marchetti, 202–5, 207
  collaborations with Rodolfo Sonego, 132, 150, 154
  Costa Azzurra, 124, 128–30, 133
  Crimen/. . . And Suddenly It's Murder! 162–4, 165
  directorial career, 176
  as a film *auteur*, 176
  films of the Fascist era, 119
  Giarabub, 24–5, 119, 183
  I quattro bersaglieri, 119–20
  I tre aquilotti, 119
  I vitelloni, 116
  Il delitto di Giovanni Episcopo/Flesh Will Surrender, 121 n.5
  Il diavolo/To Bed or Not to Bed, 124, 139, 151–4, 163
  Il tassinaro, 101, 202–6
  Il vigile, 154

Italian cinematic identity and, 6, 116, 117–18
L'Autostrada del sole, 164–5
as a mirror of Italian society, 5–6, 202–7
movement in the works of, 6–7
Oh! Qué mambo, 124, 125–7, 133
Racconti d'estate / Love on the Riviera, 124, 132–3
the Rallye del Cinema, 113, *114*, *115*, 116
on-screen persona, 116
social critique in the films of, 182–3
Thrilling, 164
Un americano a Roma / An American in Rome, 83 n.31, 117, 126, 179
Un giorno in pretura / A Day in Court, 117
Un tassinaro a New York, 83 n.31, 192 n.6, 202–5
Vacanze d'inverno, 123–4, 130–2, 133
In viaggio con papà, 201 n.1
see also *Fumo di Londra / Smoke Over London* (Sordi); *I magliari / The Swindlers* (Rosi); *Mafioso* (Lattuada); *Riusciranno i nostri eroi a ritrovare l'amico misteriosamente scomparso in Africa*; *Un Italiano in America* (Sordi)
Stefano Vanzina
Anastasia mio fratello / My Brother Anastasia, 82 n.27
Steimatsky, Noa, 57 n.14
Steno
Un americano a Roma / An American in Rome, 83 n.31, 117, 126, 179
Un giorno in pretura / A Day in Court, 117
Stewart, Susan, 48–9, 100
Strapaese, 41–2, 48, 57 n.15

Tamburri, Anthony Julian, 83 n.38
Taviani, Paolo and Vittorio
Good Morning Babilonia / Good Morning Babylon, 10 n.13, 10 n.14
telefoni bianchi (white telephones) genre, 18, 38, 85
Torriglia, Anna Maria, 124
tourism mobilities
financial factors, 124, 127–8
and Italian identities, 125
Sordi and Sonego's collaborations and, 150
see also travel comedies

transportation technologies *see also* journeys
Autostrada del Sole (aka A1), 164
Ferrovia delle Dolomiti, 132
gendered mediated mobilities, 92, *93*
identity formation and, 5
travel comedies, 134
viapolitics, 72
travel comedies
Bello, onesto, emigrato Australia sposerebbe compaesana illibata / A Girl in Australia, 155
Brevi amori a Palma di Maiorca, 124, 128, 133–6, 182
Christmas and summer romp genre, 190 n.1
Costa Azzurra, 124, 128–30, 133
explorations of Italian identity, 125, 129
financial factors, 124, 127–8
genre of, 124–5, 127, 128
Italiano all'estero (Italian abroad) tropes, 127
Oh! Qué mambo, 124, 125, 133
Parigi è sempre Parigi / Paris is Always Paris, 127, 129, 134, 136 n.4
Racconti d'estate / Love on the Riviera, 124, 132–3
sexual tourism, 125–6, 127
social mobility in, 125, 127, 131–2, 133
transportation technologies, 134
Vacanze d'inverno, 123–4, 130–2, 133
see also *Fumo di Londra / Smoke Over London* (Sordi)
Tzanelli, Rodanthi, 150

Udoff, Yale M., 166, 168–9
Un Italiano in America (Sordi)
cinematic readings of, 195–6
critique of capitalism, 195, 199–200
Italian stereotyping in, 197–8
narrative trajectory, 194–5
role of petroculture, 195, 198–201
staged reunion, 194, 197–8
as a travel comedy, 196
Vittorio De Sica in, 194, 196–7
United States of America (USA)
American organized crime, 37, 171
anti-American sentiments of the Fascist era, 53, 61, 64, 66–9, 77
cultural critiques of in *Il tassinaro*, 204
Italian cinema's transatlantic gaze, 170
Italian-American identities, 171–2

United States of America (USA) (*cont.*)
   Un americano a Roma/*An American in Rome*, 83 n.31, 117, 126, 179
   see also *americani*; *Harlem* (Gallone); *Mafioso* (Lattuada); *Un Italiano in America* (Sordi)
Urry, John, 4, 27, 72, 103 n.2
Uteng, Tanu Priya, 9 n.10, 86

Vanzina, Stefano
   Anastasia mio fratello/*My Brother Anastasia*, 82 n.27, 161–2, 169–71, 172
Verdone, Carlo, 201 n.1

Walks, Alan, 19 n.7
Walters, William, 72
Wertmüller, Lina
   Mimì metallurgico ferito nell'onore/*The Seduction of Mimi*, 10 n.13, 159 n.4

Zambetti, Sandro, 142, 148
Zampa, Luigi
   Bello, onesto, emigrato Australia sposerebbe compaesana illibata/*A Girl in Australia*, 139, 154–8
   career, 154
   Il vigile, 154

EU representative:
Easy Access System Europe
Mustamäe tee 50, 10621 Tallinn, Estonia
Gpsr.requests@easproject.com

www.ingramcontent.com/pod-product-compliance
Lightning Source LLC
Chambersburg PA
CBHW070345240426
43671CB00013BA/2410